MEGHALAYA
A Victim of Insolent Insurgencies

MEGHALAYA

A Victim of Insolent Insurgencies

Amit Kumar

CENTRUM PRESS
NEW DELHI-110002 (INDIA)

CENTRUM PRESS
H.O.: 4360/4, Ansari Road, Daryaganj,
New Delhi-110002 (In lia)
Tel: 23278000, 23261597, 23255577, 23286875
B.O.: No. 1015, Ist Main Road, BSK IIIrd Stage,
IIIrd Phase, IIIrd Block, Bangalore-560085 (INDIA)
Tel: 080-41723429
Email: centrumpress@gmail.com
Visit us at: www.centrumpress.com

Meghalaya: A Victim of Insolent Insurgencies

First Edition, 2011

ISBN 978-93-80921-74-7

PRINTED IN INDIA

Printed at Tarun Offset Printers, Delhi-110053

Contents

Preface

This book is about the prevailing insurgencies in Meghalaya. The key objective of the book is to deal with a wide range of insurgencies prevailed in this north-eastern state. At the very outset, readers are introduced with the Meghalaya and its various traits. We have also included the chapter on Meghalaya Insurgency, Politics and Peace Process which deal with the initiatives taken by the central and state government in an effort to normalize the conditions in the state.

The books also reflect the over all view on the northeastern violence that provide a wide area to understand the conflict in the state. Underdevelopment has been connected with the insurgencies and its different aspects have been dealt with utmost objectiveness. Conflicts between Khasi and Nepali have also been dealt in detail and nothing is spared in an effort to bring the real causes of the conflict.

Our objective behind writing this book is to make the readers aware about the insurgencies prevailed in the state. All kinds of politics have been raveled in a descriptive manner. Even year-wise, month-wise and date-wise events have been presented for the aid of the readers and students, that will make it easy to comprehend the situation.

Hope the book would certainly solve the purpose.

Author

1

Meghalaya: An Introduction

Meghalaya is a small state in north-eastern India. The word "Meghalaya" literally means "The Abode of Clouds" in Sanskrit and other Indic languages. Meghalaya is a hilly strip in the eastern part of the country about 300 km long (east-west) and 100 km wide, with a total area of about 8,700 sq mi (22,720 km^2). The population numbered 2,175,000 in 2000. The state is bounded on the north by Assam and by Bangladesh on the south. The capital is Shillong also known as the Scotland of the East, which has a population of 260,000.

About one third of the state is forested. The Meghalaya subtropical forests ecoregion encompasses the state; its mountain forests are distinct from the lowland tropical forests to the north and south.

The forests of Meghalaya are notable for their biodiversity of mammals, birds, and plants. Meghalaya, a hilly strip in eastern India, covers a total area of just 22,429 km^2. It was originally part of Assam, but on 21 January 1972, the districts of Khasi, Garo and Jaintia hills became the new state of Meghalaya.

Meghalaya is predominantly an agrarian economy. The important crops of the state are potato, rice, maize, pineapple, banana etc. The service sector is made up of real estate and insurance companies. Meghalaya's gross state domestic product for 2004 is estimated at $1.6 billion in current prices.

Shillong, the capital of the state, is a popular hill station. There are several falls in and around Shillong. The Shillong peak is highest in the state and is good for trekking. It is also known as the "abode of the gods" and has excellent views. If one is not in a mood for camping, the state also offers many good hotels and lodging facilities.

HISTORY

Meghalaya was formed by carving out two districts from the state of Assam: the United Khasi Hills and Jaintia Hills, and the Garo Hills on 21 January 1972. Prior to attaining full statehood, Meghalaya was given a semi-autonomous status in 1970. The Khasi, Garo, and Jaintia tribes each had their own kingdoms until they came under the British administration in the 19th century. Later, the British incorporated Meghalaya into Assam in 1835. The region enjoyed semi-independent status by virtue of a treaty relationship with the British Crown.

When Bengal was partitioned on 16 October 1905 by Lord Curzon, Meghalaya became a part of the new province of "Eastern Bengal and Assam." However, when the partition was reversed in 1912, Meghalaya became a part of the province of Assam. On 3 January 1921 in pursuance of Section 52A of the Government of India Act of 1919, the Governor-General-in-Council declared the areas now in Meghalaya, other than the Khasi States, as "backward tracts." Subsequently however, the Government of India Act of 1935 regrouped the backward tracts into two categories, namely, "excluded" and "partially excluded" areas in place of backward tracts.

At the time of Independence of the country in 1947, the present day Meghalaya constituted two districts of Assam and enjoyed limited autonomy within the state of Assam. The Assam Reorganisation (Meghalaya) Act, 1969 accorded an autonomous status to the state of Meghalaya. The Act came into effect on 2 April 1970, and an Autonomous State of Meghalaya was created within the State of Assam. The Autonomous state had a Legislature in accordance with the Sixth schedule to the Constitution. The Legislature had 37 members. In 1971, the Parliament passed the North-Eastern Areas (Reorganization) Act, 1971, which conferred full statehood on the Autonomous State of Meghalaya. Meghalaya attained statehood on 21 January 1972, with a Legislative Assembly of its own.

DEMOGRAPHICS

Tribal people make up the majority of Meghalaya's population. The Khasis are the largest group, followed by the Garos. These were among those known to the British as "hill tribes". Other groups include the Jaintias, the Koch, koch-rajbansi[part of koch tribe] and the [Hajong], Dimasa, Hmar, Kuki, Lakhar, Mikir, Rabha and the Nepali.

Meghalaya is one of three states in India to have a Christian majority with 70.3% of the population practicing Christianity; the other two (Nagaland and Mizoram) are also in the north-east of India. Hinduism is the next sizeable faith in the region with 13.3% of the population practicing it. A sizeable minority, 11.5% of the population, follow traditional animist religions (classified as other on the census). Muslims make up 4.3% of the population. In 1991 when Christians made up 65% of the population of Meghalaya the 1.1 million (11 lakh) Christians made it the state in North-east India with the most Christians. At that point more Christians lived in Meghalaya than there were people in Mizoram.

As per the census of India 2001, the sex ratio in the state was 975 females per thousand males which was far higher than the national average of 933. It has grown steadily from a 1981 level of 954. Traditionally the sex ratio in the rural areas has been higher than that in the urban areas. However, as per the census figures for 2001, the urban sex ratio of 985 was higher than the rural sex ratio of 972. This has often been attributed to the belief that, unlike most other parts of India, there is no special preference for male children in Meghalaya.

LANGUAGES

The principal languages in Meghalaya are Khasi and Garo with English as the official language of the State. Khasi is one of the chief languages of Meghalaya: Khasi, which is also spelled Khasia, Khassee, Cossyah and Kyi, is a branch of the Mon-Khmer family of the Austroasiatic stock; and is spoken by about 900,000 people residing in Meghalaya. Many words in the Khasi language are supposed to have been borrowed from Indo-Aryan languages such as Bengali and Assamese.

Moreover, the Khasi language had no script of its own in its onset. The Khasi language is believed to be one of the very few surviving dialects of the Mon-khmer family of languages in India today.

Garo language has a close affinity with the koch and Bodo language. Garo, spoken by the majority of the population, is spoken in many dialects such as Abeng or Ambeng, Atong, Akawe (or Awe), Matchi Dual, Chibok, Chisak Megam or Lyngngam, Ruga, Gara-Ganching and Matabeng. Another language of Meghalaya is the language spoken by the people of the Jaintia hills. This language, as matter of fact, is a variation of the standard Khasi language. The Jaintia language is spoken, along with the Khasi language, by the tribal groups, *viz.* Khynriam, Bhoi, Pnar and War.

CULTURE AND SOCIETY

The main tribes in Meghalaya are the Jaintias, the Khasis and the Garos. One of the unique features of the State is that a majority of the tribal population in Meghalaya follows a matrilineal system where lineage and inheritance are traced through women. The Khasi and Jaintia tribesmen follow the traditional matrilineal norm, wherein the "Kha Khadduh" (or the youngest daughter) inherits all the property and acts as the caretaker of aged parents and any unmarried siblings. However, the male line, particularly the mother's brother, may indirectly control the ancestral property since he may be involved in important decisions relating to property including its sale and disposal.

In the Garo lineage system, the youngest daughter inherits the family property by default; unless another daughter is so named by the parents. She then becomes designated as 'nokna' meaning 'for the house or home'.In case there are no daughters, then a chosen daughter-in -law (bohari) or an adopted child (deragata)comes to stay in the house as well as inherits the property. The tribal people of Meghalaya are therefore a part of what may be the world's largest surviving matrilineal culture. According to India's National Family Health Survey, Meghalaya is the state where parents have shown the least interest to have a male child—73% less than the national average.

SPIRITUALITY

According to legend, from the 13th century, a Shivalinga (called "Hatakeswarat") has existed in the Jaintia Hills under the reign of Ranee Singa. Several members of the Jaintia tribe even participate in the Hindu festival of Shivratri (Night of Lord Shiva). The ancient Meghalayans mixed their spiritual beliefs of Animism and ancestor-worship with Hinduism. In caves, the images of Shiva and Durga are visible.

GEOGRAPHY

The State of Meghalaya is also known as the "Meghalaya Plateau". It consists mainly of archean rock formations. These rock formations contain rich deposits of valuable minerals like coal, limestone, uranium and sillimanite. Meghalaya has many rivers. Most of these are rainfed and are therefore seasonal. The important rivers in the Garo Hills Region are Daring, Sanda, Bandra, Bhogai, Dareng, Simsang, Nitai and the Bhupai. In the central and eastern section of the plateau, the important rivers are Umkhri, Digaru, Umiam, Kynchiang (Jadukata), Mawpa, Umiew or Barapani, Myngot and Myntdu. In the southern Khasi Hills Region, these rivers have created deep gorges and several beautiful waterfalls.

The elevation of the plateau ranges between 150 m to 1961 m. The central part of the plateau comprising the Khasi Hills has the highest elevations, followed by the eastern section comprising the Jaintia Hills Region. The highest point in Meghalaya is Shillong Peak, which is also a prominent IAF station in the Khasi Hills overlooking the city of Shillong. It has an altitude of 1961 m. The Garo Hills Region in the western section of the plateau is nearly plain. The highest point in the Garo hills is the Nokrek Peak with an altitude of 1515 m.

DISTRICTS

Meghalaya currently has 7 districts. These are: East Garo Hills, East Khasi Hills, Jaintia Hills, Ri-Bhoi, South Garo Hills,

West Garo Hills and the West Khasi Hills. The East Garo Hills district was formed in 1976 and has a population of 247,555 as per the 2001 census. It covers an area of 2603 square kilometres. The District Headquarters are located at Williamnagar, earlier known as Simsangiri. Nongalbibra,a town in this district has a large number of coal mines. The coals are transported to Goalpara and Jogighopa via NH62.

The East Khasi Hills district was carved out of the Khasi Hills on 28 October 1976. The district has covers an area of 2,748 square kilometres and has a population of 660,923 as per the 2001 census.

The headquarters of East Khasi Hills are located in Shillong. The Jaintia Hills district was created on 22 February 1972. It has a total geographical area of 3819 square kilometres and a population of 295,692 as per the 2001 census. The district headquarters are located at Jowai. Jaintia Hills district is the largest producer of coal in the state. Coal mines can be seen all over the district.

The Ri-Bhoi district was formed by further division of East Khasi Hills district on 4 June 1992. It has an area of 2448 square kilometres. The total population of the district was 192,795 as per the 2001 census. The district headquarters are located at Nongpoh. It has a hilly terrain and a large part of the area is covered with forests. The Ri-Bhoi district is famous for its pineapples and is the largest producer of pineapples in the state. The South Garo Hills district came into existence on 18 June 1992 after the division of the West Garo Hills district. The total geographical area of the district is 1850 square kilometres. As per the 2001 census the district has a population of 99,100. The district headquarters are located at Baghmara.

The West Garo Hills district lies in the western part of the state and covers a geographical area of 3714 square kilometres. The population of the district is 515,813 as per the 2001 census. The district headquarters are located at Tura. The West Khasi Hills district is the largest district in the state with a geographical area of 5247 square kilometres. The district was carved out of Khasi Hills District on 28 October 1976. The district headquarters are located at Nongstoin.

CLIMATE

With average annual rainfall as high as 1200 cm in some areas, Meghalaya is the wettest place on earth. The western part of the plateau, comprising the Garo Hills Region with lower elevations, experiences high temperatures for most of the year. The Shillong area, with the highest elevations, experiences generally low temperatures. The maximum temperature in this region rarely goes beyond 28 degrees, whereas winters temperatures of sub-zero degrees are common.

The town of Cherrapunji in the Khasi Hills south of capital Shillong holds the world record for most rain in a calendar month, while the village of Mawsynram, near the town of Cherrapunji, holds the distinction of seeing the heaviest yearly rains. The best time to visit Meghalaya is during the months of March to July. The British and Assam Tea Estate owners would shift here during the summer months to escape the heat of the Indian Plains.

ECONOMY

Meghalaya is predominantly an agrarian economy. Agriculture and allied activities engage nearly two-thirds of the total work force in Meghalaya. However, the contribution of this sector to the State's NSDP is only about one-third. Agriculture in the state is characterized by low productivity and unsustainable farm practices, giving rise to a high incidence of rural poverty. As a result, despite the large percentage of population engaged in agriculture, the state is still dependent upon imports from other states for most food items such as meat, eggs, food grains etc. Infrastructural constraints have also prevented the economy of the state from growing at a pace commensurate with that of the rest of the country.

Meghalaya is considered to have a rich base of natural resources. These include minerals such as coal, limestone, sillimanite, Kaolin and granite among others. Meghalaya also has a large forest cover, rich biodiversity and numerous water bodies. The low level of industrialization and the relatively poor infrastructure base in the state acts as an impediment to the exploitation of these natural resources in the interest of the state's economy. However, in recent years two large cement manufacturing plants with production capacity more than 900 MTD have come up in Jantia Hills district and several more are in pipeline to utilise the rich deposit of very high quality limestone available in this district. Meghalaya also has much natural beauty and the State government has been trying to exploit this for promoting tourism in the State. However, infrastructural constraints and security concerns have hampered the growth of tourism in the state.

MACRO-ECONOMIC TRENDS

This is a chart of trends in the gross state domestic product of Meghalaya at market prices estimated by Ministry of Statistics and Programme Implementation with figures in millions of Indian Rupees.

Year	Gross State Domestic Product
1980	2,000
1985	3,930
1990	8,900
1995	19,950
2000	37,280

Meghalaya's gross state domestic product for 2004 is estimated at $1.6 billion in current prices.

INCIDENCE OF POVERTY

Planning Commission, the apex planning body under the Government of India, has estimated the percentage of population below poverty line in Meghalaya at nearly one-third the total population of the state in 2000. The incidence of poverty in rural areas at about 55% is almost double the percentage of poverty in the urban areas.

AGRICULTURE

Nearly 10% of the total geographical area of Meghalaya is under cultivation. Agriculture in the state is characterized by limited use of modern techniques and low productivity.

As a result, despite the vast majority of the population engaged in agriculture, the contribution of agricultural production to the state's GDP is low and most of the population engaged in agriculture remains poor. A substantial portion of the cultivated area is under the traditional shifting agriculture known locally as "Jhum" cultivation.

Food grains are the most important crop in Meghalaya. These are grown in over 1,330 km², nearly 60% of the state's cultivated area. The production of food grains is over 230 thousand tonnes. Rice is the dominant food grain crop accounting for over 80% of the food grain production in the state. Other important food grain crops are maize, wheat and a few other cereals and pulses. Oilseeds such as rape and mustard, linseed, soybean, castor and sesame are grown on nearly 100 km². Rape and mustard are the most important oilseeds accounting for well over two-thirds of the oilseed production of nearly 6.5 thousand tonnes.

Fibre crops such as cotton, jute and Mesta had traditionally been among the only cash crops in Meghalaya, grown almost exclusively in Garo Hills. These have been losing popularity in recent years as indicated by their declining yield and area under cultivation. Climatic conditions in Meghalaya also permit a large variety of horticulture crops including fruits, vegetables, flowers, spices and medicinal plants. These are considered to be higher value crops but traditional values and food security concerns have prevented farmers at large from embracing these crops.

The important fruits currently grown in the state include citrus fruits, pineapple, papaya, banana etc. The mandarin orange grown in Meghalaya is considered to be of very high quality. In addition to this, a large variety of vegetables are grown in the state including cauliflower, cabbage and radish.

Areca nut plantations can be seen all over the state, especially around the road from Guwahati to Shillong. Other plantation crops like tea, coffee and cashew have been introduced lately and are becoming popular. A large variety of spices, flowers, medicinal plants and mushrooms are also grown in the State.

TRANSPORTATION

The partition of the country has created severe infrastructure constraints for the Northeastern region, with merely 2% of the perimetre of the region adjoining the rest of the country. A narrow strip of land, often called the Siliguri Corridor, or the Chicken's Neck connects the region with the State of West Bengal. Meghalaya is a land locked state with a large number of small settlements in remote areas. Road is the only means of transport within the state. While the capital Shillong is relatively well connected, road connectivity in most other parts of the state is relatively poor. A significant portion of the roads in the state are still un-metalled. Most of the arrivals into the Meghalaya take place through Guwahati in neighbouring Assam, which is nearly 103 km away. Assam has a major railhead as well as an airport with regular train and air services to the rest of the country. The State still has a large number of old timber bridges.

Meghalaya does not have any railhead. It has a small airport at Umroi, about 40 km from Shillong on the Guwahati-Shillong highway. The small size of the airport does not allow the operations of large aircraft and only small aircraft operate from Kolkata and Agartala, the capital of the neighbouring state of Tripura.

FLORA AND FAUNA

As per the State of Forest Report 2003, published by the Forest Survey of India, Meghalaya has a forest cover of 9,496 km^2, which is 42.34% of the total geographical area of the state. The Meghalayan subtropical forests have been considered among the richest botanical habitats of Asia. These forests receive abundant rainfall and support a vast variety of floral and faunal biodiversity. A small portion of the forest area in Meghalaya is under what is known as "sacred groves" (see Sacred groves of India). These are small pockets of ancient forest that have been preserved by the communities for hundreds of years due to religious and cultural beliefs. These forests are reserved for religious rituals and generally remain protected from any exploitation. These sacred groves harbour many rare plant and animal species. The Nokrek biosphere reserve in the West Garo Hills and the Balaphakram National Park in the South Garo Hills are considered to be the most biodiversity rich sites in the Meghalaya. In addition, Meghalaya has three Wildlife Sanctuaries. These are the Nongkhyllem Wildlife Sanctuary, the Siju Sanctuary and the Bhagmara Sanctuary, which is also the home of the insect eating pitcher plant Nepenthes khasiana.

NEPENTHES KHASIANA

Due to the diverse climatic and topographic conditions, Meghalayan forests support a vast floral diversity, including a large variety of Parasites and Epiphytes, Succulent plants and Shrubs. Two of the most important tree varieties include: Shorea robusta (sal tree) and Tectona grandis (teak). Meghalaya is also the home to a large variety of fruits, vegetables, spices and medicinal plants. Meghalayan is also famous for its large variety of orchids–nearly 325 of them. Of these the largest variety is found in Mawsmi, Mawmluh and Sohrarim forests in the Khasi hills.

Meghalaya also has a large variety of mammals, birds, reptiles and insects. The important mammal species include elephants, bear, civets, mongooses, weasels, rodents, gaur, wild buffalo, deer, wild boar and a number of primates. Meghalaya also has a large variety of bats. The limestone caves in Meghalaya, such as the Siju cave are home to some of the rarest bat species. The prominent bird species in Meghalaya include the Magpie-Robin, the Red-vented Bulbul, the Hill Myna is usually found in pairs or in flocks in the hill forests of Meghalaya, the Large Pied Hornbill and the Great Indian, which is the largest bird in Meghalaya. Other birds include the Peacock Pheasant, the Large Indian Parakeet, the Common Green Pigeon and the Blue Jay. Meghalaya is also home to over 250 species of butterflies, nearly a quarter of all the species found in India.

The common reptile varieties in Meghalaya are lizards, crocodiles and tortoises. Meghalaya also has a number of snakes including the python, the Copperhead, the Green Tree

Racer, the Indian Cobra the King Cobra, the Coral Snake and Vipers.

EDUCATION

IIM Shillong

There are lots of good schools and colleges in Shillong. As part of developmental programme in north eastern states, ministry of human resource development opened the seventh Indian Institute of Management in Shillong which is named as Rajiv Gandhi Indian Institute of Management. This institute started admissions from the academic year 2008. Recently National Institute of Fashion Technology Shillong and NEIGRIHMS opened in Shillong. Shillong is fast turning up as the centre of learning in the North Eastern region.

Apart from Shillong, Good school and colleges are available in Jowai and Tura

TOURISM

Shillong from Shillong Peak

Earlier, foreign tourists required special permits to enter the areas that now constitute the state of Meghalaya. However, the restrictions were removed in 1955. Meghalaya is considered to be one of the most picturesque states in the country. It has enough tourism content to attract tourists of many different interests.

Tourism Content

Meghalaya has some of the thickest surviving forests in the country and therefore constitutes one of the most important ecotourism circuits in the country today. The Meghalayan subtropical forests support a vast variety of flora and fauna. Meghalaya has 2 National Parks and 3 Wildlife Sanctuaries.

Shillong Golf Course, one of the oldest golf courses of India. Meghalaya also offers many adventure tourism opportunities in the form of mountaineering, rock climbing, trekking and hiking, water sports etc. The state offers several trekking routes some of which also afford and opportunity to encounter some rare animals such as the slow loris, assorted deer and bear. The Umiam Lake has a water sports complex with facilities such as rowboats, paddleboats, sailing boats, cruise-boats, water-scooters and speedboats.

Meghalaya has an estimated 500 natural limestone and sandstone caves spread over the entire state including most of the longest and deepest caves in the sub-continent. Krem Liat Prah is the longest cave and Synrang Pamiang is the deepest cave, both located in the Jaintia Hills. Cavers from United Kingdom, Germany, Austria, Ireland and the US have been visiting Meghalaya for over a decade exploring these caves. Not many of these have however been developed or promoted adequately for major tourist destinations.

Important Tourist Spots

Cherrapunjee is one of the most popular tourist spots in North East of India. It lies to the south of the capital Shillong. The town is very well known and needs little publicity. A rather scenic, 50 kilometre long road, connects Cherrapunjee with Shillong.

The popular waterfalls in the state are the Elephant Falls, Shadthum Falls, Weinia falls, Bishop Falls, Nohkalikai Falls, Langshiang falls and Sweet Falls. The hot springs at Jakrem near Mawsynram are believed to have curative and medicinal properties. Meghalaya also has many natural and manmade lakes. The Umiam Lake (popularly known as Bara Pani meaning Big water) on the Guwahati-Shillong road is a major tourism attraction for tourist. Meghalaya has several parks; Thangkharang Park, the Eco-park, the Botanical Garden and Lady Hydari Park to name a few. Dawki, which is located at about 96 Kilometres from Shillong is the gateway to Bangladesh and affords a scenic view of some of the tallest mountain ranges in Meghalaya and the Bangladesh border lands.

Problems and Constraints

The state has a relatively poor road and communication network specially NH 62. While some of the major circuits such as Shillong-Jowai, Shillong-Tura and Shillong-Sohra are well developed; the internal road networks are rather poor and inadequately maintained. There are few markets outside the state capital Shillong. Banking facilities are also limited and only a few establishments in the state accept credit cards. The Garo Hills region which has some of the most important tourist spots is not well connected with the rest of the state.

Tourism in the North East in general has also suffered on account of years of insurgency and the resulting security concerns. Many governments had in the past issued advisories against traveling to the Northeast of India, worsening the security perception. It may however be mentioned that Meghalaya is perhaps the least affected by insurgency in the Northeast region. The current ground scenario for Shillong is one in which tourists are welcome to come and enjoy the beauty of Meghalaya.

GOVERNMENT AND POLITICS

State Government

Like most other states in India, Meghalaya has a unicameral legislature. The Meghalaya Legislative Assembly has 60 members at present. Meghalaya has two representatives in the Lok Sabha, the lower house of the Parliament of India; one each from Shillong and Tura. It also has one representative in the Rajya Sabha, the upper house of the Parliament. The ceremonial head of the State is the Governor appointed by the Government of India. However, the real executive powers are held by the Chief Minister.

Meghalaya does not have a high court of its own. The Gauhati High Court has jurisdiction in Meghalaya. A Circuit Bench of the Guwahati High Court has been functioning at Shillong since 1974.

AUTONOMOUS DISTRICT COUNCILS

In order to provide local self governance machinery to the rural population of the country, provisions were made in the Constitution of India and accordingly the Panchayati Raj institutions were set up. However, on account of the distinct customs and traditions prevailing in erstwhile state of Assam (of which Meghalaya and most of the Northeast was a part), it was felt necessary to have a separate political and administrative structure in Assam. Moreover, some of the tribal communities in the region also had their own traditional political systems and it was felt that Panchayati Raj institutions may come into conflict with these traditional systems.

To provide a simple and inexpensive form of local self governance to the tribal population, the Sixth Schedule was appended to the Constitution on the recommendations of a sub committee formed under the leadership of Gopinath Bordoloi. The Sixth Schedule provided for the constitution of Autonomous District Councils (ADCs) in certain rural areas of the Northeast including some areas that now fall in Meghalaya.

The Sixth Schedule carries detailed provisions for the constitution and management of Autonomous District Councils (ADCs) and laid down the powers of the ADCs. At present Meghalaya has three ADCs, *viz.*, Khasi Hills Autonomous District Council, Garo Hills Autonomous District Council and the Jaintia Hills Autonomous District Council.

TRADITIONAL POLITICAL INSTITUTIONS

All the three major ethnic tribal groups, namely, the Khasis, Jaintias and the Garos also have their own traditional political institutions that have existed for hundreds of years. These political institutions were fairly well developed and functioned at various tiers, such as the village level, clan level and state level.

In the traditional political system of the Khasis each clan had its own council known as the "Durbar Kur", which was presided over by the clan headman. The council or the Durbar managed the internal affairs of the clan.

Similarly, every village had a local assembly known as the Durbar Shnong, *i.e.* village Durbar or council, which was presided over by the village headman. These councils or Durbars played an administrative role in issues of common interest, such as sanitation, water supply, health, roads, education and conflict resolution. However, the inter-village issues were dealt with through a political unit comprising adjacent Khasi Villages. This political unit was known as the raid. The raid had its own council the Raid Durbar, which was presided over by the elected headman known as Basans, Lyngdohs or Sirdars.

Above the Raid was a the supreme political authority known as the Syiemship. The Syiemship was the congregation of several raids and was headed an elected chief known as the "Syiem" (or the king). The Syiem ruled the Khasi state through the State Assembly, known as the Durbar Hima. Most of the elections were through adult male suffrage.

The Jaintias also had a three tier political system somewhat similar to the Khasis. The supreme political authority was the Syiem.

The second tier of this structure was the congregation of Jaintia villages known as Raids. These were headed by "Dolois", who were responsible for performing the executive, magisterial, religious and ceremonial functions at the Raid level. At the lowest level were the village headmen. Each administrative tier had its own councils or durbars. Most elections were through adult male suffrage.

In the traditional political system of the Garos a group of Garo villages comprised the A·king. The A·king functioned under the supervision of the Nokmas, which was perhaps the only political and administrative authority in the political institution of the Garos.

The Nokma performed both judicial and legislative functions. The Nokmas also congregated to address inter-A·king issues. There were no well-organized councils or durbars among the Garos.

Frankenstein Momin, Billy Kid Sangma and Adolf Lu Hitler Marak were three men among dozens of others with equally colourful names who competed for legislative seats in Meghalaya, a remote northeast Indian state, on 3 March 2008. There were about 60 seats up for grabs, 331 candidates vying, and no shortage of unusual names it was reported on 25 February 2008. Hitler, Frankenstein battle for votes in India

FACTS AND FIGURES

- *Area*: 22,429 km^2
- *Population*: 2,175,000 (2000)
- *Ethnic groups*:
  - *Khasi*: 49%
  - *Garo*: 34%
  - *Bengali*: 2.5%
  - *Nepali*: 4%
  - *Shaikh*: 2.3%
  - *Koch*: 2.8%
  - *Hajong*: 1.8%
  - *Other*: 6.4%
- *Religion*:
  - *Christian*: 70.3%
  - *Animist*: 11.5%
  - *Hindu*: 13.3%
  - *Muslim*: 4.3%
  - *Capital*: Shillong (population 260,000)

2

Meghalaya Insurgency, Politics and Peace Process

DIPLOMATIC PROCESS

The peace process between the Government and rebels of the Hynniewtrep National Liberation Council (HNLC) in Meghalaya has received a setback with the HNLC rebuffing peace overtures made by the Church leaders, and censuring the Church in unambiguous terms for failing to protect the interests of Khasi tribals. As the Church is busy explaining its non-partisan role to the militants and civil society at large, peace attempts have floundered in the State.

The HNLC defiance was clear from its four-page brochure entitled 'We pay homage to our martyrs'. In the handout, the outfit advised the Church leaders to 'ask the government to stop creating trouble for the Khasi people in the name of governance'. The outfit also warned that it is 'identifying all those traitors who have been helping its enemies and once the process is completed, it would unleash its wrath upon them.'

These defiant words make some things clear. First, the outfit is in no mood for peace and is confident of surviving counter-insurgency operations. Secondly, it seems weary of dissent in its own ranks. The recovery of two bodies of former HNLC cadres in Shillong indicates its resolve to eradicate discord within its ranks. However, what is evident in the handout is its growing sense of alienation from dominant sections of the society. It has criticised the administrative machinery comprising of the government and the police, but has also come down harshly on the Church, the Syiems (traditional chiefs) and the Bkhraws (elders). By its own admission, it seems frustrated that in its ki khun ki hajar (sons of the soil movement), it gets little support from the society it is promoting.

However, this provides little solace for the common people who have grown accustomed to living in fear in Meghalaya. The police have been unable to arrest the slide in the law and order situation. Due to the lack of army deployment to date, the State has become a hunting ground for two insurgent outfits, the HNLC and the ANVC (Achik National Volunteers Council), and also a safe house for militants from neighbouring Assam. Life in the capital city of Shillong comes to a grinding halt before the evening hours.

But the threat perception from the two outfits in the State, by the Central and State governments is dissimilar. Both the HNLC and the ANVC were declared unlawful associations by the Union government in November 2000, but the former Chief Minister, EK Mawlong, went on record saying that his government had not made any such recommendations, and the Centre might have acted on its own. Now the tables have turned. Crime rates remain high in the State, but the Central government is in no mood to accede to the State government's demand for reinforcements.

In 2001, 40 deaths were reported from the State due to insurgency incidents. These small numbers, however, do not reflect the intensity of violence in the State. Importantly, beginning with 1998, fatalities have shown signs of escalation. Twenty deaths were reported in 1998, 22 in 1999 and 36 in 2000. The ratio of deaths of security force personnel to militants remains alarmingly high. Since 1996, when a security force person was killed in the State, 50 security personnel compared to only 27 militants have been killed. The police in this hill state are too few in number. With just two State police battalions and an additional IRB battalion to supplement the regular police force, insurgents have a free run at most times. Inaccessible terrain helps the militants to move about undetected. In the capital, too, the HNLC has engaged the police force on Republic and Independence Days in cross firing and managed to escape without casualties.

Induction of the army might not be the best solution to fighting insurgency in Meghalaya. The army is always viewed as an alien force by the people, as the army personnel, mostly, are from states outside of the northeastern region and are ignorant of local sensibilities. Hence, deployment of the army might reverse the process of alienation looming large on the insurgents. Besides, army personnel will need time to familiarise themselves with the terrain of the State.

The answer lies in the modernisation of the police force. In addition to augmenting the number of police personnel, areas like weaponry, communications and intelligence need prompt upgradation. Remote police stations need to be urgently modernised. The slide of Meghalaya from a land of peace to a safe house for insurgents must be prevented.

MEGHALAYA DEPLOYS SPECIAL ANTI-INSURGENCY POLICE TEAM

On 30th Sept. in a bid to nip in the bud the rapidly growing militancy in Meghalaya, the state government has initiated steps to negotiate with the Garo insurgent outfit of Achik National Volunteers Council (ANVC).

Several measures have been initiated at unofficial levels to hold discussions with the well-entrenched ANVC, which has spread its activities and also recently initiated alliances with several insurgent outfits from neighbouring states, according to official sources. "Feelers have been sent to top ANVC leaders for talks and to ascertain their exact demands. Though they have been active for quite some time, we don't know what exactly they want."

A major cause of worry was ANVC's recently initiated alliances with insurgent outfits of other North-East states including National Socialist Council of Nagaland (I-M), National Liberation Front of Tripura (NLFT) and United Liberation Front of Asom (ULFA), the sources said.As state Chief Secretary H W T Syiem put it, the ANVC, which has beenoperating hand in glove with NSCN (I-M), ULFA, NLFT and some insurgent outfits of Manipur, needs to be dealt with at the earliest. Added to the menace of ANVC, the state is also threatened by growing activities of Hynniewtriep National Liberation Council (HNLC), a Khasi outfit. "Though insurgency is at present in a nascent stage in Meghalaya, the problem may soon get out of control unless it is nipped in the bud," he said. Syiem said the ANVC is alarmingly growing in number and consolidating its base, while the HNLC is a comparatively smaller outfit but getting to be increasingly active. The ANVC seems to have earned considerable support among the local people. Besides fighting against alcoholism and gambling in hill areas, ANVC has also been raising its voice against atrocities against women, according to volunteers of a non-governmental organisation here. The problem has become more complicated as Meghalaya has long been used as a safe haven by underground insurgent elements from neighbouringnorth-eastern states.

Once an abode of peace and tranquility, the state now witnesses frequent abductions, killings, extortion and clashes by the local insurgents. "The state, particularly its capital city, has been a haven for underground elements of other north-eastern states who use it as a safe transit point," Syiem said, adding it was also being used as a conduit for arms flow by the ultras. Even training camps have been set up in remote and inaccessible areas of the state by certain insurgent outfits, posing a serious threat to peace and security, he said.

The state government has sought assistance from the Centre to tackle growing activities of insurgents, he said, adding "the Centre must provide necessary help before the situation worsens." Deputy Chief Minister D D Lapang said concrete action needs to be taken at the earliest to prevent the misguided youths from becoming hard-core insurgents. Coupled with the menace of nascent insurgency, the state is experiencing considerable tensionover the issue of "outsiders". Lapang said both tribals and non-tribals here are in the grip of a "fear psychosis" as they feel threatened by each other. "Continuous influx of people from outside has created a psychosis among locals who fear they would be swallowed by the outsiders," he said and suggested strengthening economic development as a step "to remove this feeling".He said political instability, unemployment, underdevelopment and activities of certain anti-national forces have been the main reasons behind the growth of militancy in Meghalaya.

The state, sharing a 423 km-long border with Bangladesh, faces influx of Muslims from neighbouring Assam, suspected to be Bangladeshi nationals, who claim to be residents of certain Assam districts and carry with them documentary evidence, senior police officials said. Syiem said the state police force is too small and ill-equipped to effectively deal with insurgency and infiltration and needs to be strengthened with acquisition of modern armsand state-of-the-art gadgets.

SANDWICHED: PLIGHT OF THE PNARS

Five thousand Khasi-Pnar tribals have fled into Sahsniang in Jainita hills of Meghalaya as a result of the atrocities inflicted upon them by the United Peoples' Democratic Solidarity (UPDS) and the Karbi National Volunteers (KNV) militants. This has added a new chapter to the narrative on ethnic conflicts in India's northeast. Earlier too, following clashes between the Dimasas and the Hmars, Pnars (the displacement figure is not available in this case) had to flee across the border. Such recurrent internal displacement and consequent misery brought about on people, who are not directly involved in the conflict underlines the need for a greater understanding and cooperation between neighbouring states.

According to the 1991 census figures, the population of Khasi-Pnars in Assam was 11,358 out of which 8,452 were in Karbi Anglong and 2,906 were in the NC Hills district. Pnars, a sub-tribe of the Khasis have been settled in the Block I and Block II areas of Karbi Anglong's Hamren subdivision and constitute a minority among the six lakh Karbi population in the district.

Intelligence reports suggest that the current problem started when UPDS cadres started their extortion activities targeting the Khasi-Pnars in the Block I and Block II areas soon after HNLC (Hynniewtrep National Liberation Council) cadres crossed borders from their makeshift camps in the Khasi and Jaintia hills and served tax notices on the Karbi population. In the absence of law enforcement agencies, insurgent outfits in remote areas have been successful in carrying the mantle of protector of civilian rights. The UPDS, with its purported objective of establishing a land for the Karbis, thus targeted its ire against the Khasi-Pnars, who appeared to be working in tandem with the HNLC.

The problem has gotten intertwined with the boundary row between Assam and Meghalaya. The official stand of the Meghalaya government which confirmed that these areas belonged to Assam has been criticised by various organisations in the state. These organisations claim the Block I and Block II areas along the border for Meghalaya. In 1951, these areas had been transferred to the Karbi Anglong (then termed as United Mikir and North Kachar Hills) after slicing them from the erstwhile Khasi and Jaintia Hills district and these remained with the state even after the birth of Meghalaya in 1972.. Since then, the Khasi-Pnars of the area have often expressed their desire to be a part of Meghalaya.

During the ongoing debate over an individual state's claim over the areas, it has come to notice that even the villagers of one particular village, Psiar, which is well inside the Meghalaya boundary have been also been affected by UPDS extortion.. The whole village was deserted as the militant cadres threatened the villagers with death unless they paid up. The entire village was set afire after the villagers took refuge in Sahsniang.

There is also a growing feeling of ethnic exclusivity among the refugees, which is likely to create assimilation problems even if they return to their original villages. A Pnar refugee was quoted saying, "we have nothing against Assam or the Karbi people but our culture, language and habit was different from them. We are Khasi-Pnar community."

Different organizations have also been opportunistic in espousing their own interests at the current juncture. The Khasi Students Union (KSU) asked the Karbis in Meghalaya to leave the state. A few attacks were also reported on the Karbis and in one instance, on 17 November, a Karbi seminarian was set afire in Shillong by a KSU activist who managed to escape the law due to pressure from a partisan administration. On 25 November, three labourers working in a coalmine in Pohkyndong village in Jaintia hills district were abducted and killed by unidentified miscreants. Till recently, the KSU refused to backtrack on its quit notice served on the Karbis and dithered on negotiating with its counterpart in Karbi Anglong.

The Meghalaya government's proposal for a joint patrol along the border has been cold shouldered by the Assam government, lest it would legitimise the unofficial claim of Meghalaya over the areas. Ambiguity of successive leaders and their procrastination has provided a fillip to intermittent clashes. The sufferers have been the tribals, who stand to gain little whichever way the issue is decided.. There are similar problems between Assam, Nagaland and Arunachal Pradesh, which in the past have resulted in the loss of several lives. Such problems are likely to recur unless addressed quickly.

INSURGENCY

Insurgency in Meghalaya started as a movement against the domination of the 'dkhars' (outsiders). The Hynniewtrep Achik Liberation Council (HALC) represented the interests of the dominant tribes of the State, the Khasis, Jaintias and the Garos. However, tribal differences led to a split in the HALC in 1992 into the Hynniewtrep National Liberation Council (HNLC), representing the Khasis and the Jaintias, and the Achik Matgrik Liberation Army (AMLA) representing the Garos. The AMLA subsequently passed into oblivion to be replaced by the Achik National Volunteers Council (ANVC).

Whereas the HNLC aims at converting Meghalaya "as a province exclusively for the Khasi tribe and free it from 'domination' by the Garo tribe", the ANVC's purported objective is to "carve out a homeland called 'Achik Land' in the areas of Garo Hills." Both outfits entered into strategic alliance with other groups like the United Liberation Front of Asom (ULFA), the National Socialist Council of Nagaland-

Isak-Muivah (NSCN-IM) and the National Democratic Front of Bodoland (NDFB), in return for allowing them safe passage as well as providing them with safe houses in the hilly terrains of the State. HNLC's activities were restricted to the Khasi hills and several of its attacks took place in the State capital Shillong. On successive years, it called for boycott of the Independence Day celebrations on August 15 and its diktats had good impact on the people. Similarly, in Garo Hills, the ANVC held sway.

Sustained counter-insurgency operations, over the years, weakened both the outfits. Since July 23, 2004, the ANVC is under an extended ceasefire agreement with the government. Still, extortion in the West Khasi Hills, East Garo Hills and South Garo Hills districts is being carried out by the group. The militants of ANVC have established a finance-sharing understanding with the NSCN-IM targeting the coal belt areas of West Khasi Hills and East Garo Hill. Both ANVC and NSCN-IM are using newly formed militant outfits, like the Atong Liberation Army (ALA) in South Garo Hills, and Achik National Security Defence (ANSD) in West Khasi Hills, to maintain extortion drives in the coal-belt areas.

However, HNLC's top leadership, based in Bangladesh, continue to resist any type of peace deals. Many of its cadres, however, have either been arrested or have surrendered. While its top leadership continues to be based in Bangladesh, the outfit has been rendered incapable of orchestrating attacks. It received further setback with the July 24, 2007 surrender of the outfit's chairman Julius Dorphang. He, along with four other militants left the outfit's camp in Bangladesh's Maulvi Bazar district and surrendered to the authorities in Shillong.

Tough counter-insurgency operations and deterioration in its cadre strength have led HNLC to join hands with the National Liberation Front of Tripura (NLFT), with which it now runs an extortion network in the West Khasi Hills. The HNLC has also renewed its alliance with the NSCN-IM, particularly to retain control over HNLC cadres on the verge of surrender. Following the ceasefire agreement between the government and the ANVC and the subsequent confinement of the ANVC cadres in the designated camps, Garo Hills of

Meghalaya has been peaceful. Since 2004, taking advantage of the vacuum left open by the ANVC, several small outfits emerged and disappeared in quick succession. Prominent among them were the Retrieval Indigenous Unified Front (RIUF), United A'chik National Front (UANF), Hajong United Liberation Army (HULA) etc.

Similarly, the Hynniewtrep National Special Red Army (HNSRA) started operations in the Khasi Hills area. In early 2006, the Liberation Achik Elite Force (LAEF) was formed by a former police commando, Peter Marak. The outfit, which is known to have linkages with the National Socialist Council of Nagaland-Khaplang (NSCN-K), has been involved in few incidents in the Garo hills area. LAEF also maintains linkages with the NSCN-IM and ULFA.

Police operations against the LAEF met with a strategic success with the arrest of the outfit's chairman Peter Marak and two of his accomplices from a place between Jorabat and Khanapara near Assam capital Dispur on August 21, 2007. On December 7, 2008, LAEF suffered a setback with the killing of its 'commander-in-chief', Kimrey K. Sangma, during an encounter with security forces at Damit village near Shahlang in the West Khasi Hills district. Earlier, on July 1, 2008, Police recovered the dead body of the then 'commander-in-chief' of the outfit, Nicheng Sangma alias Daria Sangma. He was killed during an intra-outfit clash at Parasin in the East Garo Hills district.

On November 18, 2008 nine senior LAEF cadres, including an 'area commander' were arrested from a newly set up camp at Kadambari in the Ri-Bhoi district along Meghalaya-Assam border. In 2008, a total of 23 LAEF militants were arrested and two surrendered to the security forces.

Between 1992 and 2009 (till July), at least 383 insurgency related fatalities were recorded in Meghalaya. The militancy related fatalities have been showing a continuously diminishing trend since 2003. From 79 fatalities in 2003, the number reduced to 12 in 2008. There was no civilian fatality in 2008 (Source: www.satp.org). According to police records, a total of 105 militants were neutralized in the state in 2008.

Of these, 78 were arrested, 15 surrendered and 11 others were killed.

Meghalaya continues to provide transit passage to groups like the ULFA in their journey between Bangladesh and Assam. The outfit is known to have set up safe houses in the Garo hills region and often stores arms and ammunition in the area. Further, Meghalaya's Block-I and Block-II areas adjoining Assam have witnessed extortion activities by outfits such as the United People's Democratic Solidarity (UPDS). Again, Pakistan's external intelligence agency, the Inter-Services Intelligence (ISI), is also reported to be consolidating its network in Meghalaya. The state capital Shillong is becoming a hub for trading of illegal small arms and explosives, which are brought through the Garo hills or Mizoram.

PEACE EFFORTS

The Church has played a crucial role towards peace in Meghalaya. While the Shillong Khasi Jaintia Church Leaders Forum was officially designated as the negotiator with the HNLC, the Garo Baptist Convention was instrumental in bringing the ANVC to the peace talks. In 2003, individuals like Garo politician and former speaker of the Lok Sabha P A Sangma offered to mediate between the State and the ANVC. However, the proposal was not acceptable to the state government. Similarly, in the same year, Mizoram Chief Minister Zoramthanga offered to negotiate with the State. His proposal was rejected by the state government which said that it will not allow any back door negotiation.

ANVC signed an extended tripartite ceasefire agreement with the Central and the state Government on July 23, 2004. The HNLC had come close to starting a peace process with the state government in 2006. In the last week of April 2006, the HNLC chairman Dorphang requested Chief Minister D. D. Lapang to urge the Centre to expedite the peace process. However, opinion of the state police was not in favour of starting the peace process with the outfit and it prevailed upon the Union Ministry of Home Affairs which delayed the starting of the dialogue. The outfit eventually backtracked from the process citing the state government's permission to the public sector undertaking, the Uranium Corporation of India Ltd, for uranium mining at Domiasiat in the West Khasi Hills district. Again in October 2008, the HNLC rejected an offer for peace talks by the state government saying that it has no agenda to hold talks with the state government or state police department as they are only actors of the Indian government.

However, compared to other northeastern states, Meghalaya is quite peaceful. A latest report of the Ministry of Home Affairs in June 2009 states that Meghalaya, Mizoram and Tripura are having the lowest insurgency-related activities in the Northeast.

WAR ON TERRORISM: ADDRESS THE NORTH-EASTERN CONCERNS

As the world prepares to launch a crusade against terrorism, a country like India has to ponder over a point or two before committing itself to the global war. A moment needs to be spared to take a fresh look at the multiple challenges terrorism poses to the various parts of the country, especially in the north-eastern region. The current global movement shows signs of focusing only on the Islamic aspect of terrorism and leaves untouched vast unhighlighted theatres of conflict which account for the loss of hundreds of lives and property.

Brands of insurgency or terrorism, whether actively promoted by foreign powers or clandestinely assisted by the parties having a stake in the destabilisation of the country, have a tendency to cooperate and compliment each other. In India northeast region, insurgent outfits such as the United Liberation Front of Asom (ULFA) and both factions of the National Socialist Council of Nagaland (NSCN), fighting for independent homelands, have received assistance from the neighbouring countries. The forms of assistance range from supply of arms and ammunition and other logistical support to provision of a safe haven, camping and training facilities. There have been on the record statements, in the Indian parliament, pointing accusing fingers at the role of foreign powers in fermenting trouble in the region.

The Inter Services Intelligence (ISI) of Pakistan, in the past, has been accused of promoting Islamic terrorism in the north-eastern States like Assam. Even the ULFA continues to have certain linkages with the ISI. Unconfirmed reports in December 2000 suggested that the ULFA commander-in-chief, Paresh Baruah enjoyed the hospitality of the ISI in Pakistan after the Chittagong shoot out incident earlier that month. The ULFAÃ¢â‚¬â„¢s call to all Assamese soldiers fighting in the Kargil war to return home is a pointer towards the deeper understanding the outfit enjoys with the ISI.

The Chinese army has been named by the Union Minister of State for Home Affairs, I D Swami to be providing arms to the insurgents of the NSCN-IM. ULFA along with other outfits such as the National Democratic Front of Bodoland (NDFB), the National Liberation Front of Tripura (NLFT), the Kamatapur Liberation Organisation (KLO) operate from the comfort of the camps in Bangladesh and Bhutan, away from the onslaught of the security forces. Cox Bazar in Bangladesh has emerged as a major port for supply of illegal arms and ammunition worth crores of rupees to the insurgent outfits of the region. Due to the tense terrain, even an India friendly country like Bhutan, finds it difficult to remove the camps of ULFA and NDFB from its territory. Thus, there emerges a scenario, where India is forced to confront just not a group of insurgent outfits but also of foreign assistance.

It also needs to be emphasised that the north-eastern states of Assam, Nagaland, Manipur and Tripura accounted for 1578 lives in the year 2000, in spite of the Union Government's ongoing peace talks with two prominent outfits such as the NSCN-IM and the Bodo Liberation Tigers (BLT). While the world current focus on the terrorists out of their holes genuinely accommodates the Indian concern in Kashmir, what remains unattended is a large area threatened by a conglomerate of divisive and destabilising interests.

In the grand war against terrorism, India needs to reorient its policy for a holistic fight that addresses its concerns including those in the north-eastern region. As we commit ourselves not just to address the specificity of the problem but to reach its roots, focusing only on Kashmir and the Islamic aspect of terrorism would only be a halfway approach. Our journey to the roots should take us not only to the terrorist camps of Pakistan and Afghanistan, but also to Bangladesh, Bhutan, China and Myanmar. The need is, thus, to enter into meaningful and durable dialogue with the power elites of the concerned countries for seeking their support for India integrity. As a follow up the country could plan to introduce legislation at the United Nations to cover all contingencies and threats. The ongoing wave against terrorism would then prevent the State actors from promoting terror combination of successive events has provided India with an opportunity to wipe out the evils of terrorism. While the world can afford to be partisan and to be mired in the anti-Taliban agenda, India needs to adopt a comprehensive approach that addresses its broader security concerns.

3

Insurgent Groups in Meghalaya

ACHIK NATIONAL VOLUNTEER COUNCIL (ANVC)

FORMATION

The Achik National Volunteer Council (ANVC) was formed in December 1995. It was proscribed on November 16, 2000. The outfit, signed a ceasefire agreement with the Govenrment of India on JUly 23, 2004.

OBJECTIVES

The ANVC aims to carve out a homeland called 'Achik Land' in the areas of Garo Hills. The proposed 'Achik Land' comprises the present districts of Garo Hills in Meghalaya and a large chunk of Kamrup and Goalpara district of Assam. The 'Garo majority' in these areas is used as the argument for this demand. The ANVC differs from the other Garo separatist organisation, Garo National Council (GNC), which aims for a Garo State comprising only the three districts of the Garo hills.

LEADERSHIP

Dilash R. Marak is the 'Chairman' of the ANVC. The outfit's 'Commander-in-Chief' is Jerome Momin. Among the other leaders are 'General Secretary', Wanding R. Marak, 'Publicity Secretary', Artist Sengsrang Sangma, 'Joint Secretary', Janggam Momin, and 'Finance Secretary' Rickie Sangma. The outfit divides its area of operation into several zones and each zone is headed by a 'commander'. The cadres who function as commanders of different zones are: Chenang

Marak (Eastern Zone), Goran Sangma (Southern Zone), Batjang Shera (Western Zone), Ranggam Marak (West Khasi Hills). Area commanders function below the zonal commanders in the operational hierarchy. Sohan D. Shira functions as the 'Area Commander' of Williamnagar.

The leadership maintains strict vigil on the activities of its cadres. This was manifest in the threats it issued in the year 2000 to its surrendering cadres, who were doing so under the rehabilitation package announced by the Union Government in the year 1998-99, and their family members. The outfit also warned them not to join any other outfit.

AREA OF OPERATION

The ANVC, during its active days, was active in the Garo Hills and in certain parts of the West Khasi Hills. It maintained its headquarters at Cheram in the Garo hills area. Among its activities were extortion from the business community in the name of 'fund collection'. Besides that, the outfit also pumped fake currency into circulation.

LINKAGES

The outfit was reportedly formed with the assistance of the National Socialist Council of Nagaland–Issak Muivah (NSCN-IM). However, it has severed its entire links with the Naga outfit as well as with the National Democratic Front of Bodoland (NDFB). The outfit now maintains links with the United Liberation Front of Asom (ULFA), especially after the latter wound up some of its camps in Bhutan and is in the process of relocating them in the Garo Hills. The ANVC has some of its camps in Bangladesh.

It is also involved in fake currency circulation initiated by the Inter Services Intelligence (ISI), Pakistan's external intelligence agency. In Meghalaya, ANVC, along with the other prominent outfit, HNLC, abets this infusion of fake currency and in turn receives considerable operating funds. Extortion remains the major source of funding for the ANVC. Incidents of abduction are frequent in the state. Money is regularly collected from the trading community of the area in the name of 'fund collection'. However, extortion remains the major source of funding for the ANVC. Incidents of abduction are frequent in the State. Money is regularly collected from the trading community of the area in the name of 'fund collection'.

PEACE PROCESS

On July 23, 2004 a cease-fire agreement was signed between the Government of India and the ANVC for a period of six months. A seven member ANVC team, with the notable absence of Chairman Dilash Marak and Commander-in-Chief Jerome Momin signed the agreement in New Delhi. The agreement has since been periodically extended.

A ceasefire-monitoring cell has been set up at the Coal India Complex at Araimile in Tura, headquarter of the West Garo Hills district. Two designated camps for housing the surrendered militants have also been set up at Samada and Chokpot in the Garo Hills region.

INCIDENTS

2010

- *October 6*: The State Government will submit its final views on the various demands of the ANVC to the Union Government within three months. "The Government is examining the outfit's memorandum in which the demand for creation of a Garoland Autonomous Council in Garo Hills is made," Chief Secretary W.M.S Pariat. "We will submit our views to the Centre within three months," Pariat said. The ceasefire between the Union Government and the ANVC was extended without any time frame on September 30.
- *September 14*: The ANVC said the outfit is ready to support the civic elections in Garo Hills if it did not harm the interest of the Garo people. "We may support the election provided it does not reduce the status of Garo people in the municipal areas," ANVC spokesperson Torik Jangning Marak said. He, however, said the Government should first settle the

ANVC issue before going for the civic elections in Garo Hills in view of the outfit''s demand for constitution of ''Garoland Autonomous District Council'' in the line of the Bodoland Territorial Area Council in Assam.

- *August 30*: Meghalaya Government would go for peace talks with the ANVC. State Chief Secretary W.M.S. Pariat said, "We are trying to expedite the entire talk process." While defending the Government for the delay in talks, the Chief Secretary said, "These matters require a lot of ground work and hence the delay."
- *August 29*: The Meghalaya Government assured the ANVC of releasing the funds for maintaining the outfit's designated camps. "We are committed to release the funds by Tuesday," State Chief Secretary W.M.S. Pariat said.
- *August 25*: The Union Home Minister, P. Chidambaram said that it is a matter of great satisfaction that a number of groups are engaged in talks with the Government of India. Among them are National Socialist Council of Nagaland-Isak-Muivah (NSCN-IM), pro-talk faction of the National Democratic Front of Bodoland (NDFB), Nunisa faction of the Dima Halim Daogah (DHD), Black Widow (BW), United People's Democratic Solidarity (UPDS), Achik National Volunteer Council (ANVC), Karbi Longri North Cachar Hills Liberation Front (KLNLF), Kuki National Organization (KNO) and United Peoples Front (UPF), he said. H further added, "We have appointed two Interlocutors: RS Pandey to talk to the NSCN (IM) and PC Haldar to talk to NDFB (PT), DHD (Nunisa), DHD (J), KLNLF, UPDS and ANVC, besides ULFA [United Liberation Front of Asom]."
- *August 24*: The ANVC claimed that the outfit's designated camps are in serious crisis due to non-availability of funds for several months. The ANVC

submitted a letter to Chief Minister Mukul Sangma through West Garo Hills Deputy Commissioner Sanjay Goyal to intervene in the matter. "We have not received even a single penny in the last 10 months from the Central Government to maintain our camps...The fund flow was smooth when it was coming directly from the Union Home Ministry," ANVC spokesperson Torik Jangning Marak said.

- *July 22*: A delegation of the Nongalbibra Coal Merchants Association (NCMA) met the leaders of the ANVC to clarify the recent reports about the outfit's alleged involvement in connection with the ongoing coal export trade and agreed that it was blown out of proportion, according to Shillong Times. Leaders of the NCMA, led by its president Kennedy Marak and general secretary Willibirth R. Sangma along with other office bearers called on ANVC 'publicity secretary' Arist Sengsrang N. Sangma at Williamnagar in East Garo Hills District and stated that the recent statement by the NCMA against the ANVC was created by a section of vested interest groups that were bent on creating a rift and trouble in the Garo Hills. The ANVC leader on his part reiterated that the organisation stood for the well being of the people of Garo Hills.
- *July 8*: A delegation of the ANVC met Meghalaya Chief Minister Mukul Sangma and submitted a memorandum including the key demand for creation of a Garoland Territorial Council on the lines of the Bodoland Territorial Council in Assam. ANVC spokesperson Torik Jangning Marak said, "The talks are going in the right direction and we are hopeful of an early solution to our demands."
- *June 30*: The ANVC asked for indefinite extension of ceasefire agreement with the Union Government. The ceasefire term between the Government and the outfit expires after a three-month extension in March 2010. The Union Government extended the tripartite cease-

fire agreement with the Achik National Volunteer Council (ANVC) for another three months. "It has been agreed that the SoO [Suspension of Operation] with ANVC which was expired today would be extended for a further period of three months from tomorrow," an official statement issued on June 30 said. The discussions on the demands of ANVC are on at the level of P.C. Halder, the interlocutor for peace talks with the outfit, the statement added.

- *June 29*: Shillong Times reports that the ANVC has started shifting its cadres to "undisclosed camps". ANVC spokesp-erson Torik Jangning Marak said, "The Government has not given us any clear indication on the extension of the truce and so we have shifted our cadres to undisclosed camps for their security." Admitting that they have got positive signal from the Centre for the extension of the truce, Marak said, "We are waiting for the recommendation of the State Government and will soon meet the Government." The ceasefire would expire on June 30. The report adds that there are around 175 cadres of the ANVC in outfit"s camps in different places of Garo Hills.
- *June 22*: The ANVC claimed that the outfit's cease-fire with both the Centre and the State was for an indefinite period and not for the three months agreed upon on March 23 in New Delhi.
- *June 6*: Sentinel reports that 13 militant organizations from the Northeast States of Assam, Manipur, Tripura and Meghalaya figure in the list of banned organizations as it appears in the website of the Union Home Ministry (MHA). The ULFA heads the list. The other outfits were: NDFB, People's Liberation Army (PLA), and United National Liberation Front (UNLF), People's Revolutionary party of Kangleipak (PREPAK), Kangleipak Communist Party (KCP), Kanglei Yaol Kanna Lup (KYKL), Manipur People's Liberation Front (MPLF), Revolutionary People's

Front (RPF), All Tripura Tiger Force (ATTF), National Liberation Front of Tripura (NLFT) Hynniewtrep National Liberation Council (HNLC) and ANVC. Hardly 20 days left for expiry of the cease-fire agreement between the ANVC and the Union Government, the insurgent outfit said it would prefer short-term extension of the agreement. ANVC spokesperson Torik Jangning Marak said, "We are likely to seek three months extension of the ceasefire agreement." The report adds that the next meeting between the ANVC and the Centre's interlocutor P.C. Haldar would be held in June 2010.

- *May 31*: The ANVC submitted a 12-page memorandum to the Union Government, spelling out the details of its demand for setting up a Garo Autonomous Council.
- *May 26*: Meghalaya Chief Minister Mukul Sangma met Centre's interlocutor P. C. Haldar. After the meeting, the Chief Minster said the State Government is still examining various demands of the ANVC including creation of a separate Garoland autonomous council. The report adds that the cease-fire agreement between the group and the Government was extended for another three months in March 2010 and the Garo group also had a meeting with Haldar in Shillong on March 16 to discuss their different demands. The outfit earlier had also threatened to break the tripartite cease-fire agreement with the Centre, if the latter fails to fulfill their various demands.
- *April 30*: Police sources reports that ANVC is currently divided into three groups. Police said that the first major group belongs to those cadres whose primary interest is to be rich by means of extortion. "Most of the cadres belonging to this group have already associated themselves with the new militant outfit GNLA [Garo National Liberation Army] led by Meghalaya Police 'DSP' Champion R. Marak,"

Police sources said on April 30. The GNLA has been under the Police scanner for serving extortion notes, ranging from INR 500, 000 to ten million, to petrol pump owners, coal dealers and businessmen in the coal-rich Districts of Garo Hills. Police sources said the second group includes mostly the top leaders, who are involved in peace talks with the Government. "These top leaders of the ANVC are also living lavish lifestyle," Police sources added. On the other hand, the third group with a very few numbers includes those who wanted to return to the mainstream. "Most of them are ANVC members for namesake only. They are fed up with the outfit's activities," Police sources said. Meghalaya Governor R. S. Mooshahary earlier stated that "ANVC is losing its strength and credibility."

- *April 5*: ANVC asked the Meghalaya Police to set up a cell to monitor the movement of deserters who have joined other militant groups and are allegedly engaging in extortion.
- *March 28*: Pakchara R. Sangma, a 'Deputy Superintendent of Police (DSP)' of the Meghalaya Police, who remained missing for the last many months, issued a press statement 'confirming' himself as the 'chairman' of the GNLA outfit and threatened to take on the ANVC, accusing its of 'harassing' the weaker sections of the Garo society.
- *March 22*: The meeting of the Joint Monitoring Group (JMG) on extension of cease-fire with the Meghalaya based ANVC was held in New Delhi. The Centre extended the cease-fire with the ANVC by three months. "A revised ceasefire agreement was signed by ANVC at the meeting of Joint Ceasefire Monitoring Group held in New Delhi," an official source said. Sources said ANVC assured "to adhere to the ceasefire ground rules and have better control on the camps and the cadre".
- *March 19*: The Meghalaya Governor R. S. Mooshahary

expressed concern over mushrooming of militant groups in Garo hills and the activities of Assam-based outfits along the border. The Governor said that recent developments, such as reports on the formation of militant groups in Garo hills, were a cause of concern. Other militant groups active in Garo hills are LAEF, People's Liberation Front of Meghalaya (PLF-M), Achik National Security Defence (ANSD), Atong Liberation Army (ALA), and United Achik National Front (UANF). ULFA and NDFB are also active in Garo hills and border of Ri Bhoi District. The Governor said that the Government was committed to contain militancy at all costs. The Governor added that the security establishment of the State has acted swiftly to break up and contain the activities of the Hynniewtrep Liberation Front (HLF) in Khasi hills, and LAEF in the Garo hills. He said the activities of the local militant organisations like the HNLC and ANVC have been substantially controlled.

- *March 18*: A senior Police Officer of Meghalaya in the rank of Deputy Superintendent of Police (DSP) joined the GNLA, the newly formed militant outfit in Garo Hills. According to sources, DSP Champion R. Marak recently joined the outfit after he had gone missing for quite sometime. He joined the Police Force in 2004 and belonged to Songsak region of East Garo Hills. The report adds that GNLA is being led by the DSP Champion Marak while former ANVC 'area commander' of East Garo Hills, Sohan D. Shira, is believed to be the 'commander in chief'. The group is also said to be in close ties with the NSCN-IM and presently has 20 well-armed cadres who have recently served extortion notes demanding huge amounts of ransom in East and South Garo Hills. The group is also trying to wean away many of the disgruntled ANVC cadres who are annoyed with their leadership over the handling of the ongoing peace process.

- *March 17*: The Centre has expressed concern over violation of conditions of the cease-fire with the ANVC. Meghalaya Chief Minister D.D. Lapang, who called on Union Home Minister P. Chidambaram in New Delhi, apprised him of the outcome of March 16 talks between the ANVC and Centre's interlocutor P C Haldar. Chidambaram told the Chief Minister that there had been instances of violation of conditions of the suspension of operation (SoO). But at the same time the Centre would like to continue the SoO with the outfit, he said. Chidambaram assured that all necessary steps would be taken by the Centre to maintain peace and tranquillity in Meghalaya. The Home Minister asked Lapang to assess the ground realities and suggest suitable measures for the successful culmination of the peace process. The ANVC said that the group would seek public opinion whether the group would go for periodic cease-fire or indefinite cease-fire.
- *March 16*: The ANVC, after meeting the Centre's interlocutor P.C. Haldar in Shillong, withdrew the threat of pulling out from the cease-fire agreement and agreed to Centre's proposal for periodic agreement with a validity of three months. After the talks, ANVC "spokesperson" Torik Jangning Marak said the outfit would not pull out from the ceasefire as "it would affect the prevailing peaceful atmosphere of Garo Hills". "ANVC is not pulling out from the agreement yet we are not happy about as it was a unilateral decision which was taken in the last meeting to have periodic ceasefire," he said. Meanwhile, Telegraph reports that the Centre decided to examine the ANVC's demand for an autonomous body like a Garoland Territorial Council.
- *March 15*: The ANVC agreed to sit for peace talks with the Union Government in Shillong, capital of Meghalaya. The ANVC 'publicity secretary' Arist Sangma said they had agreed to come to Shillong

for the talks with the Centre''s interlocutor P. C. Haldar following a request from the Meghalaya Government.

- *March 14*: The ANVC asked for holding the peace talks at Tura in West Garo Hills District instead of capital Shillong. "We have received a letter from the government that the talks with Haldar will be held in Shillong, but we want the meeting to be held in Tura," the ANVC publicity secretary Arist Sangma said. "As our demands are concerning Garo Hills, the interlocutor should come to Tura instead of Shillong to hold the discussion," he explained. "There is a need to have a change in the venue and we hope that the government will look into the matter," Sangma said.
- *March 13*: The ANVC denied its involvement in the abduction of a coal trader Nokma Chongrin Marak of Garo Hills and instead accused the GNLA outfit of attempting to derail the ongoing peace process. The ANVC 'spokesperson' and 'chief organising secretary' Torik Jangning Marak said, "We are in the negotiating table for the last 6 years having shunned the path of violence with a positive attitude and opting for a permanent solution. The allegation (by GNLA) is a desperate attempt to derail the peace process." "ANVC chairman Dilash Marak has no hand in the abduction of Nokma Chongrin Marak and most of the extortions and demand notes are being served by the new outfit (GNLA). Soon we will send representatives to the government for a joint operation in Garo Hills," Torik Jangning Marak said.
- *March 11*: Meghalaya Deputy Chief Minister Mukul Sangma asked Union Home Minister P. Chidambaram to initiate all steps for peace and development of the Garo Hill Districts for a logical conclusion of the tripartite accord with the ANVC. After meeting Chidambaram, the Deputy Chief Minister said following the suspension of operations

against the militants way back in July 2004, there was an overall improvement of law-and-order situation in the region. "But there is confusion and uncertainties in Garo Hill due to the indication of expiry of the 'suspension of operation' (SoO) on March 31 by the Home Ministry," he pointed out.

- *March 8*: The ANVC said that it would seek a plebiscite on whether to continue with the tripartite peace talks, after the Centre took an 'arbitrary' decision to extend the cease-fire only periodically.
- *March 7*: A three-day conclave of the ANVC concluded at Balonggre, in the outskirts of Tura town in West Garo Hills District. The conclave was attended by a conglomerate of Non Governmental Organisations, student and social organizations, church elders, senior citizens, public representatives from Assam and political activists from Meghalaya to discuss ways to push forward the tripartite peace talks. The people who attended the conclave expressed apprehension over the last Joint Monitoring Group (JMG) meet between the ANVC, Meghalaya Government and Union Government at Tura in which the central delegation was in favour of a periodical cease-fire extension in place of an indefinite one citing violation of ground rules. In the JMG meeting, the Government delegation had accused the ANVC of giving its support to a new militant group- Garo National Liberation Army (GNLA) and engaging in sporadic extortion, an accusation the outfit denied. The ANVC, on the other hand, has expressed disappointment that its charter of demands with its main focus of creating a Garoland Territorial Council has not been seriously considered which, according to the group, is a 'benign' and 'reasonable' demand within the ambit of the Indian Constitution.
- *February 23*: The Union Government modified the previous decision of indefinite cease-fire extension

with the ANVC to that of periodical extensions in a Joint Monitoring Group (JMG) meeting at Tura.

- *February 7*: Meghalaya Chief Minister D.D. Lapang in the Conference of Chief Ministers on Internal Security asked the Centre to go for a tripartite political and development accord with the ANVC to bring the ongoing peace process to a logical conclusion. He also stated that insurgent outfits like ULFA, National Socialist Council of Nagaland, NDFB and UPDS are not only supporting groups like LAEF, but also providing them arms, ammunition and training. He said that insurgent outfits both from the Northeast and adjoining Bangladesh were also using the peaceful State of Meghalaya both as temporary sanctuary and corridor. Lapang further claimed that both ANVC and HNLC have been largely neutralised with a sustained Police operation. But passive militancy is still a cause for concern, he further added.
- *January 3*: The ANVC accuses the Union Government of delaying discussion on its demand for constitution of a separate Garoland Autonomous Council (GAC), a self-governing body for the Garo Hills. The ANVC 'publicity secretary' Arist Sengsrang Sangma said, "We have come down from our demand for a separate Garoland and now the Centre should initiate discussion to facilitate the creation of the council."

2009

- *December 11*: The ANVC outfit states that its fight for a separate Garoland would gain momentum with the Centre initiating the process for the creation of Telangana. The outfit's 'publicity secretary', Arist Sangma, said with the Centre taking steps to create a Telangana State, the outfit's demand would also be justified in the days to come. "Our demand is very much genuine and we are not asking for the sun or moon, but a separate state within India unlike other militant groups, which are demanding sovereignty," Sangma said.

- *September 29*: Meghalaya Police has reportedly sought the help of the ANVC to neutralise other militant groups in the Garo Hills. The ANVC leader Arist Sangma said that the outfit was ready to help the Meghalaya Police.
- *September 14*: The ANVC demanded an autonomous status for the Garo hills with "less or no interference" from the Meghalaya Government. The 'publicity secretary' of the ANVC, Arist Sengsrang Sangma, suggested the creation of an autonomous body like "Garoland Territorial Council" which can govern itself without any interference from the State Government. According to Sangma, the idea of formation of a "Garoland Territorial Council" for Garo hills, in line with the Bodoland Territorial Council (BTC), was welcome, but there should be less interference from the State Government and more autonomy to the body, unlike the BTC. "We are yet to suggest any name for the autonomous body, which can politically safeguard the interests of the people of Garo hills with more powers, wider functions and without the interference of the state government," Sangma said. "By autonomy to Garo hills, we do not mean the one prevailing in the existing Garo Hills Autonomous District Council, which is still under the direct supervision of the state government," he added. He also said that once autonomy for Garo hills was realised, the militant group would demand direct funding from the Centre, unlike the present District Councils in the State which get funds from the State Government. Responding to a suggestion made by the Joint Secretary (in charge of Northeast) of the Union Ministry of Home Affairs to abandon the outfit's demand for a separate State, Sangma said that though there was no change of stand on the statehood demand, the outfit was open to talks for

the autonomous status to Garo hills. "The joint secretary, home, in charge of Northeast, told us that the Centre does not want to divide the Northeast further," he adds. To some extent, the ANVC agreed to this, but the militant group would negotiate with the Centre on what arrangement it would provide to the Garo hills for the outfit to give up its demand for a separate Garo State, he mentioned.

- *September 10*: The Centre is reported to have rejected a demand for a separate Garo State by the ANVC, when the Joint Secretary (in-charge of Northeast) of the Union Ministry of Home Affairs, Naveen Verma, held a series of meetings with senior State Government officials and discussed a rehabilitation package for the ANVC. Verma is understood to have made it clear that if the ANVC wants a rehabilitation package, it has to leave aside its demand for Garoland, a separate State comprising three Districts of Garo Hills region in Meghalaya. The Centre has asked the group to furnish a fresh list of demands concerning rehabilitation of its cadres. The Centre has also asked the State Government to monitor whether the insurgent group was adhering to the cease-fire ground rules.

2008

- *December 3*: Shillong Times quoting police source reports that the ANVC is carrying out an extortion drive with support from the NSCN-IM in the coal belt areas of West Khasi Hills and East Garo Hills. According to police sources, the activities of ANVC and NSCN-IM are at their peak during the winter season as this is the period when a large quantity of coal is exported to Bangladesh resulting in a huge business transaction. "The ANVC and NSCN (IM) equally share the extorted amount," police sources state.
- *November 23*: Meghalaya Police said that the newly

formed militant outfits, the Atong Liberation Army (ALA) in South Garo Hills, and Achik National Security Defence (ANSD) in West Khasi Hills, are being used by the NSCN-IM and ANVC for carrying out an extortion drive in coal belt areas. Police sources said the ALA and ANSD were extorting money from coal-laden trucks and coal exporters in West Khasi Hills and South Garo Hills. "We have already started our operations to destroy these two militant outfits before they could manage to make their presence felt in the State," sources said.

- *October 17*: Police recover explosives, a camera, CDs and incriminating documents, including demand notes, belonging to ANVC from a rented house at Chinengree village near Shahlang in the West Khasi Hills district. The documents recovered from the house indicate that money was extorted by the outfit from various parts of the district. The ANVC cadres, however, manage to escape from the incident site.
- *July 23*: The Union Government extends the cease-fire with the ANVC for an indefinite period for the first time, unlike the earlier periodical review of the cease-fire with the militant group.
- *May 29*: Surrendered ANVC cadres asked the Meghalaya Government to provide them with recruitment in 5th India Reserve Battalion and monetary assistance. They also alleged that the former State Government did not have the commitment to rehabilitate all surrendered insurgents. They say that the previous D.D. Lapang-led Government had given "more importance" to the Shillong-based former cadre of the HNLC than those from the Garo Hills. The former ANVC cadres have sought Government jobs for at least 25 of them and financial assistance for the others to start their own entrepreneurship.
- *May 28*: The LAEF's new 'commander-in-chief' Daria Sangma, while speaking to the media over phone,

reconfirms the Meghalaya Police's claim that the LAEF has forged ties with the Assam-based Black Widow (BW) outfit. He said that it was in the interest of consolidating LAEF to pursue its goal of a 'separate Garo state'. The report added that a group of five LAEF cadres recently returned from arms training organised by the BW in Assam. Daria also said the Garo outfit had recently held a general council meeting in the West Khasi Hills in which he was appointed the new 'army chief' in the presence of LAEF 'chairman' Darong T. Marak who, according to police, had been killed by his own colleagues long ago. The LAEF general council meeting is said to have also appointed one Khanam D. Shira as 'general secretary' of the outfit, besides a former ANVC cadre Nikseng Sangma holding an important portfolio within the group. Nikseng had deserted the ANVC and joined with former ANVC 'eastern area commander' Sohan D. Shira to help the LAEF during the early days of its formation. Following the killing of the then 'chairman' Peter Marak in the hands of police and subsequent surrender of Sohan before the government, Nikseng reportedly fled into the LAEF stronghold of West Khasi Hills. Daria also says tells the media that the general council meeting had taken up several resolutions one of which was to turn 'pro-active' in its operations against certain organisations aligning with the government to wipe out the outfit.

- *April 7*: One ANVC militant, Amjad A. Sangma, is arrested by the Meghalaya Police during a search operation at Williamnagar in the East Garo Hills district. One 9-mm pistol was recovered from his possession.
- *February 29*: The Congress party candidate Mukul Sangma complained to the Returning Officer that the ANVC and police are aiding the National Congress Party candidates from Ampati constituency in the Garo Hills. Mukul said that ANVC cadres led by

Ronald Sangma threatened people and Amapati police station officer in-charge A.M. Sangma had taken no cognizance of the offence. He mentioned that his supporters were also assaulted.

- *February 28*: The ANVC said that it will remain neutral in the Legislative Assembly elections scheduled to be held on March 3, 2008. In a letter signed by 'chairman' Dilash Marak alias S. M. Marak, the outfit stated: "Rumours will always be there and the ANVC respect and recognise the people's 'Right' to choose their own representatives and shall remain neutral as far as the 2008 assembly elections are concerned."
- *January 20*: One ANVC cadre, Dorang G. Momin, is arrested by the Meghalaya police personnel when they neutralise a hideout at Tarajak village in the West Khasi Hills district. However, 10 militants, including two persons belonging to the Naga community, managed to escape from the incident site. An AK-47 rifle and an M-16 rifle, other arms and ammunition are recovered from the hideout.

2007

- *December 12*: The Joint Monitoring Committee meeting of the representatives of the ANVC, Meghalaya Government and Union Ministry of Home Affairs (MHA) was held in the national capital New Delhi. The meeting expressed concern over the reported extortion being carried out by the outfit and stressed the need to strictly adhere to ground rules of the cease-fire agreement signed on July 23, 2004.
- *November 22*: Shillong Times reports that the 'organising secretary' of the ANVC, identified as Bernard N. Marak alias Torik Jangnang, is released. On August 17, he was arrested for his involvement in extortion at Tura market in the West Garo Hills district, and was later lodged in the Jowai jail under the Meghalaya Preventive Detention Act for almost three months.

- *September 9*: An unidentified civilian is shot dead by suspected militants at Chachatgre in the East Garo Hills district. He was reportedly working as a domestic help of Sohan D. Shira, a surrendered ANVC leader.
- *September 6*: One Achik National Liberation Front Army militant, Nabat Marak, is shot dead by suspected ANVC militants at Chidimit village near Songsak in the East Garo Hills district. Meghalaya Police stated that ANVC militants after killing Marak buried his body at the village. He reportedly deserted the ANVC in 2005 and later joined the Achik National Liberation Front Army outfit.
- *August 25*: A self-styled 'area commander' of the ANVC, identified as Sohan D. Shira, surrenders in an unspecified place in Meghalaya.
- *August 17*: The organising secretary of the ANVC, Bernard Marak, is arrested from Tura in the West Garo Hills district on charges of extortion. Police said several complaints had been lodged against Marak, also known as Torik Jangang, by the truckers. Three of his associates arrested on August 16 had also confessed to their involvement in the racket. They had been collecting INR 20 each from each truck plying in Tura posing themselves as members of the truckers' association. Marak was also manning the liaison office of the militant group at Tura.
- *May 23*: The Unlawful Activities (Prevention) Tribunal extended the ban on the ANVC and HNLC for two more years due to their continued anti-national and anti-social activities. The new order will remain in force till May 15, 2009.
- *April 14*: The two-day meeting of the Tribunal to look into the proscription on the HNLC and ANVC concluded. Official sources said that there was no representation from the HNLC and only the ANVC contested the case aiming at lifting the proscription.
- *January 17*: An ANVC cadre, Onkang Sangma, who

had deserted the camp at Chokpot in the South Garo Hills district in 2006, surrenders at Williamnagar in the East Garo Hills district.

2006

- *November 9*: The Union Government extends the proscription on ANVC.
- *October 25*: The ANVC fails to respond to the appeal made by Meghalya Chief Minister, J. D. Rymbai, and Home Minister, R. G. Lyngdoh, to lay down arms, before the State Government could convince the Union Government to lift the ban imposed on the outfit, indicates report.
- *September 28*: The ANVC decides to discuss with the Meghalaya Government the conditions of disarmament for lifting the ban on the outfit. "We will have to discuss the matter before taking any decision in this regard," said 'publicity secretary' Arist Sangma.
- *September 11*: The newly formed Garo outfit, Achik National Liberation Front Army (ANLFA), allegedly accuse the Meghalaya Government of being soft on the ANVC, which is currently under a cease-fire with the Union and State Governments. The ANLFA alleges that the State Government is turning a blind eye to the 'atrocities' committed by the ANVC cadres in Garo Hills.
- *August 31*: The self-styled 'chairman' of the ANVC, Dilash Marak, figures in the list of wanted militants, residing in Bangladesh, handed over by the Border Security Force (BSF) to the Bangladesh Rifles (BDR) during their meeting in Shillong.
- *August 31*: Two political parties, the Hill State People's Democratic Party from Khasi Hills and Garo National Council from Garo Hills, at a joint statement demand the creation of separate provinces for the two major tribes of the State. Both the parties are opposed to the idea of 'Greater Garoland' demanded

by the ANVC. However, the ANVC criticizes the joint proclamation of the two parties as a "political propaganda".

- *August 28*: The ANVC states that it has discussed the issue of Garo Hills with the Union Government in New Delhi in July 2006. The 'publicity secretary' of the outfit, Arist Sangma, said, "We submitted our memorandum and said separate Garoland was our demand."
- *August 8*: Meghalaya Government starts the Disaster Awareness and Search and Rescue Traning programme for ANVC cadres at Tura in the West Garo Hills district.
- *July 11*: The cease-fire agreement between the Government and ANVC is extended by one more year. An agreement to this effect is reached during the Joint Monitoring Group held in New Delhi on an unspecified day. The ANVC entered into a tripartite cease-fire agreement on July 23, 2004.
- *May 30*: Meghalaya Home Minister H. Donkupar R Lyngdoh, while responding negatively on the request of the ANVC to the Union Government to lift the ban imposed on it, says, "Let people be satisfied with their non-violence and peaceful existence." "No doubt, the illegal activities of the ANVC has reduced to a great extent; but until people are satisfied, the ban should continue," adds the Home Minister.
- *May 28*: The ANVC asks the Union Government to withdraw its ban on the outfit to facilitate peace talks.
- *May 10*: The ANVC, while criticizing other Garo outfits such as the ANLF and United UANF, terms them as "group of extortionists and dacoits who have no ideology or principle." "Both UANF and ANLF are only after money and they are not fighting for the cause of the people of Garo Hills," said ANVC 'publicity secretary' Arist Sengsrang Sangma. "We are fighting for a separate state and our demand is very much within the framework of the Indian constitution while the so called UANF has claimed

that the organisation is fighting for independence which is not at all acceptable both to the government of India and the Garos as well," he added.

- *May 1*: Chief Minister D. D. Lapang, while expressing the State Government's willingness to hold talks with the militant outfits, says, "But we have no say on the issues, which are totally depended on the initiative of the Union Home Ministry." He further adds, "We have to patiently wait and see things to happen because whatever steps that have been followed with the ANVC, the same thing will be done with HNLC."
- *April 7*: An ANVC cadre is killed by three of his colleagues at Tura in the West Garo Hills district.
- *April 5*: The JMG meeting held at the BSF premises in Guwahati decides to conduct a joint survey for setting up a designated camp for the ANVC cadres in the South Garo Hills of Meghalaya by the end of April 2006. The existing camp at Jetra in the Ri Bhoi district will be dismantled following complaints from paramilitary forces.
- *March 27*: Meghalaya Chief Minister D.D. Lapang, while responding to the issue of negotiations with militant outfits, informs the Legislative Assembly that a "Joint Monitoring Group (JMG) has been formed to monitor the cease-fire with the ANVC. The next JMG meeting will be held on April 5 in Guwahati, said, while adding that, "We are thinking of adopting similar pattern as the first step to initiate dialogue with HNLC."
- *March 24*: The ANVC calls for the formation of a separate state known as the 'Garoland State' for the Garos in Meghalaya. The 'publicity secretary' of the outfit, Arist Sengsrang Sangma, says that it is high time for all Garos to come under one umbrella and demand a separate state.

2005

- *December 14*: Union Minister of State for Home

Affairs, S. Reghupathy, while speaking in the Rajya Sabha (Upper House of Parliament), says that cease fire and suspension of operations is on with ANVC along with certain other militant outfits of the North East.

- *November 16*: Police kills Tiko Areng, a militant belonging to the ANLF, a splinter faction of the ANVC at Dongranggre near Shallang in the West Khasi Hills district. One 9mm pistol and a grenade are recovered from the incident site.
- *November 9*: ANVC 'publicity secretary', Arist Sengsrang Sangma, says, "We have told the cadres that those who are willing to leave can do so without deserting or running away from the camps." Commenting on reports that some former ANVC cadres have formed a new outfit, the ANLF, he says, "We will try to neutralise ANLF with the police, otherwise there will be law and order problem in Garo Hills." He further says that the relation between the police and the ANVC has improved considerably over the past few months.
- *November 6*: Two ANVC cadres, M. Marak and N. Momin, who have escaped from the Chokpot cease-fire camp, are killed by a joint team of Meghalaya Police and the army near Thapha in the East Garo Hills district. Three Chinese-made hand grenades and three rounds of AK-47 ammunition, besides documents such as extortion notes and money receipts are recovered from the incident site.
- *November 4*: Meghalaya Police kills two hardcore ANVC cadres, Rarik Sangma and Rabi Marak, and arrests two others at Bangsiminol under Mendipather police station in the Garo Hills district. Police sources informed that the slain militants are part of a group of nine ANVC cadres who have deserted the outfit's camp at Samanda in East Garo Hills and Chokpot in South Garo Hills and have made attempts to form a new outfit, the AN LF. Police also recover an AK-56

rifle with 20 rounds of ammunition, three hand grenades and an SLR with 17 rounds of live ammunition from the incident site.

- *September 4*: ANVC threatens to call off the cease-fire agreement with the State Government protesting against the latter's constant allegation of truce violation by the outfit. The outfit's 'Publicity Secretary' Arist Sangma said, "We express concern over the state government's often repeated statement that the ANVC is engaged in extortions... If the government continues with its wild allegations, we will be forced to go back to the jungle."
- *July 18*: The cease-fire between ANVC and the Union Government is extended for a year with effect from July 23, 2005. The decision is taken following a meeting between the ANVC leaders and MHA officials at Patgaon in the Guwahati city of Assam. The ANVC is asked to submit names of its cadres taking shelter in the two designated camps in East and South Garo Hills to the Union Government and also keep its arms and ammunition in safe custody.
- *July 6*: Meghalaya Government sends a note to the Union Government detailing the acts of cease-fire violation by the ANVC. Chief Secretary P. J. Bazeley said that the State Government would agree to extend the cease-fire agreement beyond July 23 provided the truce ground rules are framed and strictly adhered to. He says, "We have told the Centre that we will not be a party to the cease-fire with the ANVC if there are no proper ground rules."
- *May 11*: Two ANVC cadres, Ganesh Sangma and Nicholas Sangma, and one of their associates are arrested from Borsora in the West Khasi Hills district of Meghalaya.
- *April 19*: Meghalaya Chief Minister, D D Lapang, while addressing a press conference in Shillong, said the ANVC is violating the cease-fire agreement.
- *April 14*: Meghalaya Home Minister, Mukul Sangma,

says that failure to settle issues relating to the cease-fire ground rules have led to the delay in starting the peace process with the proscribed ANVC.

- *March 30*: A tribunal makes recommendations for the extension of the proscription on the HNLC and ANVC for another year.
- *March 8*: Meghalaya Home Minister, Mukul Sangma, says that the State Government will begin peace talks with the ANVC only after the outfit adheres to the principles of the cease-fire.
- *January 17*: The ceasefire agreement between the Government and the ANVC is extended by six months. The agreement is reached during the JMG meeting held at Tura in the West Garo Hills district. The duration of the present ceasefire is set to expire on January 23.

2004

- *December 23*: As a first step towards fulfilling the cease-fire ground rules, the ANVC submits a list of 100 of its cadres to the State Government. Informing this in Shillong, the State Home Minister, H.D.R. Lyngdoh, says that these cadres will be accommodated in the two designated camps. However, the outfit is yet to submit the list of arms and ammunition, adds Lyngdoh.
- *December 22*: Union Government extends the ban on two militant outfits of Meghalaya, the ANVC and HNLC. In an official notification in Shillong, the MHA cites the reasons for extension stating that although the ANVC agrees to abjure violence and expresses willingness for talks within the framework of Constitution, it continues "collection of funds and extortion, acquisition of sophisticated weapons and recruitment of new cadre."
- *December 10*: Meghalaya Government asks the ANVC chairman Dilash Marak and 'commander-in-chief' Jerome Momin to confine themselves to the Garo Hills area.

- *December 9*: The JMG meeting between the banned ANVC and the representatives of the MHA and the Meghalaya Government takes place in New Delhi to discuss the 'ground rules'. Following the second round of the tripartite talks of JMG, the ANVC agrees to submit the full list of its cadres to the State Government by December 20 to facilitate the implementation of cease-fire ground rules. The cadres will stay in two designated camps in the Garo Hills region.
- *July 23*: ANVC signs a tripartite agreement with the Union and Meghalaya Governments for immediate suspension of hostilities. The agreement is signed by the Secretary, Border Management in the MHA, A.K.Rastogi, Chief Secretary of Meghalaya, P.J. Bazely, and representatives of the ANVC led by its 'General Secretary' Wanding K Marak.
- *July 2*: The abducted Indian Forest Service official, D Sathyen, is released unharmed in the South Garo Hills district of Meghalaya after about a fortnight amidst claims by the State Government that no ransom was paid to the abductors.
- *June 24*: ANVC denies any links to the abduction of D. Sathiyan, Indian Forest Service officer posted at the Balpakram National Park. The outfit's 'publicity secretary', Arist Sengsrang Sangma, says that the outfit does not have any connection with the incident.
- *June 22*: ANVC demands Rupees 15 lakh as ransom for the release of abducted D. Satyan.
- *June 18*: Suspected ANVC terrorists abduct Forest Officer, D. Satyan, from his house at Baghmara in South Garo Hills district.
- *June 1*: Suspected ANVC terrorists shot dead a trader from Tura in Meghalaya for failing to pay extortion money demanded by them.
- *June 1*: Suspected ANVC terrorists kill a trader from Tura in the West Garo Hill district.
- *May 10*: Suspected ANVC cadres kill a schoolteacher at Kukurmara in the Kamrup district of Assam.

- *May 6*: Meghalaya Police arrests an ANVC terrorist, involved in truck burning incidents at Borsora on April 28, from Nonghyllam in the West Khasi Hills district.
- *March 16*: One ANVC terrorist is killed in an encounter with the security forces at Kajinagar in the West Garo Hills district.
- *February 20*: Suspected ANVC cadres release Borsora Land Custom Station Superintendent, L.H. Faihrem, from captivity at Tila Basti in the East Khasi Hills district. He was abducted on October 9, 2003.
- *January 19*: One police personnel is killed and four others are injured when an Improvised Explosive Device (IED), allegedly planted by ANVC terrorists went off at Tapadarengchi in the East Garo Hills district.
- *February 13*: Four ANVC terrorists are killed by SFs in an encounter near Phulbari in the West Garo Hills district.
- *February 10*: Meghalaya Police arrests an ANVC terrorist, identified as Jubi R Marak, from an unspecified location in the State.
- *February 6*: Meghalaya Chief Minister, D D Lapang, accuses former Lok Sabha Speaker and Nationalist Congress Party (NCP) leader P A Sangma of conniving with the proscribed ANVC to remain in State politics.
- *January 7*: Two ANVC 'sympathizers' are arrested for distributing extortion notes bearing the signature of R Marak of the ANVC 'finance wing' at Mendipathar in the East Garo Hills district.

2003

- *December 15*: A woman ANVC cadre, identified as Tresy Sangma, wife of the Mendipather 'area commander' of the outfit, is arrested near Mendipather in the East Garo Hills district.
- *November 16*: Meghalaya Police arrest a self-styled

corporal of the ANVC, identified as Havel Sangma, from Bologgitok village in the West Garo Hills district and recover a Japanese wireless hand-set and a tape recorder from his possession.

- *November 10*: Suspected ANVC terrorists kill three civilians at Rajapal in the East Garo Hills district.
- *October 28*: ANVC 'commander-in-chief' Jerome Momin indicates that the outfit "would continue its struggle for a greater Garoland and not give in to any moves initiated by the government towards a reconciliation."
- *October 1*: Two Achik National Volunteer Council (ANVC) terrorists surrender before the police in Shillong, and at Baghmara in South Garo Hills respectively.
- *September 30*: ANVC decides not to participate in the Meghalaya Government backed peace talks with the Garo Baptist Convention (GPC) after the September 26 incident.
- *September 26*: Security force personnel kill eight ANVC terrorists in two separate encounters in the West Garo Hills district and recover one AK-56 rifle with twelve rounds of live ammunition, one Pakistan-made.32 pistol with seven rounds of ammunition, two Chinese hand grenades and some incriminating documents from the encounter site.
- *September 24*: Meghalaya Chief Minister Lapang offers truce to the ANVC and HNLC.
- *September 10*: ANVC terrorists in Meghalaya release abducted Bajengdoba SBI Branch Manager after nine days of captivity.
- *August 7*: An ANVC sympathizer alleged to be involved in supplying arms to the outfit is killed during an encounter at Rewak in the South Garo Hills district.
- *July 16*: Two ANVC terrorists, including a 'commander', are killed during an encounter at Bikonggre village in the West Garo Hills district while three others escape from the incident site.
- *June 27*: Meghalaya Police arrests former State

Minister and senior Nationalist Congress Party (NCP) leader Adolf Lu Hitler Marak at Laban in Shillong for his alleged links with the ANVC.

- *June 24*: ANVC terrorists ambush a police patrol party near Borsora in the West Khasi Hills district killing two police personnel and injuring three others.
- *June 19*: Two women ANVC cadres surrender before the State Home Minister R G Lyngdoh at Shillong.
- *May 20*: At least five ANVC terrorists are arrested from Ampati in the West Garo Hills district.
- *May 15*: Four ANVC terrorists are arrested from a hideout at Ampati in the West Garo Hills district.
- *May 4*: Meghalaya Police unearths an ANVC 'finance cell' at Asimggre village in West Garo Hills district and seizes incriminating documents indicating to an extortion racket being run by the outfit in the area.
- *May 01*: Suspected ANVC cadres abduct two persons from Balachand, West Garo Hills district.
- *April 29*: Three ANVC terrorists, including an 'area commander', surrender before the State police at Sonapahar village in West Khasi Hills district with two AK-56 rifles, two wireless sets, four grenades and 216 rounds of AK-47 ammunition.
- *April 28*: ANVC 'area command headquarters' in the Garo hills area is reportedly dissolved and brought under the single command of 'commander-in-chief' Jerome Momin.
- *April 26*: Suspected ANVC terrorists release two abducted Meghalaya Government officials after 26 days of captivity near Willamnagar, East Garo Hills district. ANVC abducts a State Government official from Dadenggri in West Garo Hills district.
- *April 23*: Reports indicate that 'preliminary talks' were held between the Union Government and the ANVC on an unspecified date in Bangkok, Thailand.
- *April 15*: Suspected ANVC terrorists abduct a local businessman from Jhanjhani market, Mancachar police station-limits, in Assam's Dhubri district.

- *April 13*: ANVC releases three of the five Assam-based businessmen abducted on April 7, near Phulbari in West Garo Hills district.
- *April 7*: Meghalaya police arrest two ANVC terrorists at Weiloi village, East Khasi Hills district, from the vehicle of a former Legislator Adolf L. Hitler Marak.
- *April 2*: Four suspected ANVC terrorists, including a woman cadre, abduct a businessman at Ampati, West Garo Hills district.
- *March 31*: The Assam-based NDFB releases Customs officer Dipak Mahanta near Williamnagar in South Garo Hills district. Terrorists had abducted him on February 28, 2003.
- *March 24*: NDFB sets free the four remaining coal exporters, following the escape of two other exporters from its unidentified hideout in Meghalaya. ANVC and NDFB terrorists abducted the six coal exporters and a customs official Dipak Mahanta from Gasupara in South Garo Hills district on February 28.
- *March 6*: ANVC terrorists ambush a vehicle of the Border Road Organisation killing three persons on the spot in the East Garo Hills district. They also loot Rupees seven million and two self-loading rifles before escaping. A group of six ANVC terrorists abduct two teachers of a local school at Katuligaon near Ampati in the West Garo Hills district.
- *February 28*: ANVC and NDFB terrorists abduct six coal exporters and a customs official from Customs station at Ghasuapara in South Garo Hills district.
- *February 26*: Security forces rescue four abducted persons, including the Subsidiary Intelligence Bureau Assistant Director Deben Singh Rana at Damalgiri, Garobada police post limits in Tura, West Garo Hills district.
- *February 13*: Union Minister of State for Home Affairs, I D Swami, says peace initiative with ANVC is in progress. ANVC terrorists abduct a Government official at Bajengdoba in East Garo Hills district.

- *February 2*: ANVC terrorists kill Santhosh Hajong, a retired Meghalaya Police Battalion personnel at Ampati, West Garo Hills district.
- *January 22*: ANVC terrorists abduct a Government official from his residence at Bajendoba, East Garo Hills district.
- *January 14*: Suspected ANVC terrorists kill three persons in Songsak, near Williamnagar, East Garo Hills district, for allegedly using the outfit's name to extort money from local residents.
- *January 3*: The Union Home Ministry extends ban under the Unlawful Activities (Prevention) Act of 1967 on the ANVC and the Hynniewtrep National Liberation Council (HNLC) in Meghalaya.

2002

- *December 31*: ANVC demands ₹two million as ransom for medical practitioner P. Bezbaruah's release.
- *December 19*: ANVC terrorists abduct medical practitioner P. Bezbaruah in Williamnagar, East Garo Hills district.
- *December 12*: A businessman abducted from Nidhanpur, Assam, flees from an ANVC hideout despite being hit by bullet in the leg.
- *December 9*: Union Ministry of Home Affairs (MHA) establishes contact with ANVC and confirms the possibility peace talks in the future, most likely in Delhi in the year 2003.
- *December 1*: Terrorist-attack on a passenger bus in West Garo Hills, Meghalaya, injures two passengers. The ANVC's hand is suspected in the attack.
- *November 12*: ANVC relates the 1996-Wakabua raid to the rise of terrorism in Garo Hills. At the same time, the outfit's southern command in-charge and publicity-wing head Sohan D Shira says the September 9, 2002-killings of Deputy Superintendent of Police Paichon Sangma and five others, near Chokpot, was in retaliation to the Wakabua camp

raid.

- *October 05*: Meghalaya Chief Minister F A Khonglam discloses he is in possession of certain evidence against three Ministers from the Garo Hills region having nexus with the proscribed ANVC terrorist outfit. He says they all belong to the Congress and the Nationalist Congress Party (NCP).
- *September 24*: An ANVC terrorist is killed and another arrested by security forces (SF) in Dobu, East Garo hills district, following a prolonged gun-battle between group of five terrorists and a joint team of Police and Central Reserve Police Force (CRPF) personnel. Three more terrorists escape. A 9mm carbine, 11 rounds of ammunition and a US-made carbine are recovered from the clash-site.
- *September 9*: Six Meghalaya police personnel, including a Deputy Superintendent of Police (DSP), are killed in an ambush laid by ANVC terrorists at Chocpot, in the Garo Hills of Meghalaya.
- *July 1*: An ANVC terrorist is killed in an encounter with police near Dudhnoi in Assam. Five ANVC terrorists surrender at the Mendipather police station in the presence of Church leaders, in East Garo Hills.
- *June 30*: Meghalaya Forest Minister Monindra Rava's son, Devajyoti Rava, and four others are killed by unidentified, armed-men at a place between Belguri and Abhiram Para near Tikrikilla. Police suspect the ANVC's hand in the attack.
- *June 11*: Two ANVC terrorists are killed in an encounter at Amarsang village, near Kulung, under Borsora police station limits, West Khasi Hills district. Two AK-47 rifles, a Self-Loading Rifle (SLR), a Chinese rifle, two 12-bore guns and a large quantity of ammunition are recovered from the site of the encounter. ANVC terrorists injured in an encounter in South Garo Hills. Police recovered ₹1,54,000 in cash from the clash-site.
- *May 12*: Three Nepalese settlers are, and seven more

injured in an attack by the ANVC terrorist outfit at the Tinali settlement near Phulbari in the West Garo Hills district of Meghalaya.

- *April 1*: ANVC terrorist killed in encounter near Rangagre village under Tura police station limits.
- *March 14*: Suspected ANVC terrorists kill eight persons, including four policemen in West Garo Hills.
- *March 1*: ANVC terrorists abduct a leading businessman and a manager of a construction company from Chibinang, West Garo Hills.
- *February 16*: An ANVC terrorist attempting to cross over to Bangladesh killed in an encounter by security forces at Chadogre village in West Garo Hills.
- *January 31*: ANVC terrorist and two Border Security Force (BSF) personnel killed in an encounter at Phanda in South Garo Hills district.
- *January 22*: ANVC conducts a joint attack with National Democratic Front of Boroland (NDFB) terrorists on a security forces camp using rocket-propelled grenades (RPGs) at Tikrikilla in South Garo Hills.

2001

- *December 26*: ANVC terrorist escapes from the Williamnagar district Jail, East Garo Hills district.
- *November 25*: ANVC terrorist arrested from a dwelling at Sonatala near Ranikota
- *November 22*: ANVC terrorist surrenders to the South Garo Hills District police.
- *November 20*: ANVC terrorists abduct a Sub-Divisional Officer from Waribok, near Rongrang, in West Garo Hills.
- *October 20*: Three ANVC terrorists arrested from Doldegre area in West Garo Hills district by a joint team of Meghalaya police and Central Reserve Police Force (CRPF).
- *October 9*: Two ANVC cadres injured in an encounter on the outskirts of Williamnagar.

1999

- *August*: Two policemen killed when suspected ANVC terrorists blow up two jeeps at Aniaga village in the East Garo hills.

1998

- *October*: Five security force personnel killed and over `100,000 looted during an attack in East Garo hills.
- *February*: Two police personnel killed and `800,000 looted in an ambush laid by ANVC terrorists, the East Garo Hills.

HYNNIEWTREP NATIONAL LIBERATION COUNCIL (HNLC)

FORMATION

The Hynniewtrep National Liberation Council (HNLC) is a product of a 1992 split in the Hynniewtrep Achik Liberation Council (HALC), the first militant tribal outfit in Meghalaya. The HALC split due to inter-tribal antagonisms leading to the formation of the HNLC and the Achik Matgrik Liberation Army (AMLA). In the erstwhile HALC, the Hynniewtreps (Khasis, who trace their origin to seven celestial families) represented the Khasi and Jaintia tribes and the Achiks represented the Garos in the common fight against the Dkhars or 'outsiders'. The HNLC was proscribed on November 16, 2000.

OBJECTIVES

An important objective of the HNLC is to transform Meghalaya as a province exclusively for the Khasi tribe and free it from 'domination' by the Garo tribe. Another objective is to fight against the presence of 'outsiders', as the HNLC feels that Khasi youth are deprived of the fruits of development in the state.

LEADERSHIP

Julius K Dorphang is the 'Chairman' of the HNLC.

Cheristerfield Thangkhiew functions as its 'General Secretary'. Among the other leaders are 'Publicity Secretary' M. Diengdoh, 'Commander-in-chief' Bobby Marwein.

The HNLC 'Operations group' consists of Khraw Bian, Shining Star Synkhli, Shynshar Nongbri, Bantei Kharkongor, Raju Blah and Kynteilang Kharkongor. The top leadership of the outfit is based in the Bangladeshi capital Dhaka. Some of HNLC's camps too are located in that country, mostly in the Chittagong Hill Tracts (CHT) region.

Chairman Julius Dorphang surrendered to the government on July 24, 2007. This surrender was reportedly a result of the internal differences within the organsiation. A group of HNLC cadres was also sent by the outfit's leadership in Bangladesh to eliminate Dorphang. An October 30, 2007 encounter in a locality in Shillong led to the killing of five cadres of the group.

AREA OF OPERATION

The HNLC primarily operates in the Khasi Hills of Meghalaya. A number of its activities has been reported from the capital city of Shillong.

LINKAGES

The HNLC is closely linked with the National Socialist Council of Nagaland–Issak Muivah (NSCN-IM). HNLC's nexus with the Tripura based National Liberation Front of Tripura (NLFT) was revealed with the December 17, 2007 neutralisation of a joint HNLC-NLFT camp in the Narpuh reserve forest in the Jaintia Hills district.

Accoridng to Meghalaya police souces, both the outfits have been found to be engaged in extortion in the Jaintia Hills coal belt.

The HNLC also has a front organisation called the HSDF (Hynniewtrep State Democratic Front), whose 'Commander-in-Chief' Dominic Kharpuli and three other cadres were arrested on October 20, 2001. HNLC promotes the circulation of fake currency in the State, at the behest of Inter Services Intelligence (ISI), Pakistan's external intelligence agency.

INCIDENTS

2010

- *December 16*: The Ministry of Home Affairs extended its ban on the HNLC terming all wings and factions of the outfit as unlawful. "The insurgent group is detrimental to the sovereignty and integrity of the country and if it's not controlled, they would re-group and cause heavy loss of civilian and security forces lives," a Ministry statement said. The outfit, though considerably reduced in strength, is still active in parts of the State. Some of its top leaders including "chairman" Cheristerfield Thangkhiew are still believed to be operating from Bangladesh.
- *October 8*: The law-enforcing agencies over the last seven years are not taking action against surrendered HNLC cadres who are involved in killing, abduction and extortion cases. The Police records said that most of the HNLC cadres who surrendered before the Government during 2003 and 2007 were behind heinous crimes committed in the State. The report adds that the surrendered HNLC leaders like Khainborlang Wanniang, Kynsai Jyrwa, James Sylliang, K. Tongwah, Herman Pakyntein, Lung ktung and others have not been booked for their past criminal activities except a couple of cases filed against surrendered HNLC cadres for their 'misadventures' on certain occasions. The report reveals that not a single case has been registered against surrendered HNLC 'chairman' Julius Dorphang so far. The report also mentions that there are 300 surrendered HNLC cadres in the State.
- *October 1*: A HNLC cadre, Richarbor alias Juban, surrendered before the Border Security Force (BSF) at Dawki in Jaiñtia Hills District.
- *September 21*: BSF troops of the Assam and Meghalaya frontier killed four militants of ULFA and Military Council of the KLNLF, arrested 17 militants

belonging to the HNLC, KLNLF, People's Liberation Army (PLA), Military Council faction of the Kangleipak Communist Party (KCP), UNLF, MULTA and Harkat-ul-Jihad-al-Islami (HuJI) among others. They also got nine militants of ULFA, NDFB and All Adivasi National Liberation Army (AANLA) to surrender along with arms and ammunition.

- *September 12*: The HNLC threatened the people against participating in the municipal elections scheduled to be held in Meghalaya on September 14 and 15.
- *August 30*: The HNLC refuted reports that the outfit had borrowed arms from other militant groups for their activities.
- *August 29*: The HNLC is borrowing arms from other militant groups and pay in return after doing the "job" (extortion) with the "instrument". "The delivery power of the banned outfit has decreased so much that it is borrowing arms from others to carry out operations," said S.K. Jain, Additional Director General of Police (ADGP), Special Branch. "We had inputs about the outfit borrowing arms from Silchar ahead of the Independence Day, but the sources could not be specified," he added. The fact was revealed after the arrest an HNLC cadre, identified as Aibor alias Saddam Hussein, from Pynthorsale village in Jaintia Hills District. He confessed that the outfit borrowed some weapons including six AK-47 rifles, four revolvers and two grenades during that time. Two of the borrowed sophisticated rifles were seized from Aibor. The HNLC maintains an on-and-off relationship with the NSCN-IM, NDFB and NLFT, according to the ADGP who also said the outfit's nexus with ULFA is not yet ascertained. At present, the HNLC has around 50 active cadres, but each one of them does not have arms and ammunitions. "The figure might not be accurate as it is based on our assessment on sightings and technical intercepts,"

Jain said. The outfit has its camps at Maulvi Bazar, Sylhet and Chittagong Hill Tract of Bangladesh. Many of its leaders are into betel nut plantations and own stone quarries in the neighbouring country.

- *August 23*: Surrendered HNLC cadre, James Sylliang, refuted allegations leveled by his former chairman Julius K. Dorphrang that he was behind alleged irregularities in the tender process for the North-Eastern Hill University (NEHU) construction work in Shillong. He also demanded an apology from the former HNLC chairman for his "irresponsible remark".
- *August 20*: Meghalaya Chief Minister Mukul Sangma has sought a status report on the allegations against surrendered HNLC militants interfering into affairs of the North-Eastern Hill University (NEHU) in Shillong and also being involved in cattle smuggling. "We are taking seriously the inputs received about the alleged illegal activities of the SHNLC men. The government is committed to ensuring that lawlessness does not prevail and will not allow anyone to indulge in activities that will go against the interest of the people of the State," Sangma said.
- *August 19*: Shillong Times reports that the surrendered HNLC cadres are slowly taking charge over some crucial business interests in Meghalaya. Sources said the surrendered cadres are also getting the bulk of contract works in North-Eastern Hill University (NEHU). The unemployed youths in the State allege that the Government is tilted towards the surrendered militants instead of encouraging educated youths for productive growth. Sources said that whenever any tenders are floated by NEHU the officers of the construction wing direct the youths to meet and seek permission from Julius Dorphang, the former self-styled HNLC 'chairman' and his associates. Incidentally Dorphang is also a seasoned businessman now. Some registered contractors of

NEHU on request of anonymity said, "Surrendered HNLC cadres are the bosses in NEHU and they are the ones who control the tendering process now." According to these contractors, the surrendered HNLC has formed its own association of contractors particularly for NEHU construction works. All registered contractors seeking work in NEHU have been advised to seek membership of the association or they would not be allowed to participate in the tendering process. "We are required to pay a commission ranging from two to five per cent of the total value of the project to the surrendered HNLC association for each and every contract allotted to us," a contractor said. The report adds that the surrendered militants take full charge during the submission of tenders. They are at the gate to scan all tenderers and oversee the entire tender process. Contractors are actually short listed and selected by these former militants. Sources have also informed that most of the parking bays under the Meghalaya Urban Development Agency (MUDA), too, are controlled by the surrendered HNLC cadres. The Special Operation Team (SOT) personnel arrested nine cattle smugglers from Pynursla area in East Khasi Hills District in the night of August 19. The Police had also seized 16 cattle heads, INR 265000, one truck, five light vehicles and nine cell phones from their possession. Besides having link with the surrendered HNLC cadres, they are close to certain top politicians including a Cabinet Minister of the State, sources said. "Though the Home Minister HDR Lyngdoh was informed about the serious matter, he did not initiate any action since there was pressure on him from various quarters to overlook the issue," sources claimed.

- *August 16*: The HNLC reiterated its desire to hold talks and asked the Meghalaya Government to "show seriousness for lasting peace" in the State. HNLC 'general secretary' Cherishstarfield Thangkhiew said the outfit was willing to hold a political dialogue with the Government on various demands. However, Thangkhiew deplored that the Government had made statements on the need to have peace only in the media and was yet to take any pro-active steps on the issue. Meghalaya Chief Minister Mukul Sangma said his Government was always ready to have a political dialogue with the HNLC. Responding to the statement issued by the HNLC reiterating the outfit''s desire to hold talks "provided there is seriousness on the part of the government," the Chief Minister said the Government would be pleased to have the modalities for the dialogue.

- *August 15*: Meghalaya Chief Minister Mukul Sangma expressed concern over the activities of new militant outfits and those from Assam as a 36-hour shutdown by the HNLC paralysed life in four Khasi-Jaintia Districts of the State on Independence Day. The report adds that a group of HNLC cadres armed with AK56 rifles and grenades had entered Meghalaya from Bangladesh to strike in the capital town of Shillong.
- *August 13*: The HNLC reiterated its objection to holding of civic polls in the State saying the elections would snatch away the power of the traditional institutions. In a press statement issued, HNLC 'publicity secretary' Sainkupar Nongtraw said, "Has the Indian government taken the prior consent of the people to conduct the civic polls or does it intend to go ahead with the polls by discounting the will of the people?". The outfit also termed the celebration of Independence Day in Hynniewtrep land as 'illegal' and asked the people to refrain from the celebrations.
- *August 12*: Meghalaya Minster in-charge of Home H.D.R. Lyngdoh said that the Police have intelligence inputs of 10 to 12 HNLC militants managing to infiltrate into the State from Bangladesh with weapons. "Police is on their look-out," Lyngdoh said.

- *August 11*: The HNLC called for a 36-hour bandh (general shut down) from 6 pm on August 14 to 6 am on August 16, in protest against the Independence Day celebrations on August 15 in Meghalaya. Meanwhile, several prominent citizens of the State criticized the call for bandh.
- *August 9*: The HNLC warned the Residential Director of a cement factory in Jaintia Hills for his "ill behaviour" and asked the company to take corrective measures. A statement issued by HNLC 'publicity secretary' Sainkupar Nongtraw also asked the official, Divander Bhansal, "not to confront" with the sentiment of the local population.
- *August 6*: The HNLC has adopted the jehadi style to disrupt the Independence Day celebrations in a shocking way, intelligence sources revealed, reports Shillong Times. "HNLC cadres are moving in groups of three to four people similarly like the jehadis during any operations. There is even similarity to the Mumbai attack as far as movements of militants are concerned," intelligence sources said. Intelligence sources confirmed that the HNLC cadres in smaller groups have already sneaked into Meghalaya from Bangladesh. Referring to the recent arrest of HNLC's Aiborlang Khartani alias Saddam Hussein, sources said, "Police have managed to nab one of them, but could not get all the facts from him as in this kind of situation no one really knows about the whole operation since every group is given specific tasks," the sources added. The intelligence sources confirmed that the HNLC is planning "something big" which might shock the Shillong city this time. The outfit, after losing its ground a few years ago, is desperate to make its presence felt once again in the city, sources said. "Once it is able to develop the fear psychosis in the minds of the people, they would be able to extort money from the city's non-tribal businessmen," sources said claiming that extortion

drive by HHLC has been totally wiped out. Meanwhile, the sources have not denied any nexus between HNLC and jehadi outfits like al Qaeda for subversive acts. There is also strong suspect about HNLC getting arms from the National Democratic Front of Bodoland (NDFB) and National Socialist Council of Nagaland-Isak-Muivah (NSCN-IM). "As per our information, HNLC does not have enough arms," the sources said.

- *August 4*: The Jaintia Hills District Police arrested a HNLC cadre, identified as Aibor alias Saddam Hussein, from Pynthorsale village about 30 kilometres from Jowai. Police recovered two AK-47 rifles from his possession.
- *July 18*: A HNLC 'sergeant major' Joplin Pohtam alias Jop, a key aide of the outfit's 'commander-in-chief' Bobby Marwein, was arrested by the BSF near Umngot River in Dawki of East Khasi Hills District. The BSF said Joplin, who hails from of Sokha village in Jaintia Hills, was arrested while trying to cross over to India from Bangladesh. However, sources claimed the HNLC top leader was not arrested and that he was handed over by Bangladeshi nationals after making him drunk.
- *July 5*: HNLC runs a stone quarry in Jafflong District of Bangladesh. The outfit is also believed to own several betel nut plantations besides running other business in Bangladesh. A senior Police official confirmed the presence of the stone quarry at Jafflong near the India-Bangladesh border. "We came to know about the existence of a stone quarry owned by the HNLC in Bangladesh from the arrested and surrendered militants," the official said. According to sources, the outfit's daily earning from the quarry amounts to INR 30,000 to INR 40,000. "Inability of the group to carry out extortion drives in Shillong has prompted it to find a new means of earning," the sources claimed. The sources further revealed that

HNLC cadres often come through Umngot river to Dawki along with Bangladeshi labourers in boats to collect boulders for the stone quarry. Sources said the vital confessions were made by HNLC's self-styled 'sergeant major' Pariston Pakyntein, who was arrested by the Border Security Force (BSF) near Dawki recently. Pakyntein told the police that the stone quarry had been in operation for the last two years and many cadres of the outfit are "engaged" there. The Police sources believe that strength of the outfit has reduced considerably after many of its senior leaders and cadres were either arrested or surrendered before the Police. The State Police claim that the present cadre strength of the HNLC is below 50. The HNLC top leaders, including 'general secretary' Cherishsterfield Thangkiew and 'commander-in-chief' Bobby Marwein are still at large and believed to be remote controlling the outfit from Bangladesh.

- *June 6*: Sentinel reports that 13 militant organizations from the Northeast States of Assam, Manipur, Tripura and Meghalaya figure in the list of banned organizations as it appears in the website of the Union Home Ministry (MHA). The ULFA heads the list. The other outfits were: NDFB, People's Liberation Army (PLA), and United National Liberation Front (UNLF), People's Revolutionary party of Kangleipak (PREPAK), Kangleipak Communist Party (KCP), Kanglei Yaol Kanna Lup (KYKL), Manipur People's Liberation Front (MPLF), Revolutionary People's Front (RPF), All Tripura Tiger Force (ATTF), National Liberation Front of Tripura (NLFT), HNLC and Achik National Volunteer Council (ANVC).
- *May 20*: The 12-hour general shut down called by the HNLC, in protest against the May 14 killing of villagers at Langpih along Assam-Meghalaya border, affected normalcy in capital Shillong and other Districts of the State.

- *May 15*: The HNLC called a 12-hour bandh (general shut down) on May 20 in Meghalaya in pretest against the May 14 killing of four persons belonging to Khasi community by the Assam Police at Langpih village along Assam-Meghalaya border. "The unfortunate incident took place only because neither the Centre nor the state governments are interested to resolve the long-pending boundary disputes," the outfit's publicity secretary Sainkupar Nongtraw said.
- *May 12*: The HNLC reiterated its denial of any involvement in the killing of Khasi Students Union (KSU) leader Phershal Kongwang in 2007.
- *May 11*: HNLC was involved in the abduction and subsequent killing of the Khasi Students Union (KSU) leader Phershial Kongwang in 2007. The slain KSU leader's father Gabriel Kharmawshun said, "Some surrendered HNLC cadres had informed us that our son was killed by the outfit." Self-styled 'sergeant major' of the outfit Poniston Pakyntein, who was arrested by the Border Security Force from Dawki in Jaintia Hills District in May 2010, had confessed before the Police that he was involved in the abduction and killing of Phershial on December 16, 2007. He disclosed that he and some of his accomplices took the KSU leader to Radhanagar Bagan in Jaflong area of Bangladesh and killed and buried him there. Meanwhile, KSU general secretary Hamlet Dohling said, "HNLC should clarify as to why was he kidnapped and killed."
- *May 2*: Four cadres of the HNLC were convicted of arms smuggling and imprisoned for 17 years in Bangladesh, said Additional Director General of Meghalaya Police (Special Branch) S. K. Jain. "Sketchy reports from various networks confirmed that the four convicted Indians in Bangladesh are members of the outlawed HNLC," said Jain. On April 29, the court of Additional District and Sessions Judge of Sylhet-I convicted Robin (35), Mill (28), Over (25) and

Star (24) - all hailing from Shillong - in a five-year-old case of arms smuggling. All the four, Jain said, were wanted by the Meghalaya Police for their involvement in the biggest bank robbery in Jaintia Hills District on January 24, 2005. On July 15, 2005, Bangladesh Rifles (BDR) troopers arrested the four HNLC militants from Karaballa point under Sylhet District after they entered Bangladesh through Karimganj sector in Assam. The BDR recovered from their possession an AK 56 rifle, three grenades, two 9-mm pistols, 316 bullets and four magazines of AK 56 rifle, 328 bullets and three magazines of 9-mm pistol, INR 3,000 and BDT 2,700. According to the Police official, the HNLC is closely linked to the National Socialist Council of Nagaland- Isak-Muivah (NSCN-IM) and the National Liberation Front of Tripura (NLFT).

- *April 30*: Meghalaya Home Minister H.D.R. Lyngdoh asked leaders of the proscribed HNLC to give up armed struggle for a Hynniewtrep homeland and join the mainstream.
- *April 28*: A HNLC cadre, Wilfred Syiem alias Bah Grik, surrendered at Amlarem Police Station in the night. Superintendent of Police of Jaintia Hills District O. Pasi informed that Wilfred had joined the outfit in 2001 and had undergone arms training in the Chittagong Hill Tracts of Bangladesh. Wilfred, a resident of Mawlai Nongpdeng in Shillong, did not deposit any arms. He revealed that he had worked as a daily labourer at Panai, a Khasi village in Sylhet District of Bangladesh.
- *April 9*: Two suspected HNLC cadres were arrested by the Border Security Force personnel near Dawki in Jaintia Hills District along India-Bangladesh border. They were identified as Rishot Lyngdoh and Suk Kharakor.
- *April 8*: The HNLC slapped a demand of INR three million on a local car dealer. Sources said that the

HNLC is taking advantage of the turmoil prevailing in the State and the resurgence of militancy in Garo Hills to send a message that the Khasi and Jaintia Hills are its turf and no one can operate in that space. The report adds that several others, including coal traders and businessmen, received extortion notes in recent times but they all decided to remain silent and negotiate with the outfit. Sources said that many of these businessmen who have received extortion notes do not have enough faith in the system to seek for any kind of help. They preferred to negotiate and pay some amount to the outfit and continue with their businesses than counter the militants. Sources said that HNLC remained immobile for sometime but a senior Police official said, "it is a matter of time before they resurface because the State does not seem to have a policy to deal with them." Several young recruits have joined the outfit in recent times and negated the efforts of the State Police to immobilize the outfit, said sources.

- *March 19*: The Meghalaya Governor R. S. Mooshahary expressed concern over mushrooming of militant groups in Garo hills and the activities of Assam-based outfits along the border. The Governor said that recent developments, such as reports on the formation of militant groups in Garo hills, were a cause of concern. Other militant groups active in Garo hills are LAEF, People's Liberation Front of Meghalaya (PLF-M), Achik National Security Defence (ANSD), Atong Liberation Army (ALA), and United Achik National Front (UANF). ULFA and NDFB are also active in Garo hills and border of Ri Bhoi District. The Governor said that the Government was committed to contain militancy at all costs. The Governor added that the security establishment of the State has acted swiftly to break up and contain the activities of the Hynniewtrep Liberation Front (HLF) in Khasi hills, and LAEF in the Garo hills. He said the activities of the local militant organisations like the HNLC and ANVC have been substantially controlled.

- *February 8*: Three suspected HNLC militants, identified as Ribonlang Nongbri (21), Ekliar Nongbri (26) and Thringstar Nongbri (35), were arrested by the Police from Lewduh area in Shillong city.
- *February 7*: The former chairman of the HNLC, Julius Dorphang, demanded a review of the rehabilitation package for surrendered militants, saying there were many drawbacks in the system. Dorphang said many surrendered militants wasted the INR 150000 given to them after the rehabilitation period, ranging from three to nine months, at Mawiong. As the Government has no proper policy to help the militants sustain themselves in the long run, the one-time financial assistance has not paid off. The money is deposited in the bank in the name of the surrendered militant and is often withdrawn soon after the rehabilitation period, he said. He said though there is an official-level committee supervising the rehabilitation package, it has no say regarding the withdrawal of the funds. According to Dorphang, there should be a committee to monitor the release of the funds and they should also change the current system of allowing the surrendered militants to withdraw the money deposited in the bank. "I am not in favour of providing cash to the surrendered militants directly. The money can be put to use to start a small business with the knowledge of the monitoring committee," he said. There are at least 200 surrendered HNLC militants in Shillong who have completed the rehabilitation. Dorphang said senior members like him should also be part of the monitoring committee so that the genuine beneficiaries are not deprived of the cash incentives. He also pointed out that among the 200 surrendered militants, some were yet to get the rehabilitation

package. "Some of the boys said they are yet to get the rehabilitation package though they had surrendered several years ago," Dorphang said, adding that the Government should process their cases. Meghalaya Chief Minister D.D. Lapang in the Conference of Chief Ministers on Internal Security asked the Centre to go for a tripartite political and development accord with the ANVC to bring the ongoing peace process to a logical conclusion. He also stated that insurgent outfits like ULFA, National Socialist Council of Nagaland, NDFB and UPDS are not only supporting groups like LAEF, but also providing them arms, ammunition and training. He said that insurgent outfits both from the Northeast and adjoining Bangladesh were also using the peaceful State of Meghalaya both as temporary sanctuary and corridor. Lapang further claimed that both ANVC and HNLC have been largely neutralised with a sustained Police operation. But passive militancy is still a cause for concern, he further added.

- *January 31*: A senior Police official said that with coal business thriving in West Khasi Hills, the HNLC is luring innocent young men to work for the militant outfit taking advantage of the large scale unemployment and backwardness of the District. The boys act as couriers to distribute demand notes and collect money from the coal barons on behalf of HNLC. "We are concerned over the attempt of HNLC to recruit the illiterate, impressionable boys from West Khasi Hills border", the official said. The HNLC has gone on a massive recruitment drive along the Meghalaya-Bangladesh border to meet the huge vacuum in the organisation, he added. In recent times, the HNLC has suffered a rapid attrition in its manpower strength. HNLC 'area commander' Alex Hahshah, who was arrested along with eight other new recruits from a house at Parmowda village in

West Khasi Hills District on January 27, has been in the coal belt areas for the last five years and was instrumental in recruiting the boys in that area to join the outfit. According to police, Hahshah was wanted in connection with several killings and extortion in different parts of the State in the last six years. The nine member group of militants was operating in the coal-rich areas of Parmowda, Borsora, Nongjri, Nonghyllam and Rajaju for the past several days. Their sole purpose was to extort money from the coal barons, before they landed up in police custody. As this is the peak season for coal export, several coal laden trucks move from the coal rich areas of West Khasi Hills to different destinations, Police said. The HNLC is taking advantage of the situation to extort money, Police added. According to Police, constant vigil in Shillong has made it difficult for the HNLC to operate within the city so they have now focused on the coal belts and other mineral-rich borders areas as a safe haven for carrying out extortion. He also said that the ongoing extortion in the border areas is a cause of concern but efforts are on to check this trend.

- *January 27*: The Meghalaya Police arrested nine HNLC cadres, including an 'area commander' Alex Hahshah, during a search operation at Parmodan village in West Khasi Hills District. "We had been looking for the area commander for the last six years," Superintendent of Police of West Khasi Hills District M. Kharkrang said. The group was planning to embark on an extortion spree. The report adds that in 2009 there were nearly 50 incidents in which the HNLC was involved and in all five persons were killed. Police sources said in 2009, 62 militants had been neutralized and of these, 48 were arrested, 10 surrendered and four were killed.
- *January 23*: A National Youth Award winner, Andreas H. Marwein, was arrested by the Meghalaya Police

in capital Shillong for his linkage with the HNLC. Police said Marwein, who had received the National Youth Award in 2009, was recently arrested for working as an over ground worker of the militant outfit. According to Police, Andreas had collected nearly INR 10 million over the last five years for the HNLC and helped mobilize youths to join the outfit.

- *January 15*: Meghalaya Chief Minister D.D. Lapang rejects media reports that HNLC's top leaders, including the outfit's 'general secretary' Cheristerfield Thangkhiew and 'spokesperson' Sainkupar Nongtraw, were about to surrender before the State Police. There were reports that the two top HNLC leaders had managed to escape from their base in Bangladesh to Meghalaya to surrender. "We have not received any information about their surrender from the police," Lapang said. He also added that the Government had not made any contact with the cadres of the proscribed militant outfit. There were also reports that the two top militants of the outfit are likely to surrender following an ideological difference with the outfit's 'commander-in-chief' Bobby R. Marwien over a Government invitation for talks, but the militant outfit had earlier refuted the reports saying that all was well within the outfit. The report adds that the Chief Minister had asked the HNLC cadres to surrender "honourably" and also offered them safe passage after the recent arrest of ULFA 'chairman' Arabinda Rajkhowa.
- *January 4*: Superintendent of Police of East Khasi Hills District Claudia Lyngwa denying the reported revival of the HNLC in Meghalaya said, "One swallow doesn't make a summer....The outfit is down and its dares to operate only in areas where the businessmen receiving demand notes don't cooperate with the police out of fear." The former HNLC 'chairman' Julius Dorphang said that to use the surrendered militants was not a right approach and instead he

asked the Government to initiate peace talks directly with the outfit. After the December 23, 2009 hit-and-run by the HNLC militants in East Khasi Hills, which left a coal baron dead and his wife injured, Meghalaya Director General of Police S.B. Kakati had suggested that the Police might ask surrendered HNLC militants for their help to search for the hideouts. The Police wanted to take the help of surrendered cadres to track the militants who take shelter with Khasi villagers inside Bangladesh after carrying out criminal activities in the State. The Police thought the surrendered HNLC militants, who are familiar with the terrain, would be of great help to them. However, terming the move as not acceptable, Dorphang said this would create bad blood between the HNLC and the surrendered militants. "The idea of seeking the help of surrendered militants to hunt for the HNLC is not desirable," Dorphang said. He said if the Government wants to bring the HNLC to the negotiation table, the help of their relatives can be sought. There are around 200 surrendered militants in Shillong and Dorphang who is one among them warned that the present law and order situation might worsen if the Police sought the help of the surrendered militants to neutralise the HNLC. He, however, criticised the HNLC for killing the coal exporter. "This act is that of petty robbers and if the HNLC wants to fight, it should directly wage war with the security forces and should not target innocents," Dorphang added.

2009

- *December 29*: The Meghalaya Police decides to seek the help of surrendered HNLC cadres to track down the militants who are provided shelter by villagers residing in Bangladesh after carrying out criminal activities in the State. "We are developing a strategy of engaging the surrendered militants to tackle the

HNLC militants in the border," said Meghalaya Director General of Police (DGP) S.B. Kakati. There are more than 150 surrendered HNLC militants who had narrated to the police in the past that majority of the HNLC cadres stay with Khasi villagers inside Bangladesh. The militants also assist the Khasi villagers in the betel nut plantations. A major disadvantage for the Meghalaya Police is its inability to build up an effective intelligence network along the border areas of the Khasi hills region where the HNLC has a significant presence. Unable to extort money from Shillong due to constant vigil of the Police, the HNLC militants are carrying out large scale extortion from the coal exporters in the remote borders, Police said. "We need effective co-ordination of the police forces of East Khasi Hills and the Jaintia Hills to tackle militant activities in the borders," said Kakati, adding that more forces will be deployed in the border to tackle insurgency related crimes. "We had deployed some personnel of the Special Operations Team (SOT) in East Khasi Hills border, but we did not have actionable intelligence about the attack on December 23 [killing of a coal trader]," the DGP said. Kakati also admitted that police were aware of the threat to the coal baron from HNLC through intelligence inputs but the slain coal trader's family members had not divulged anything. The Meghalaya Government orders a magisterial inquiry into the death of an inmate of the Jowai District Jail, Pynhunlang Kharbani (33), who was declared 'brought dead' at Jowai Civil Hospital on December 26 after he suddenly fell sick in his prison cell. Kharbani was reportedly booked under the Meghalaya Detention and Prevention Act (MPDA). "A magisterial inquiry into the death of the prisoner is already on to find out the exact cause of death," Jaintia Hills District Deputy Commissioner T. Dkhar said. He said a 15-day time was given to the

Additional District Magistrate Sainkupar Syiemlieh to investigate into the incident. Meanwhile, the HNLC claims that Kharbani was a cadre of the outfit.

- *December 28*: The HNLC militants are taking shelter in Khasi villages well inside Bangladesh after committing crime in Meghalaya. "The HNLC militants mingle with the Khasi villagers staying in Bangladesh thereby making it impossible either for Meghalaya police or Bangladesh security forces to track down the militants," a senior Police Official said. The report adds that four HNLC militants who shot dead a coal trader, Raja Khongsit, in the East Khasi Hills border area, had infiltrated from Bangladesh into Pomshutia village in Meghalaya and exfiltrated to Bangladesh after committing the crime.
- *December 23*: A coal trader, Raja Khongsit (45), is shot dead by four suspected HNLC militants at Pomshutia village in East Khasi Hills District. His wife is injured in the attack.
- *December 19*: Meghalaya Chief Minister D.D. Lapang criticizes the HNLC for creating confusion by resorting to a general shut down even after the Union Home Minister P. Chidambaram cancels his visit to the State. The outfit reportedly called the 24-hour general shut down, beginning 6.30pm on December 18, to protest against the Home Minister's visit, alleging that India was adopting double standard on human rights issues. The former 'chairman' of the proscribed HNLC Julius Dorphang said the outfit's insistence on going ahead with the general shut down even after the Union Home Minister had called off his visit to the State was a major blunder in the history of the outfit. "It shows the leadership vacuum in the HNLC," the surrendered militant mentioned.
- *December 15*: An HNLC cadre, Badonsing Lyngdoh Marshillong, who surrendered before the Dawki Police in the evening of December 13, reveals that the outfit still had over 100 cadres and most of them

were wandering in Bangladesh to earn for their livelihood. He mentions that while leaders of the proscribed outfit were leading a luxurious life in Bangladesh, its common cadres were facing a lot of difficulty to make their both ends meet. He said the cadres of the outfit were working as labourers in the Khasi Pnar villages of Bangladesh. Marshillong, who joined the militant group in 2003, is a school drop-out. A resident of Pyndengsohsaw villager under Mawsynram Police Station in East Khasi Hills District, Marshillong crossed over to Bangladesh via Balat and completed his training at Arusumen Camp in the same year. After his training, the leaders gave him no assignment and had to spend his time with no responsibility. Later, he worked as a labourer at betel leaf garden of some of the Khasi-Pnar people residing at Nonsara village in Bangladesh earning BDT 100 per day. In 2006, he married one local Nonsara girl, Syntiew Dkhar. They now have a two-year-old daughter. In 2007, Marshillong had informed the 'area commander' of the banned outfit in writing that he was not willing to remain in the group. But he did not get any response. In the early part of December 2009, the group asked him to leave Bangladesh at once or face death. He was forced to leave Bangladesh. He crossed over to India on December 13 and surrendered at Dawki Police Station.

- *December 16*: The HNLC calls for a 24-hour general shut down during Union Minister of Home Affairs P. Chidambaram's visit to the State on December 19. The HNLC spokesman Sainkupar Nongtraw said that the shutdown will come into effect from 6 pm on December 18 in the entire Khasi-Jaintia Hills. "The bandh will be organised to show to the Union Home Minister the opposition by people of 'Hynniewtrep Land' against forceful occupation of land by the armed forces, human rights abuse and attempt to forcefully extract uranium from West Khasi Hills," Nongtraw said.

- *December 13*: A senior HNLC cadre, Badonsing Lyngdoh, who hails from Pyndemsohsaw in West Khasi Hills District, surrenders at Dawki Police Station in Jaintia Hills District. He surrenders along with his wife and two-year-old daughter. His wife is identified as Syntiew Dkhar hailing from Nonsara village near Maulari Bazar of Sylhet District in Bangladesh. Badonsing had joined the outfit in 2003. Police subsequently take the militant and his family to Jowai for interrogation.
- *December 6*: The HNLC rejects Meghalaya Chief Minister D. D. Lapang's appeal to 'surrender' and his offer for 'safe passage'. The outfit accuses the Government for not being sincere by solving political problems raised by it. "Mr Lapang's statement was only to frighten us and dampen the patriotic spirit in the history of Hynniew-trep", the HNLC says. In an e-mailed statement issued to a section of the media, HNLC says, "The organisation will not entertain the personal appeal of Mr Lapang for safe passage."
- *December 5*: Meghalaya Chief Minister D. D. Lapang appeals to HNLC leaders 'general secretary' Cherishterfield Thangkhiew and 'commander-in-chief' Bobby Marwein to come over ground and also offers them 'safe-passage.'
- *August 12*: The HNLC calls for a boycott of the Independence Day celebrations on August 15 saying "it is against the Indian colonialism for denial of the basic human rights (national existence) which is our birth right". In an e-mailed statement, the HNLC spokesman Sainkupar Nongtraw says the outfit had formed the council to "fight with arms towards the freedom of our people from the clutches of forgiveness in the Hynniewtrep land".
- *May 20*: A senior militant of the banned HNLC,

identified as Phikerlang Majaw alias San, surrendered before the East Khasi Hills District Police. He had joined the HNLC in 2002. He crossed over to Indian territory from Bangladesh after deserting the outfit's camp at Arisuma in Chittagong Hill Tracts (CHT) area a few days ago. Phikerlang's primary job was to ride a boat, a three-hour journey, carrying food items, including rice and vegetables, to the HNLC camp from Borkhaghat market. Phikerlang said he decided to surrender after being fed up with the hardship he had to endure in the HNLC camp in CHT. He said he had stayed with HNLC leader Hep Khoit and his wife in the camp, adding that about 50 HNLC militants were still living in the camp at Arisuma under the command of one Kambes. He, however, said there were only two weapons, one AK47 and the other AK 46, in the camp. Meanwhile, Superintendent of Police of East Khasi Hills District, Claudia A. Lyngwa, said other militant groups, including the NLFT, KYKL and NDFB, had set up base in CHT area and was providing arms training to the HNLC militants.

- *May 1*: Meghalaya Police revealed that militants of the banned HNLC, who surrender before the Security Forces without depositing any arms and ammunition, are being offered the Government's rehabilitation package. An unnamed Meghalaya Police official said the Government has laid down guidelines that only in exceptional and deserving cases militants who surrender without arms and ammunition may be considered for rehabilitation under the Government package. However, most of the recent surenderees who did not deposit arms and ammunition, the official maintains, were far from "exceptional and deserving" cases, but provided with the rehabilitation package. Only the outfit's chairman Julius K. Dorphang, who surrendered with four of his bodyguards in July 2007 without arms or ammunition, was an "exceptional case", the Police official says. The militants who surrender with at least one weapon are shifted to a transit camp and given counseling and later training on a vocation with a monthly stipend of INR 2,000 and daily perks of INR 50 as part of the rehabilitation. After three months, the surrendered activists are released and given INR 150000 in three installments over a period of six months for self-rehabilitation and joining the mainstream. "The Government policy is okay, but the militants are trying to take the money and many go back to their old ways indulging in extortion and intimidation," the Police official adds. Apart from the rehabilitation package, the Government has laid down monetary incentives for laying down arms and ammunition during surrender. Deposit of a rocket launcher fetches a militant INR 25,000, while an AK-assault rifle INR 15,000. The other incentives include INR 10,000 for a deposited carbine or SLR, INR 5,000 for a stengun and long-range wireless set. INR 3,000 each would be given for laying down.303 rifle, pistol, revolver or any other service weapon, remote control device and improvised explosive device. INR 1,000 for a rocket, short-range wireless set, explosive material and INR 500 for each grenade deposited are the other Government incentives.

- *April 13*: The HNLC calls for a 24-hour general shutdown in protest against the visit of the president of the Congress party, Sonia Gandhi, to address a public meeting at Shillong, for the elections scheduled to be held in Meghalaya on April 16.
- *April 6*: Two HNLC militants, Andreas Sangma alias Bush and his wife Angelina Shylla, surrender before Police at Shillong. Andreas along with seven others joined the HNLC in 2001. They had undergone arms training at Chittagong Hills Tract in Bangladesh. Angelina along with another girl, Rishalin Syiemlieh, joined the outfit in 2003. Angelina reveals that

Rishalin and another girl from Mawlai called "Bih Rit" are still in Bangladesh.

- *March 31*: Sentinel reports that illegal traders along the Khasi-Jaintia hills are victims of an extortion drive carried out by the HNLC. The report states that after the Police's success in curbing extortion activities of the proscribed outfit, the HNLC has now begun focusing on local traders across the India-Bangladesh border.
- *March 10*: A 'corporal' of the HNLC, identified as Kordor Lyngdoh Mawlong alias Sumar, surrenders before the Superintendent of Police of East Khasi Hills District. He reportedly joined the outfit in 2002 and underwent arms training at the Chittagong Hill Tracts in Bangladesh.
- *March 1*: Three HNLC female cadres surrender before the Superintendent of Police of Jaintia Hills District, M.K. Singh, at Dawki. They are identified as Josephine Rynjah, Kalbi Dora Snaitang and Philda Shylla. They reportedly received arms training at Chittagong in Bangladesh, and used to stay at Lamapunji and Maulwi Bazaar areas in the neighbouring country.
- *February 22*: A civilian, Kolar Suting, is shot at and injured by five suspected HNLC militants at his residence in Mawriang in the East Khasi Hills District.
- *February 12*: A 25 year-old woman cadre of the HNLC, identified as Marbilas Syiemlieh, surrenders before the East Khasi Hills District Police in capital Shillong. She revealed that economic hardship in the HNLC camps in Bangladesh forced her to return to the mainstream. Marbilas was attached to the 'Army Wing' of the HNLC and had undergone arms training in Chittagong Hill Tracts in Bangladesh since 2003. She hails from Manad village under Mawkyrwat Sub-Division in the West Khasi Hills District and is reported to have said that the HNLC is facing a serious financial crisis.

- *January 23*: The HNLC has called for a boycott of the Republic Day (January 26) celebrations in the Khasi and Jaintia Hills areas.
- *January 4*: A NDFB cadre, Guatam Boro, is arrested after being injured in an encounter with Police in Shohksih coal mining area of Jaintia Hills District a day earlier, subsequently succumbs to his injury. Guatam, hailing from Churachi village of Nalbari District in Assam, is involved along with other militants of the HNLC in extortion drive in coalfields of Jaintia Hills District.

2008

- *December 20*: A HNLC sympathiser, Pilot Shylla, is arrested from Brishyrnot village of Jaintia Hills District. "An SBBL gun was also recovered from his possession," said Police. Shylla confesses to have supported the militant outfit by providing information about the movement of Police in Jaintia Hills.
- *December 5*: Police foil an extortion drive of the HNLC in the Borsora –Nongjri-Nonghyllam coal belts—following interception of calls from Bangladesh. The HNLC leadership, based in Bangladesh, sent three cadres to Borosra-Nongjri areas for the collection drive but they were arrested by the police on December 1. According to police sources, the trio was asked to collect extortion money from the coal barons, and it was confirmed on the basis of the phone calls intercepted by a senior cadre, identified as Alex Hahshah. "Alex Hahshah made calls to the prominent exporters in Borsora-Nongjri area asking them to pay around ₹1.5 lakh to ₹2 lakh each", stated the Police sources, adding, "This was revealed by the arrested HNLC cadres during the course of interrogation." Alex Hahshah hailed from Nongjri area and he had all the phone numbers of the coal traders and exporters. The report adds that following

a break of some time, the HNLC had launched its extortion drive in the coal belts of West Khasi Hills along the India-Bangladesh border, after the three platoons of the State Police Battalion were withdrawn from Nonghyllam, 25 miles and Rajaju in November 2008.

- *December 3*: A senior cadre of the HNLC, identified as Marshal Roy Kharkongor alias Bah Arol, surrenders before Umkiang police at Jowai in the Jaintia Hills district. During the course of his interrogation, Marshal confesses that he had joined HNLC in 2001 and had completed three months training at Chittagong in Bangladesh. He is a resident of Madanriting in capital Shillong. He further discloses that the group of five cadres had entered Jaintia Hills through Hingaria village bordering Bangladesh and had halted at Umsona-Raja for about two weeks. Marshal, finding an opportunity, deserts his fellow cadres and surrenders before the police.
- *November 25*: A cadre of the 'finance wing' of the HNLC, identified as Wanpalei Ryngkhlem alias Palei, is arrested by the Meghalaya Police from Polo area in capital Shillong. Police said the outfit is conducting an extortion drive in various parts of Shillong. The modus operandi, according to police, is that HNLC 'authorises' certain people to collect money and then send it to its leaders who are camping in Bangladesh. The coal belt regions in Jaintia Hills and West Khasi Hills are the other areas where the HNLC has launched extortion drive to fill its coffers. Police sources say the HNLC had struck deals with the NSCN and NDFB for such a drive. The report adds that top HNLC leaders holed up in Bangladesh are reportedly facing severe crisis of cash and cadres, forcing them to join hands with the NSCN and NDFB and rope in certain individuals who can help the Khasi outfit in extorting money from businessmen, coal traders and others in the State.

- *November 12*: The Cabinet Committee on Security (CCS) extends the ban on HNLC by two years for its involvement in many recent cases of militancy in Meghalaya. The ban is also extended on ULFA and NDFB for their involvement in October 30 serial bomb blasts. The existing ban on the HNLC expires on November 15. Over the years, the Centre has banned 34 militant outfits, of which 13 belong to the Northeast.
- *November 3*: Meghalaya Police arrest 'second lieutenant' of the HNLC, identified as Shandor Phanbuh alias Antony, from Jingkieng Mawlai. Shandor is also the 'camp commander' of the outfit in Chittagong Hill tracts of Bangladesh. The report adds that the arrested militant along with two other cadres of the NDFB had infiltrated into India before the Durga Puja (a Hindu Festival). All the three had even abducted a Guwahati-based trader and confined him at an unspecified place in the Ri-Bhoi district. Later, the trader was released after the relatives paid a huge amount of ransom as demanded by the trio, which was equally shared by them.
- *October 24*: The HNLC 'publicity secretary' Sainkupar Nongtraw, rejects the talks offer made by Meghalaya Director General of Police B. K. Dey Sawian, who has recently stated that the doors are open for the Khasi outfit to come to the negotiating table. "HNLC has no agenda to hold talks with the State Government or its Police Department as they are only actors of the Indian Puppet Government," Nongtraw says. He adds that the State Government's invitation to HNLC for talks was aimed at creating "mistrust and confusion among the people." The HNLC says that it had sent a letter to the Union Ministry of Home Affairs (MHA) in 2003 offering to hold talks, adding the outfit was yet to get a reply from the Centre. The report adds that the HNLC had earlier prioritised six points to be included in the cease-fire

agreement with the Centre. They include lifting of the ban on the outfit, talks in a "neutral" country with safe passage to its cadres, supporters and sympathisers and a transparent agenda for talks.

- *October 15*: A HNLC cadre, Kyntiew Kupar War, surrenders before Meghalaya Police at Dawki. He is involved in a number of extortion ceases in the coal belt region at Lyngngam in the West Khasi Hills district. According to police source, Kyntiew joined the HNLC in 2001 and received arms training at Chittagong Hill Tracts in Bangladesh. Later in 2007, he was shifted to West Khasi Hills.
- *October 6*: A HLNC cadre, Bantei Sohtun alias Pyrkhat, surrenders before the Border Security Force (BSF) Inspector General P.K. Mishra in the Shillong city. He is involved in abduction and extortion in the East Khasi Hills district. He had joined the outfit in 2003, and had undergone arms training along with four others in Chittagong Hill Tracts in Bangladesh. After completion of his training, he was asked to stay with a few other members of HNLC at a Khasi village in Bangladesh. Bantei said the struggle to earn his livelihood forced him to come overground. P.K. Mishra says HNLC was still operating from its camps at Islapunji, Baramchal, Nooncherapunji, Panai, Amoli, Rangki, Begunchera, Nirlapunji and Niharpunji/Nihari under Maulavi Bazar district of Bangladesh.
- *September 16*: The HNLC opposes the municipal elections in Shillong. The outfit states that with the traditional institutions like the rangbah shnong (headman) already existing in Shillong, there is no question of having another authority.
- *August 28*: One HNLC militant, Lidon Syrti, surrenders before the Border Security Force. Syrti hailed from Rattachera village under Khlehriat police station in the Jaintia Hills district. During interrogation he revealed that he was the body guard

of the 'commander-in chief' of the HNLC, Bobby Marwine..

- *August 27*: One HNLC cadre, Phyrnailang Swer, is arrested from a place in the Jaintia Hills district. He confessed to having extorted huge amounts of money from traders in the area. Following his confession, police recovered two Chinese 9-mm pistols and four rounds of ammunition from a place in Mankijai.
- *August 25*: One HNLC cadre, Fullman Khongthohrem alias Dum, surrenders before the Meghalaya Police in capital Shillong. Fullman hails from Lapalang village near Dawki in the East Khasi Hills district. He had joined the outfit in 2002 and was trained in Chittagong Hills in Bangladesh. He has, however, not laid down any arms.
- *August 20*: One surrendered HNLC militant Tyngshain Lyngdoh Sohïong, involved in the August 12 killing of his colleague Kerlang Laitstep and his brother Philip Laitstep, surrenders before the Assam Rifles.
- *August 18*: One Pynhunlang Swer, claiming himself to be an HNLC cadre, is arrested by the Meghalaya Police on for demanding money from a trader of Jaintia Hills District. According to police sources, Pynhunlang, along with two other accomplices, have demanded INR 2500000 from a prominent businessman and citizen of Shangpung area in the name of the HNLC.
- *August 17*: Two HNLC cadres, including one identified as Command Lytan alias Commando, are arrested by police from Shillong Club for attempting to extort money from some traders. They have demanded money from INR 300000 to INR 500000 from the traders of Jaintia Hills.
- *August 14*: The HNLC proposes to hold talks with the Union Government on its '21st raising day'. The outfit's 'general secretary' Cheristerfield Thangkhiew says that they were ready to initiate a dialogue with

the Government to end the armed struggle, provided the Government was sincere.

- *August 12*: The HNLC calls for a general strike from August 14 in Meghalaya in protest agonist the Independence Day celebrations on August 15.
- *July 10*: One surrendered NDFB militant belonging to the Khasi tribe, identified as Jaklis Mawpniang alias Jimmy Momin, confesses before the Meghalaya Police during his interrogation that he was a former police constable of the first Meghalaya Police Battalion. "Mawpniang, hailing from Umsaw village of Meghalaya's Ri Bhoi district, deserted the battalion in 1983 to join the NDFB," an unnamed senior police official says. Mawpniang became the NDFB 'area commander' in Assam's Kokrajhar district and later became a trainer for the HNLC in Chittagong Hills Tracts in Bangladesh. "According to our information, he is the only Khasi in the NDFB outfit though there are many Garos in the NDFB and Ulfa," the official said.
- *July 24*: The HNLC said that the black flag march of the Khasi Students' Union (KSU) to protest the abduction of its circle president Fairshall Kongwang was a "blind experience." Denying its involvement in the abduction and killing of the student leader, the HNLC publicity secretary Sainkupar Nongtraw, in a statement to the press, stated that the KSU must understand that the surrendered cadres and the police have hatched a 'game plan.' The student body observed June 23 as black flag day protesting the abduction of Kongwang, who disappeared from Shyiap, a picnic spot near the Indo-Bangladesh border on December 16, 2007.
- *June 29*: Two HNLC militants, who infiltrate from their hideouts in Bangladesh, are arrested from Mawkyrwat village in the West Khasi Hills district. One revolver and five live rounds of.22 ammunition, cellphone and incriminating documents are recovered

from their possession. Police say both the militants were sent to India by their outfit to extort money from coal exporters and other businessmen in the district.

- *June 12*: Four surrendered cadres of the HNLC confess that Phershal Khongwang, Dawki unit president of the Khasi Students' Union (KSU), was abducted and later killed by HNLC cadre, Hep Khoit, along with two of his accomplices, Bol Khonglah and Jop Lamin, in Bangladesh in 2007. The HNLC cadres also unsuccessfully tried to kill former Khasi Hills Autonomous District Council (KHADC) chief H.S. Shylla.
- *June 6*: Four HNLC cadres, who were earlier remanded to police custody, are released for "lack of evidence". They were arrested by the Border Security Force (BSF) personnel in Tripura while entering Indian territory from Bangladesh without passport on May 16. They later revealed that they had deserted a HNLC camp in Bangladesh to surrender before the government.
- *May 31*: Intelligence sources said that seven former Naga insurgents, who deserted the NSCN–IM and NSCN-K, continue to maintain links with the HNLC and LAEF to extort money from coal exporters and other traders in the coal belts of West Khasi Hills and Garo Hills. "The Naga men normally go back to their State after collecting huge amount of money through extortion in Meghalaya," the sources say. Intelligence sources also said that former NSCN cadres involved in extortion in Meghalaya were planning to form a new militant outfit that could be more powerful than the NSCN-IM and NSCN-K. Many coal exporters from and outside the State have incurred huge losses due to the ongoing extortion drive jointly launched by cadres of the NSCN, HNLC and LAEF. Militants' threat is reported to have forced several coal exporters to leave the coal belt areas

recently. There are reports that the Tripura-based NLFT was supporting the HNLC's extortion drive in the district where coal exporters and managers of various cement plants were made to pay money to militants.

- *May 29*: Surrendered ANVC cadres asked the Meghalaya Government to provide them with recruitment in 5th India Reserve Battalion and monetary assistance. They also alleged that the former State Government did not have the commitment to rehabilitate all surrendered insurgents. They say that the previous D.D. Lapang-led Government had given "more importance" to the Shillong-based former cadre of the HNLC than those from the Garo Hills. The former ANVC cadres have sought Government jobs for at least 25 of them and financial assistance for the others to start their own entrepreneurship.
- *May 26*: Meghalaya Police said that militants belonging to the BW, HNLC and NLFT have demanded huge amounts of ransom from several cement companies in the Jaintia Hills district.
- *May 21*: Meghalaya Police arrests one hardcore HNLC cadre, Banteiborlang Lyngdoh Nonglait, from the coal belt areas at Nongjri near Borsora in the West Khasi Hills district. He was arrested while entering the export coal depot belonging to one Control Marbaniang. Ten live ammunitions of AK-47 are seized from his possession. According to police sources, he had recently returned from Bangladesh to carry out an extortion drive in the coal belt areas.
- *May 16*: The HNLC says in an e-mail statement that it has expelled four of its cadres, Heplung alias Judas, Mardor, Baiar, Pyndap alias Morning and Raimon, for allegedly 'breaching' the model code of conduct of the outfit. Four HNLC cadres are arrested by the Border Security Force personnel at Joshitilla village in the Dhalai district of Tripura along the India-

Bangladesh border. They confessed that they deserted their camp in the Moulavibazaar district of Bangladesh following acute shortage of food and medicine. They also mentioned that 182 HNLC cadres are now staying in that camp.

- *April 5*: One HNLC cadre, Ossomon Rynjah alias Belu, is arrested by the Border Security Force (BSF) personnel from Andermanik border outpost in the Mamit district while trying to cross over to Mizoram from Bangladesh. He confessed that the HNLC has maintained links with the Tripura-based NLFT since 2001. He also stated that the strength of HNLC in the Bangladesh camp located under Baghachuri police station in the Rangamati district was about 100 in 2001. As many as 26 NLFT cadres also stayed in the HNLC camp at that time, he added. Rynjah confessed that since most of the cadres deserted the camp the strength has been reduced to 26, and the camp is left with one.303 rifle. He said that he deserted the camp due to forced labour detention and ill treatment by the HNLC commanders.
- *April 3*: Meghalaya Police arrested six persons, including rangbah shnongs (members of the traditional local-self government institutions) and businessmen, from different parts of the Jaintia Hills district for their suspected links with the HNLC. They were identified as Phon Syih, Welcome Dkhar, Lambha Dhar, Susil Dkhar, Pyntngen Bareh and Rangbahduh Khonglah. According to police sources, they were arrested following confession of the HNLC militants who were arrested during the recent encounter at Wahlymbong. They are accused of giving shelter, money and other goods to the HNLC cadres. Two arrested HNLC cadres, Willender Diengdoh Marngar and Riskin Phawa, had reportedly collected INR 50000 from them.
- *March 30*: The Superintendent of Police (Special Branch), Claudia A. Lyngwa, while terming the

HNLC as "an organisation of a few vested interests," said that deteriorating cadre strength of the outfit had forced it to join hands with the Tripura-based NLFT. She stated that the outfit's cadre strength could be between 70 and 80, including a few senior members camping in Bangladesh. "These (few) vested interests (HNLC activists) are very much aware that they are losing their strength every day and the best option for them is to surrender," she said, adding, "Deteriorating cadre strength has forced HNLC to join hands with the NLFT."

- *March 27*: The HNLC 'camp commander' at Chittagong Hill Tract, Syrpailin Mawlong, is arrested at Umkiang in the Jaintia Hills district. He confesses before police that the outfit was facing a funds crisis and he had been asked by his leaders to carry out an extortion drive in the Jaintia Hills. He also said that after the surrender of former Chairman Julius Dorphang, the outfit is yet to nominate any other leader as the chairman. He added that 100 cadres, including eight to nine women, were based in Bangladesh. Two HNLC militants, Vicky Majaw and Leader, are shot dead by Meghalaya Police during an encounter at Umkiang in the Jaintia Hills district. However, three NLFT militants who along with the HNLC militants opened fire on the police personnel manage to escape from the encounter site. Four SBBL shot guns, two AK-56 assault rifles and 33 rounds of live ammunition, a country-made.22 revolver, two Chinese hand grenades and two sets of Japanese-made wireless handsets, three torches, a mobile handset and two authorisation letters for extortion were recovered from the encounter site. According to police sources, the HNLC and NLFT ran a joint camp at Wahlymbong for about two months to extort money from coal traders and businessmen of Jaintia Hills. The encounter occurred when police raided a militant hideout in the Umkiang area following the arrest of six HNLC militants, including an 'area commander' Syrpailin Mawlong alias Bhalang, and a courier Riskin Phawa, during a search operation in Malidor area and Umkiang village on March 26. Four others were identified as Emanuel Umthlu alias Shwa, L. Marngar alias Willinder Marngar, Aibor Sawian and Chedrak Wanniang.

- *March 19*: One HNLC militant, identified as Gedolf Nongrem of Mawkhar, surrendered before the Border Security Force (BSF) at the Umsyiem border outpost near Dawki. During interrogation, Nongrem told the BSF that he, along with five others, was lured by one HNLC activist Lungtung of Mawlai to join the banned outfit and had undergone arms training at an HNLC camp in Chittagong, Bangladesh. "I left for Bangladesh in June 2003 and underwent training along with others, including eight female activists, at an HNLC camp in Chittagong," Nongrem said.
- *March 14*: The surrendered HNLC militants decide to ask the Meghalaya Government for general amnesty. The decision was taken at the first meeting of the surrendered militants, chaired by its former chairman Julius Dorphang, at Mawlong. "We have decided to urge the Centre and the state to grant general amnesty to all the surrendered HNLC militants. We want the government to provide a better rehabilitation package to prevent them from going astray," Dorphang said. There are more than 100 surrendered HNLC militants in capital Shillong. "Most of these boys are poor and are finding it difficult to sustain themselves," he said, adding that many of them are yet to receive the rehabilitation package. Dorphang said. He also refuted allegations that the surrendered HNLC militants had campaigned for the ruling Congress party in the recently-concluded legislative Assembly elections. "The allegations are not true. The surrendered militants were free to support any candidate," he added.

- *February 27*: Normal life in the capital Shillong and other parts of the State was affected due to a general strike called by the HNLC in protest against Prime Minister Manmohan Singh's State visit.
- *January 26*: The HNLC calls for a 24-hour strike in the Khasi and Jaintia Hills in protest against the celebration of the Republic Day.
- *January 24*: The 'publicity secretary' of the HNLC, Sainkupar Nongtraw, accuses some politicians of playing the 'religious card' to win the elections. The outfit asked the church bodies to initiate steps to prevent such activities.

2007

- *December 30*: Meghalaya Police stated that Phersial Kongwang, the Khasi Students Union's (KSU) Dawki Circle president, was abducted and later taken to Bangladesh by the HNLC militants. "We have thoroughly investigated the matter. We have no doubt that HNLC men have taken the victim (Mr Kongwang) to Bangladesh," police say. Police add that HNLC cadre, Bah Hep alias Hep Khoit, and two other unidentified armed persons were involved in the abduction
- *December 28*: One surrendered HNLC cadre, Stephan Rymbai, is arrested from his rented house at Salini Colony in Mihmyntdu of Jaintia Hills district. Police said that Rymbai had been involved in a number of crimes even after he came over-ground.
- *December 26*: Meghalaya Police said that the HNLC is being helped by the NLFT in Jaintia Hills, the NSCN-IM in West Khasi Hills and the NDFB in areas of Ri-Bhoi district. The HNLC's declining manpower and continued failure to start an extortion drive in Shillong city has forced the outfit to seek help of other outfits and extort money from businessmen, especially coal traders, in other districts of the State bordering Bangladesh. "The firepower of HNLC is

less at present and the outfit cannot buy more weapons due to financial constraints. It has to borrow arms from other militant groups," said an unnamed source.

- *December 19*: The surrendered 'chairman' of the HNLC, Julius Dorphang, said that the HNLC maintains a fleet of boats to ferry ration and other items to its cadres at their camps in the Chittagong Hill Tracts of Bangladesh. Dorphang also said that since the Chittagong Hill Tracts is surrounded by deep jungles and criss-crossed by rivers, a boat was the easiest mode of transport. He added that most of the items were collected from different places from where they were taken to loading points along the Feni, Karnaphuli, Sangu (Sankhu) and Matamuhuri rivers. From the offloading points, the ration was carried to the camps. One HNLC cadre, who had escaped during the December 17 police raid on the camp jointly set up by the HNLC and NLFT inside Narpuh Reserve Forest of Jaintia Hills, surrenders before East Khasi Hills Superintendent of Police, A.R. Mawthoh.
- *December 17*:Meghalaya Police neutralizes a joint camp of the HNLC and the NLFT during an operation at Narpuh reserve forest in the Jaintia Hills. A number of 9-mm live cartridges.22 live cartridges, one very high frequency handset, six micro cassettes, a prescription of a Bangladeshi doctor, photographs, a diary and four butts of AK-56 rifles are recovered. However, no arrests were made.
- *December 15*: Meghalaya Police stated that one suspected HNLC militant, while trying to hijack a Jeep belonging to a coal exporter, Milan Khongsit, was assaulted by civilians at Mawngap in the East Khasi Hills district.
- *December 7*: Nagaland Post reports that the Meghalaya Police has launched a flush-out operation targeting HNLC extortionists in the coal belt area.

- *December 6*: Shillong Times, quoting intelligence sources, reports that the HNLC has resumed its extortion drive in the coal belt of Borsora in the West Khasi Hills district. The HNLC demanded INR 500000 from coal exporters owning ten or more trucks. Those having five and more than five trucks were asked to pay ransom between INR 250000 to 300000.
- *November 24*: Shillong Times reports that at least eight senior cadres of the HNLC will desert their camp in Bangladesh and come overground and surrender in protest against the system of functioning and policy of the HNLC 'commander-in-chief' Bobby Marwein.
- *November 19*: Shillong Times reports that the Meghalaya Police are investigating the alleged nexus between teer (a traditional form of gambling that sustains the age-old sport of archery) bookies and the HNLC, which reportedly helps the militant outfit to strengthen its coffer. After a gap of four years, Meghalaya Police have reopened the file related to the teer bookies-HNLC nexus. Police had unearthed the nexus between teer bookies and HNLC in 2003 and arrested some office bearers of the Archery Sports Association. Four years later, the file, in this regard, was reopened following the encounter on October 30 at Cleve Colony in which five HNLC militants were killed. Manbha Rynjah, one of the slain militants, was a teer bookie and contractor.
- *November 11*: Meghalaya Police said that the NDFB has continued to help the HNLC since 2005 by supplying weapons to the outfit. They claimed that the HNLC militants, who are camping in Paham-Umdoh forest, maintain links with the NDFB. An unnamed senior police official stated: "NDFB leaders used to make periodic visits to the make-shift camps of the HNLC in the Ri-Bhoi district".
- *November 7*: Deputy Superintendent of Police Raymond P. Diengdoh was killed when a team of

police personal attacked a HNLC hideout at Paham Umdoh forest near Byrnihat in the Ri-Bhoi district. One militant, identified as Salin alias Jockey, of Mawsynram in the East Khasi Hills district, was also killed in the encounter. Police arrested two HNLC cadres, Sharailang Raiwan and Andy Lyngdoh, from the encounter site. Two Kalashnikov rifles, a pistol and some cartridges are recovered from the incident site.

- *November 6*: The Khasi Hills Autonomous District Council (KHADC) chief, H.S. Shylla, accuses the non governmental organisations and a political party of having nexus with the HNLC. The KHADC chief accused the Khasi Students' Union, the Federation of Khasi, Jaintia and Garo People and Khun Hynniewtrep National Awakening Movement party of having a nexus with the outfit.
- *November 4*: Meghalaya Police stated that the HNLC is using women as agents to extort money from places where the finance wing of the organisation fails to penetrate. "Even after the arrest of a few women who worked for the HNLC in the past, some women are still helping the outfit in collecting money in Shillong and Dawki in Jaintia Hills," a senior unnamed police official disclosed. He said that before going on an extortion drive, the women make 'missed calls' to top HNLC leaders based in Bangladesh, who help them with ways and means to negotiate the amount. A prepaid mobile phone having a balance of INR 800 to INR 900 is used by the women to send "missed calls" to Bangladesh. The report adds that the arrest of a woman, Velvet Rose Jana, who accompanied HNLC militants to assassinate HS Shylla, the Chief Executive Member of the Khasi Hills Autonomous District Council, in August 20074, has revealed that she had extorted money on behalf of the outfit from businessmen. She confesses to have worked in tandem with her husband, Tome Jones Rynjah, to spread the activities of the HNLC,

including extortion in Shillong. Police had arrested the couple from Mawlai Syllaikriah locality of Shillong for their role in leading the HNLC cadres to the house of Shylla. According to A.R. Mawthoh, the Superintendent of Police of the East Khasi Hills district, the HNLC courier recently sent INR 400, 000 to Bobby Marwein, 'commander-in-chief' of the outfit, who is based in Bangladesh.

- *October 30*: Five HNLC militants, one of them identified as Safir Hashah, are shot dead by police personnel during an encounter at Cleave Colony under Laitumkhrah police station in the East Khasi Hills district. The incident occurs when a police team tries to intercept a vehicle carrying the militants. Two police personnel are also injured in the exchange of fire. An AK-47 rifle, a double barrel gun, a single barrel gun, one grenade and some ammunition are recovered from the slain militants. The East Khasi Hills district Superintendent of Police, A.R. Mawthoh, informs that the militants entered Meghalaya from Bangladesh to kill the outfit's surrendered chairman, Julius Dorphang.
- *October 29*: One courier of the HNLC, Rimen Rymbai, is arrested by police personnel at Dawki in the Jaintia Hills District. Rymbai was sent by his seniors from Bangladesh to collect the demanded amount from a prominent businessman of Dawki. Sources add that Rymbai hails from Lamapunji under Gowainghat police station in the Sylhet district of Bangladesh.
- *October 29*: Two HNLC cadres, Rajesh Lamin and Lyli Lamin, surrender before the East Khasi Hills district-Superintendent of Police.
- *October 17*: Meghalaya Police chief, B.K. Dey Sawian, said that the HNLC is carrying out an extortion drive at Laitumkhrah and Nongthymmai areas in capital Shillong. He also stated that though the cadre strength of the HNLC is reducing, the possibility of the outfit's cadres regrouping cannot be ruled out.

- *September 11*: Two persons, identified as Wanwarting Pathaw alias Perry and Suk Nongrang, are arrested from Nongmynsong in capital Shillong. They are involved in the September 9-abduction of John Alex Dohkrud, the brother of a surrendered HNLC cadre Amos Dohkrud, from Lad Mawlai Motsyiar.
- *August 24*: Meghalaya Police arrest the mother of Bobby Marwein, the 'commander-in-chief of HNLC, from an unspecified place in the East Khasi Hills district. Superintendent of Police A.R. Mawthoh said, "The police are investigating the involvement of Marwein's mother, wife and Thangkhiew's sister in the extortion racket."
- *August 23*: Police arrests the sister of Cherishstarfield Thangkhiew, 'general secretary' of the HNLC, and wife of Bobby Marwein, 'commander-in-chief'' of the same outfit, for their involvement in extortion at Jaiaw Langsning in the East Khasi Hills district.
- *August 22*: Police arrest a HNLC cadre, identified as Phrangsngi Hahshah, from Motphran in the East Khasi Hills district. He is suspected to be the linkman behind the extortion drive of the outfit.
- *August 21*: Five HNLC cadres, while extorting from traders, are arrested at Dawki in the Jaintia Hills District. They were identified as Ispon Khonglah, Donbok Kongwang, Teiborlang Kongwang, Dominic Rangjem and Wansalan Khonglah.
- *August 21*: Four suspected HNLC cadres are arrested from various parts of the capital Shillong. They came from Bangladesh recently to carry out an extortion drive.
- *August 16*: One senior HNLC cadre, Aral Mango alias Heh, surrenders before the Ri-Bhoi district Superintendent of Police J. Rymmai. Heh was reportedly a linkman between the HNLC and NDFB.
- *August 15*: The HNLC expresses its willingness to sit for tripartite talks involving both the Union and State governments. 'General Secretary' Cheristerfield

Thangkhiew said in a statement on the 20th raising day of the HNLC that the group was keen to end bloodshed and is willing to sit for talks.

- *August 12*: The HNLC calls for a 24-hour bandh (strike) from August 14 in protest against the Independence Day celebrations on August 15. A statement issued by the outlawed group's 'publicity secretary' Sainkupar Nongtraw said that it would continue its "20-year-old armed struggle for political and socio-economic development of the people". The strike exempts patients and hospital attendants and milkmen from its purview.
- *August 6*: The HNLC 'publicity secretary' Sainkupar Nongtraw alleged that 'chairman' Julius Dorphang, who had recently surrendered, had been bought over by Chief Minister D. D. Lapang. A statement said that by coming over-ground, Dorphang had undermined his own position as a top leader of the outfit. "Dorphang must know the kind of action that the HNLC would take against deserters who took away its properties," the HNLC statement added. It also said that by surrendering, Dorphang had 'stabbed the HNLC from the back'. The HNLC also said that Dorphang is earlier authorized by the outfit's leadership to speak to Lapang over phone regarding the peace initiative "but the outfit did not expect that he would be bought over by Lapang to the extent that he deserted his own colleagues."
- *August 3*: A surrendered HNLC cadre, Bitkhotal Khongkip, who disrupted the Elector's Photo Identity Card programme at Nongskhen village in the East Khasi Hills district on July 30, is arrested by the police from an unspecified location.
- *August 2*: The surrendered 'Chairman" of the HNLC, Julius Dorphang, has decided to resign from the top post of the group. He admitted that personality conflicts among the top HNLC leaders had eroded the image of the group. Dorphang, however, denied

the allegations made by the HNLC of taking away INR 20 million before his surrender and also rejected other charges of selling weapons and assets of the outfit.

- *August 1*: The Deputy Commissioner of the East Khasi Hills district, Bhalang Dhar, ordered the police to arrest surrendered HNLC cadre, Bitkophal Khongkip, for his alleged misbehaviour with the Election department officials during an electorate photo identity card programme at Nongskhen in the East Khasi Hills district. The HNLC 'publicity secretary', Sainkupar Nongtraw, in a press statement alleged that the surrendered chairman of the group, Julius Dorphang, has decamped with the outfit's money amounting to INR 20 million. He added that Dorphang has sold away properties of the organization, including the arms of his security personnel. The statement also denied Dorphang's claim that the HNLC general secretary and 'Commander-in-Chief' did not understand the meaning of peace.
- *July 24*: Julius K. Dorphang, chairman of the outlawed HNLC, along with his four bodyguards, identified as Teilang Wanniang, Salonsar Thongni, Bima Suting and Rit Lakashiang, surrendered to the security forces at an unspecified location in the capital city of Shillong. Dorphang accepted an offer of safe passage from the State Government and decided to join the mainstream, indicating a major setback to the Khasi outfit formed in 1988. However, no weapon is deposited by the HNLC cadres. Dorphang and the four cadres arrived in Shillong on July 23-night by road through Lyngkhat village near the India-Bangladesh border under tight police security.
- *May 28*: One HNLC cadre, identified as Trustman Roy Lyngdoh Nonglait belonging to the Mawlai Kynton Massar area, surrendered before the police at an unspecified location.

- *May 23*: The Unlawful Activities (Prevention) Tribunal extended the ban on the ANVC and HNLC for two more years due to their continued anti-national and anti-social activities. The new order will remain in force till May 15, 2009.
- *May 17*: One Hynniewtrep National Liberation Council (HNLC) cadre, identified as 'sergeant major' Andy Roy Lartang alias Bahdeng, surrendered to the security forces at an unspecified location.
- *May 7*: Two surrendered HNLC cadres, Mayborn Rapthap and Victor Rumnong, are booked under the Meghalaya Prevention Detention Act for their suspected involvement in cases of abduction and murder. A woman cadre of the HNLC, identified as Lanosha Kharkulia, surrenders before A.R. Mawthoh, the Superint-endent of Police of East Khasi Hills district.
- *April 14*: Six HNLC cadres, identified as Kitbakmar Baniang, Amos Khamnaior, Teidur Kharsahnoh, Orrissal Ynsatlang, Ricky Kharjana and his wife Baitbianglen, surrender before the Border Security Force at Panisagar in the North Tripura district of Tripura. The two-day meeting of the Tribunal to look into the ban on the HNLC and ANVC concludes. Official sources said that there was no representation from the HNLC and only the ANVC contested the case aiming at lifting the proscription.
- *April 12*: Three surrendered HNLC cadres, Khainborlang Kharwaniang, Mayborn Rapthap and Victor Rumnong, were arrested from different parts of the Shillong city in connection with the abduction of six persons on February 22.
- *February 20*: Two HNLC cadres, Lord Canning Thongni and Everywell Leroy, who surrendered in Shillong confessed that they used to hand over the extortion money to a Bangladeshi national, Abdus Salam. Police suspect that the top HNLC leaders are using Bangladeshi nationals as couriers to bring

extortion money, since they had lost faith in the lower rung cadres. Superintendent of Police of the East Khasi Hills district, A. R. Mawthoh, disclosed that around 130 militants had so far surrendered in East Khasi Hills. "More and more cadres are leaving the outfit as the extorted money has been pocketed by the top leaders," Mawthoh added.

- *February 10*: Nine HNLC militants, including its senior leader Herman Pakyntein, surrender along with a rifle and two shot guns at Panisagar in the North Tripura district of Tripura. They escaped from their hideout in Bangladesh. According to police sources, the present cadre strength of the HNLC is estimated to be around 60 to 70, following the surrender.
- *January 2*: A court in the East Khasi Hills district remands a former HNLC cadre, Samborlang Kharlyngdoh, to three-day police custody. Jhalupara police arrested him a day earlier for illegally possessing a 9-mm pistol along with six rounds of ammunition.

2006

- *December 25*: An extortionist, Asuk Amyrsong, is arrested from Kharkhana village in the Jaintia Hills district along the India-Bangladesh border. However, two others manage to escape. They reportedly served extortion notes of INR 25,000 to a lady, Mala Pohlong, in the guise of HNLC cadres.
- *December 20*: One HNLC cadre, Aimos Khonglaban, surrenders at Pynursla police station in the East Khasi Hills district.
- *November 27*: A HNLC cadre, Tensing Khonglah, surrenders before the Superintendent of Police of Shillong City. According to police sources, Khonglah was operating from Sanatula near Silchar in the Cachar district of Assam.
- *November 20*: Responding to the offer made by the

HNLC for peace talks with the Union Government, the Meghalaya Home Minister, Robert G. Lyngdoh, stated that the State Government should be involved in the peace talks "so that it won't be held responsible for any failure in the process." "We are ready to hold talks at any moment and our door for negotiation is always open. But the talks should be a tripartite one like what was done with the ANVC," he added.

- *November 9*: The Union Government extends the proscription on HNLC.
- *October 31*: HNLC has started setting up camps at Block I in the Karbi Anlong district of Assam. Reports added that five hardcore cadres belonging to the "Action Group (Army Wing)" of the outfit set up a camp in Assam.
- *October 4*: A senior HNLC cadre, Mon Pohrmen, who was the 'commander' of the camp at Panai in Bangladesh, surrenders before Meghalaya Police at Jowai in the Jaintia Hills district. He deposits some sample demand notes before the police.
- *September 28*: A HNLC cadre, Dap Singh Ritshong alias Syrpai, surrenders before the Meghalaya Police at an unspecified place.
- *September 25*: Meghalaya Police recover dead bodies of two former HNLC cadres, Philio Hashah and his brother Anthony Hashah, from Wah Khri near Mairang in the West Khasi Hills district. They were killed en route to appear in the district court for a pending case relating to their earlier linkages with the HNLC.
- *September 25*: Meghalaya Police arrests a HNLC cadre, Tom Jones Rynjah, from Mawlai Syllaikriah in the capital Shillong, and seizes some incriminating documents from his possession.
- *September 20*: A HNLC cadre, Krinding Lyngdoh, surrenders before the Meghalaya Police at an unspecified location. According to police sources, the surrendered militant, who confessed to having

recently returned from Bangladesh, did not deposit any arms.

- *September 20*: Meghalaya Police kills a HNLC cadre, Bankit Khonjee, and arrests another during an encounter at Umkrem in the East Khasi Hills district. A modified sten gun of 9 mm caliber, one 9 mm carbine, 40 rounds of ammunition and eight empty cases of assorted ammunition are recovered from the incident site. Following the incident, one surrendered HNLC cadre is also arrested for sheltering the HNLC cadres.
- *September 10*: The Union Government authorises the Meghalaya Government to directly negotiate with the HNLC. Meanwhile, State Chief Minister J. D. Rymbai and Home Minister R. G. Lyngdoh ask the cadres of the outfit to give up arms and return to the mainstream.
- *August 30*: Disillusioned women cadres of the HNLC, who are in an isolated camp in Bangladesh and are desperate to leave the outfit to join the main stream, are reportedly being prevented from deserting the militant camp. At least eight women cadres, including six from Shillong and West Khasi Hills and two from Pynursla in East Khasi Hills, have remained in Bangladesh, according to police sources. "But they are prevented by their top leaders," police say.
- *July 15*: A HNLC cadre, Diam Salon, surrenders at Jowai police station in the Jaintia Hills district. The surrendered militant escaped from his camp in Bangladesh.
- *July 6*: At least 435 HNLC cadres were killed, surrendered or arrested by the police personnel so far, says Inspector General of Police, B. L. Buam. Out of the total, 289 were arrested, 27 died in encounters, while 119 surrendered.
- *June 29*: At least three HNLC militants, including one of their leaders identified as Khrawbor Lartang alias Kordor, Lumbor Nongneng alias Pdit and Precious

Star Lamare alias Kos, surrender before the East Khasi Hills district police in Shillong, the State capital.

- *June 25*: At least ten HNLC cadres, who surrender in the North Tripura district of Tripura on June 21, are brought back and remanded to ten-day police custody at Shillong, the State capital.
- *June 23*: Two unidentified HNLC cadres are shot dead in an encounter with the police at Nonghyllam near Nongjri village in the West Khasi Hills district. While another militant manages to escape, one carbine, one pistol and few rounds of ammunitions are recovered from the encounter site. According to intelligence reports, the HNLC militants infiltrated into the Indian territory from Bangladesh.
- *June 21*: At least ten HNLC cadres, including a senior leader, surrender before the Border Security Force personnel at an unspecified place in the North Tripura district of Tripura. The surrendered militants, who desert their camp in Bangladesh, were identified as West Syngkli, Bamut-lang Chyne, Coverland Lartang, Oswald Nengnong, Erest Wanshnong, George Tang-sang, Peter Kharmawphlang, Fullmoon Nongsiej, Shemphang Syiem-iong and Larsemson Jala.
- *June 19*: Two suspected HNLC cadres, Minot and Tensing, are arrested at an unspecified place under Halidayganj police station in the Dhubri district along the India-Bangladesh border, while infiltrating.
- *June 15*: Two HNLC cadres, Minit Lang and Tensing Khngla, are arrested by the BSF personnel near Makamtilla under Patherkandi block in the Karimganj district while crossing the India-Bangladesh border. Both reportedly were trying to reach the Khasi hills of Meghalaya through the adjoining Cachar district. They reveal during interrogation that most militant outfits with camps in Bangladesh are planning to push in more cadres

to the Indian territory through the border during the monsoon.

- *June 2*: A HNLC cadre, Tibor Dkhar alias Ban, who left his hideout at Puthisara in Bangladesh, surrenders at Shillong before the Superintendent of Police of the East Khasi Hills district. An AK 47 rifle, suspected to be abandoned by the HNLC cadres, is recovered from the forest area of the North-Eastern Hill University near Mawlai.
- *May 31*: The HNLC threatens against persons participating in the forthcoming Municipal elections at Shillong, the State capital. The outfit also expresses 'concern' about ongoing influx into the Jaintia Hills.
- *May 24*: The MHA asks for the estimation of assets of the top leaders of the Hynniewtrep HNLC including its 'chairman' Julius K Dorphang, 'general secretary' Cherishsterfield Thangkhiew and self-styled 'Commander -in-Chief" Bobby Marwein. Official sources say that the MHA is also assessing the activities of the outfit to ensure that it does not indulge in extortion from the businessmen.
- *May 1*: Chief Minister D. D. Lapang says that the proposal for peace talks with the HNLC is a better option than seeing the outfit members surrendering. Lapang, while expressing the State Government's willingness to hold talks with the militant outfits, said, "There is nothing to hide and it is true that I had a telephonic conservation with HNLC Chairman Julius Dorphang on the issues related to peace talks."
- *April 30*: The Meghalaya Home Department says that insincerity of the 'commander-in-chief' of the HNLC is the main reason for the State Government delaying the peace process. According to Home Department sources, "We have no doubt about the sincerity of the outfit's chairman Julius K Dorphang; but we have got some doubts about Bobby Marwein, who often indulges in illegal activities despite making the initial move for peace process." The sources add that the

Union and State Governments are keen to have a cease-fire with the banned outfit, but given the present situation, "both are of the view that the process should be re-examined before arriving at any decision".

- *April 27*: The Chief Executive Member of the Khasi Hills Autonomous District Council, H. S. Shylla, criticizes the threat of the HNLC to pull out of the proposed peace talks with the Meghalaya Government in protest against the latter's permission for Uranium mining at Domiasiat in the West Khasi Hills district.
- *March 27*: Meghalaya Chief Minister D.D. Lapang, while responding to the issue of negotiations with militant outfits, informs the Legislative Assembly that a "Joint Monitoring Group (JMG) has been formed to monitor the cease-fire with the ANVC. The next JMG meeting will be held on April 5 in Guwahati, said, while adding that, "We are thinking of adopting similar pattern as the first step to initiate dialogue with HNLC."
- *March 27*: A former HNLC cadre, Aibor Marwein, is shot at and wounded at Mawlai Nongkwar Block III in the Shillong city. Marwein was arrested in 2002 while being an active HNLC cadre.
- *March 24*: The Union Home Minister Shivraj Patil, while responding at Shillong to the issue of the reported willingness of the proscribed HNLC to negotiate with the Government, says, "Doors are open for dialogue with any militant group."
- *March 21*: An HNLC cadre, Khrawkupar Shylla alias Khro, is arrested from Mawlai Nongk-war in the East Khasi Hills district. He confesses about the involvement of HNLC in arms smuggling in Meghalaya.
- *March 17*: Meghalaya Director General Police, W.R. Marbaniang, says that an unspecified number of misguided youths from West Khasi Hills and other areas have joined the banned HNLC.

- *February 21*: The Jaintia Hills district police arrest three HNLC cadres, Arwat Kharumnuid alias Jo Swer, Robert Jiteng alias Bah Bah and Khlainbor Pakyntein alias Heprit, from a camp of coal miners at Jaliaphet. However, two of them subsequently escaped from police custody.
- *February 21*: The Church leader, Rev. Basaiawmoit, who was appointed by the State Government to broker peace with the HNLC, establishes contacts with the top leaders of the proscribed outfit and intimates about the Government's desire to have a dialogue with them. He says, "Today (Tuesday) evening, I conveyed the HNLC leadership the outcome of my meeting with the Chief Minister and the State Home Minister."
- *February 18*: A HNLC cadre, Pynshngaiñlang Lyngdoh Mairang, surrenders before Mairang Police in the West Khasi Hills district.
- *February 3*: A suspected HNLC cadre, who is arrested from Jowai in the Jaintia Hills district, manages to escape during an accident involving the security convoy carrying him near Mawryngkneng.
- *January 30*: Hardcore HNLC militants take shelter in the Block-I areas along the Assam-Meghalaya border for raising funds for the outfit. The militants have reportedly sneaked into the State from Bangladesh for revitalising the outfit. A militant, Hopeborn Shangpliang, who has surrendered during the second week of January, confesses to have regrouped the militants in the Jaintia Hills district for extortion from the coal traders. A senior police officer says, "The HNLC militants chose Block-I as their area of operation so that the Meghalaya police would not be able to know about their movements."
- *January 20*: A HNLC militant, Hopeborn Shangpliang, surrenders before police personnel at Jowai in the Jaintia Hills district. He deposits a 9mm pistol and 10 rounds of live ammunition. Police sources say that

the militant, a self-style sergeant of the outfit, had joined the HNLC in 1999. He left the outfit's camp in Bangladesh in 2005 and since then has been operating from Psiar in Block I area of the Jaintia Hills district.

- *January 16*: The 'publicity secretary' of the HNLC, Sainkupar Nongtraw, expresses doubts over the seriousness of the Meghalaya Government in dealing with the issue of illegal migrants. Nongtraw claims that the action of the State police in flushing out illegal immigrants as published in newspapers is "an eyewash" and a "fashion show". He further says: "If the State and the Central governments had the responsibility to flush out immigrants who have illegally entered the State, why they took 34 years to initiate measures. May be it is the government which has provided them with land, houses, jobs and at the same time recognised them as the legal immigrants settled in Umpling, Pynthor, Mawprem and other localities of Shillong".
- *January 8*: A senior HNLC cadre, Bashembha Pathaw, is arrested from Psiar village on the Meghalaya-Assam border in the Jaintia Hills district. Ten AK-47 ammunition are recovered from his possession.

2005

- *December 23*: Meghalaya Police arrests 'vice-chairman' of the HNLC, Teilang Thangkhiew, from a hideout at Pohkseh in the capital Shillong. Police sources say that Thangkhiew returned from Bangladesh a few days back to revitalise the outfit following the arrest and surrender of more than hundred cadres during the recent years.
- *December 2*: Church leader, Rev. Basaiawmoit, says that the proscribed HNLC is awaiting an official response either from the Prime Minister's Office or the Union Home Ministry to initiate peace talks. "After proper consultation with the Home Ministry

officials I created a channel through which the HNLC was immediately contacted with the hope of ending the decade-long insurgency problem and bring peace and normalcy back to the Khasi-Jaintia Hills and the State as a whole. I have communicated HNLC's views to the Centre but the latter is yet to respond to it", he says.

- *November 3*: HNLC is reported to be involved in extortion activities targeting coal traders of the Jaintia Hills district. The police arrest two persons, president of the Meghalaya Transporters and Suppliers Union, Jamrist Rymbai, and his colleague, Chamik Nongpluh, from Lad Rymbai for their connivance with the outfit's extortion activities. Police sources say that the arrested persons have served an extortion note of Rupees 16 lakh (INR) on a coal merchant on behalf of the outfit.
- *November 1*: The proscribed HNLC, in an e-mail to the local media in Meghalaya's capital Shillong, refutes reports that speculate the surrender of the outfit's 'commander-in-chief' Bobby Marwein and some other cadres. The 'publicity secretary' of the outfit, Sainkupar Nongkhlaw, says, "There are forces who want to create cracks in our organization and the reports are at their instance... Reports about our c-in-c's surrender is part of the propaganda waged by the forces against the council."
- *September 27*: Julius K Dorphang, 'chairman' of the HNLC, expresses his keenness for peace talks with the Union Government. The surrendered 'publicity secretary' of the outfit, Mihsalan Kynjing, says that HNLC has made some attempts in the past to initiate peace talks and some members of the group have reportedly met officials of the Union Home Ministry in 2004.
- *July 27*: The surrendered 'finance secretary' of the HNLC, Yitjanai Sunn alias Iainehskhem Shylla, reports that 200 HNLC cadres, including 10 women,

presently camping in Bangladesh, are in a state of disarray. He also claims that the outfit is going through a major financial crisis and at present it has only Rupees 20 lakh in its coffers. He also says that 20 cadres have become victims of fratricidal clashes in Bangladesh and five to six of them died due to malaria. He also confirms that there is a tie-up between the HNLC and NDFB.

- *July 25*: Six HNLC cadres, including the outfit's Finance Secretary Yit Sun alias Iaineh Skhem Shylla, surrender before the police in Shillong. The others are identified as Donald Wann alias Lumlang from Jaiaw Mawbynna, Elvin alias Treng Saw from Mawlai Syllaikariah, Kohbah from Mawlai Mawtawar, Hamar Ropmay alias Hep Tatoo from Mawlai Nongpdeng and Phyrnai Nongrum alias Bahlieh from Mawlai Umjaiur. The HNLC, however, in a statement issued by 'Information Secretary' Mangkara Dkhar claims that the six have "deserted" its temporary camp. It also charges them with indulging in misuse of power, stealing of official property and violating the principles of the outfit.
- *July 22*: The police arrest a surrendered cadre of the HNLC, James Sylliang, from Mawlai in the capital Shillong. According to police sources, Sylliang is arrested after complaints are lodged against him for involvement in criminal activities, including extortion.
- *July 12*: Meghalaya Police says that HNLC leaders are living safely in Bangladesh and are also involved in business activities in that country. The East Khasi Hills district Superintendent of Police, A. S. Rynjah, says, "They (leaders of the banned Hynniewtrep National Liberation Council (HNLC) militant outfit), are living in safe rented houses in Dhaka, Maulavi Bazar and Panai areas." Citing intelligence inputs, he further said that insurgent leaders are also engaged in business activities by acquiring farms of betel nuts, betel and arecanut in the border villages.

- *July 11*: Meghalaya Police rescues a trader, Mainak Dey, who was abducted two days earlier from Lawbah village in the East Khasi Hills district. Official sources said that subsequent to an encounter with HNLC cadres, he was rescued. An unidentified HNLC cadre is killed in the encounter and another is arrested while four others manage to escape. One rifle, one shotgun, one country-made pistol, one hand grenade and some incriminating documents are recovered from the incident site.
- *June 29*: Unknown assailants kill a surrendered HNLC militant, Oli Syiemlieh, near Mawsynram in the East Khasi Hills district. The victim was missing since June 27 and his body with several injuries was recovered from a forest area in Nongtrai.
- *June 21*: A hardcore HNLC cadre, Forekest Hahshah, surrenders before the Superintendent of Police of West Khasi Hills district at Nongstoin. According to official sources, Hahshah has fled form his camp in Bangladesh recently.
- *June 11*: A group of unidentified gunmen kill a surrendered HNLC cadre, identified as Pyngtngenlang Tariang alias Bah Bah Panai, near Umkrem village in the East Khasi Hills district. The dead body of Tariang is recovered on the next day.
- *June 3*: Meghalaya Chief Minister, D. D. Lapang, assures all possible help to Church leader P. B. M. Basiawmoit in his efforts to bring the HNLC to the negotiating table. The Chief Minister says, "We appreciate and admire the move of Mr Basiawmoit and the government will extend all possible helps for him." Lapang further indicates that he has requested the Union Government to speed up the process with the HNLC.
- *May 25*: Suspected HNLC and NDFB cadres abduct a trader from Moosyiem village in the Jaintia Hills district. They also shot at and injured the trader's brother before escaping.

- *April 27*: A HNLC cadre belonging to the 'finance wing' of the outfit, identified as Teiskhem Sun, is arrested from the Mawlai area. Subsequent to information provided by Sun, police recover an AK-47 rifle along with 30 rounds of ammunition from a forest area near Umsning in the Ri-Bhoi district.
- *April 26*: Two HNLC cadres belonging to the 'finance wing' of the outfit, identified as David Mylliem Umlong and Golden Pathaw, are arrested from the Lewduh and Mawlai Umjaipur areas respectively.
- *March 30*: HNLC approaches the Union Government for peace talks and in this regard, sends four cadres of the outfit to New Delhi to initiate the peace process. Confirming this, State Home Minister, Mukul Sangma says, "We are expecting some positive outcome regarding the latest development. Details will be made available at the right time."
- *March 30*: A tribunal makes recommendations for the extension of the proscription on the HNLC and ANVC for another year.
- *March 28*: Bangla Dhar alias Biang, a senior HNLC cadre, allegedly involved in extortion activities in Dawki and other border areas, surrenders before the Superintendent of Police of East Khasi Hills district.
- *March 25*: Suspected HNLC cadres abduct Man Bahadur Pradhan, manager of a coal export firm of Sutnga in the Jaintia Hills district.
- *February 16*: An unidentified 'area commander' of the HNLC is lynched by villagers of Sohkynphor in the Jaintia Hills district. He was allegedly involved in extortion activities in the area.
- *January 30*: A suspected HNLC cadre is arrested at Jowai in the Jaintia Hills district.
- *January 24*: An eight-member group suspected to be linked to the HNLC loot Rupees 93 lakh from the Meghalaya Co-operative Apex Bank branch at Khliehriat in Jaintia Hills district. The Meghalaya Director-General of Police, L. Sailo, confirming the

link between the group and the HNLC says, "They owe allegiance to the HNLC in some form or the other."

- *January 14*: Meghalaya Police arrests a HNLC militant, Kobarlan Snaitang, from Pyndensohsaw near Mawsynram in the East Khasi Hills district.
- *January 7*: Seven HNLC cadres, who surrendered before the Border Security Force authorities at an unspecified place in the State of Mizoram, are likely to be brought back to Shillong on January 8.

2004

- *December 22*: The Union Government extends the ban on two militant outfits of Meghalaya, the ANVC and HNLC. In an official notification in Shillong, the Union Home Ministry cites the reasons for extension stating that although the ANVC agrees to abjure violence and expresses willingness for talks within the framework of Constitution, it continues "collection of funds and extortion, acquisition of sophisticated weapons and recruitment of new cadre." For HNLC, the notification says, it openly declares its "secessionist" objective, engaged in armed means to achieve the objective, indulged in intimidation, extortion and looting of civilians for collection of funds for the organisation. Both the outfits, according to the notification, maintain links with other insurgent groups of the North-east region for collecting weapons, carrying out violence, extortion, intimidation and looting besides having camps in some neighbouring countries for "sanctuary, training and clandestine procurement of arms and ammunition."
- *December 19*: Two surrendered HNLC cadres, Barlin Kharnoir and Firestar Rapsang, are arrested on charges of car-lifting from the Bara Bazaar area of capital Shillong.
- *December 15*: A HNLC cadre, Spurfield Suting alias

Phlex, surrenders before the police at Borsora in the West Khasi Hills district.

- *December 13*: A hardcore HNLC cadre, Deningstar Rapsang, surrenders before the Meghalaya Home Minister, H.D.R Lyngdoh. He deposits one AK-56 rifle along with three magazines, one M-20 pistol and another 73 rounds of live ammunition. According to police sources, the outfit's 'commander-in-chief', Bobby Marwein, deputed Rapsang to raise extortion money from the capital Shillong.
- *December 10*: HNLC blames its surrendered cadres for the killing of five HNLC activists in its Bangladesh camps. A statement issued by its 'secretary of information and communication', Mangkara Dkhar, said: "Such policy by the authorities would lead to problems in bringing peace in the State."
- *November 17*: Meghalaya Police arrests a senior HNLC cadre from Pyndensohsaw near Mawsynram in the East Khasi Hills district.
- *November 4*: Four extortionists with alleged links with HNLC arrested in the capital city of Shillong.
- *October 15*: A security guard of the HNLC 'General Secretary' C Thangkhiew surrenders before the police at Pynursla outpost in East Khasi Hills district along with two hand grenades and one SBBL gun.
- *October 1*: HNLC terrorists shot at a taxi driver at Cheruphi in Jaintia Hills district.
- *September 29*: Police arrest three suspected HNLC cadres, who claimed to be members of the newly formed Hynniewtrep National Youth Front Tiger Force, from Ladthalaboh in Jaintia Hills district.
- *September 16*: Security forces arrest an HNLC cadre, Shanbor Warjri, from the Mawlai Mawdatbaki area in the capital city of Shillong.
- *September 3*: A HNLC cadre surrenders to the police at Jowai in the Jaintia Hills district.
- *August 30*: Police recovers 10 rounds of AK

ammunition from the house of a HNLC cadre at Mawlai Motsyiar in the capital city of Shillong.

- *August 30*: A HNLC cadre, identified as Khlainbor Pakyntein, is arrested from Mawlai Motsyiar in the East Khasi Hills district.
- *August 29*: Unknown miscreants damage the vehicle of a surrendered HNLC cadre at Jaiaw Langsning in Shillong.
- *August 24*: A HNLC terrorist, identified as Sadelbert Thongni, surrenders before the police at Nongstoin in the West Khasi Hills district.
- *August 3*: Twenty-eight HNLC militants surrender before Chief Minister D. D. Lapang in Shillong.
- *June 28*: Meghalaya Police arrests three HNLC terrorists who crossed over to Meghalaya from the West Khasi Hills border of Bangladesh to extort money from coal exporters of the Borosora area in the State.
- *May 18*: Five HNLC cadres surrender in Mizoram before the Border Security Force.
- *May 3*: Reports indicate that the HNLC charges its surrendered cadres for extorting money from the people in the name of the outfit in collusion with the State police.
- *March 31*: A surrendered HNLC terrorist, identified as Ibor Marwein, is arrested from the Khasi Hills Autonomous District Council office in Shillong along with one.9 mm pistol and some ammunition.
- *April 30*: At least eleven HNLC cadres surrender at a Border Security Force camp in Mizoram, bordering Bangladesh.
- *March 16*: 28 HNLC terrorists, including two women cadres, lay down arms before Meghalaya Chief Minister D D Lapang at the Meghalaya Police Training Centre at Mawiong in the East Khasi Hills district.
- *January 30*: Eight HNLC cadres, including top leaders Armstrong Lyngdoh and Kitdor, surrender before the Home Minister RG Lyngdoh.

- *January 14*: Fourteen HNLC cadres surrender before the Meghalaya Chief Minister D.D. Lapang in Shillong.

2003

- *December 30*: Two HNLC terrorists are arrested near the Bangladesh-Tripura border while on their way to Meghalaya via Tripura.
- *November 3*: Meghalaya Police arrest two office bearers of the Archery Sports Association (ASA) in the capital Shillong for reportedly contributing money to the proscribed HNLC after collecting funds illegally.
- *November 2*: A hardcore HNLC terrorist is arrested from the Mawlai Syllaikariah area near capital Shillong.
- *October 17*: Meghalaya Police arrests one HNLC terrorist during a raid in the premises of North Eastern Hill University (NEHU) at Shillong.
- *October 15*: HNLC 'publicity wing' chief, Edward Charles Synder, is arrested, from a cyber café in the capital Shillong.
- *October 1*: Meghalaya Police arrests three HNLC terrorists from a hideout near Umium River in the East Khasi Hills district.
- *September 27*: HNLC 'commander-in-chief (Western Command), Delphinus Myrthong alias Khraw is killed during an encounter near Nongstoin in the West Khasi Hills district.
- *September 24*: Meghalaya Chief Minister Lapang offers truce to the ANVC and HNLC.
- *September 22*: Union Government blocks an HNLC discussion group on the Internet through which the outfit was circulating its newsletter, The Voice.
- *August 20*: Meghalaya Police arrests Mardor Bamon, 'political secretary' of the HNLC from Mawlai.
- *August 16*: Suspected HNLC terrorists attack police training school at Golf links, Shillong, with hand grenade.

- *July 29*: HNLC 'chairman' Julius Dorphang refutes Government's claim over surrender of top cadres and asks the police to reveal the identity of its cadres who have either surrendered or are arrested.
- *July 9*: Police file FIR under the Unlawful Activities Act for funding the proscribed Hynniewtrep National Liberation Council (HNLC) against 79 businessmen in Meghalaya.
- *June 14*: Meghalaya Police arrests Paul Lyngdoh, second in command in the finance wing of HNLC, from a hideout near Nongthymmai in Shillong.
- *June 7*: Meghalaya Police arrests two HNLC terrorists, including the 'general secretary' of HNLC's finance wing, at the Nongrim Hills locality, responsible for spreading the extortion network in the Khasi hills and Ri Bhoi districts.
- *May 22*: Security force personnel arrest a woman HNLC cadre identified as Blister Mary Kurbah from Mawngap in the East Khasi Hills district.
- *May 14*: HNLC 'assistant finance secretary' Heston Bohphang is arrested from his residence at Umpling in the capital Shillong.
- *April 19*: Two HNLC suspects are killed and three more arrested following an encounter at Mawpud village, East Garo Hills district.
- *April 23*: Security forces apprehend two unidentified HNLC terrorists near Williamnagar, East Garo Hills district.
- *March 17*: Media reports indicate that HNLC has resumed its extortion drive in the Garo Hills area after maintaining a low profile for approximately a year.
- *March 22*: Security forces arrest two HNLC terrorists at Mawlai, East Khasi Hills district, and recover three AK 47 rifles, 24 rounds of live cartridges and five magazines.
- *March 24*: The Shillong Khasi-Jaintia Church Leaders' Forum (SKJCLF) Chairman Bishop Purely Lyngdoh

announces that the forum is likely to discuss, among others, a peace initiative with the HNLC during a meeting on March 27.

- *March 4*: HNLC suspects kill a police personnel at Wahthapabru, near Mission compound area, Shillong, in East Khasi Hills district.
- *February 12*: Police unearth a HNLC arms dump, including a carbine, a stengun, 48 bullets of M-16 rifle, 48 rounds of AK series and 103 rounds of hunting rifles, among others, near Wahingdoh, Shillong, East Khasi Hills district.
- *February 5*: A HNLC arms dump is unearthed near Wahumkhrah River in Shillong. Two AK 56 rifles, an AK 47 rifle, three carbines and unspecified quantity of ammunition are seized from the dump.
- *January 29*: Police recover arms and ammunition, including an M-16 rifle, a semi-automatic rifle, 41 rounds of M-16 ammunition, 15 rounds of 7.62 ammunition and some incriminating documents, among others, from a HNLC terrorist at Distar Marbaniang, in Wahingdoh, Shillong, East Khasi district.
- *January 18*: Reports indicate that 15 HNLC terrorists have sneaked into Meghalaya from Bangladesh to carry out terrorist strikes ahead of the Republic Day on January 26.
- *January 10*: The SKJCLF urges both the Government and HNLC to hold unconditional talks.
- *January 4*: In a New Year message, the HNLC reiterates its aim to achieve 'freedom' for the Hynniewtrep people.
- *January 3*: Union Home Ministry extends ban under Unlawful Activities (Prevention) Act of 1967 on the ANVC and HNLC in Meghalaya.

2002

- *December 23*: One HNLC terrorist is killed during an encounter at Qualapatty, East Khasi Hills district.

- *December 9*: Some 20 HNLC terrorists sneak into Meghalaya, armed with sophisticated weapons, through the porous Indo-Bangladesh border in West Khasi Hills to carry out subversive activities in the region.
- *December 7*: Meghalaya police arrest four HNLC terrorists from Jaiaw and Mawlai areas and recover a Sten gun and 20 rounds of live ammunition from one of the hideouts of the outfit at Jaiaw.
- *December 3*: Police arrest Welcome Nongkynrih, a trusted associate of HNLC area commander James, in Mawlai Umjaiur, Meghalaya.
- *November 27*: A Special Operations Team of Meghalaya police arrests two Hynniewtrep National Liberation Council terrorists identified as Roland Syiemlieh and Banwansuk Nongkseh in Lower Lachumiere area, and recovers a huge cache of arms and ammunition after raiding a hideout, in Mawlai Nongpdeng. The catch includes 591 rounds of M-16 ammunition, two Chinese made hand grenades, a.32 pistol, 5 rounds of SLR ammunition and an AK-47 magazine.
- *November 4*: HNLC warns the Nationalist Congress Party (NCP)-led government in Meghalaya against counter-terrorism measures and police excesses
- *November 1*: HNLC suffers setback following the largest arms seizure by Meghalaya police. State police unearth a hideout at Khlaw Roman, in Mawlai Nongpdeng, Shillong, and seize 663 ammunition rounds of various makes. The seizure includes 460 rounds of M-16 and 169 rounds of Ak-47 ammunition, two Chinese-made high-explosive grenades, a round of SLR 7.62 (self loading rifles).27 bore cartridges and three rounds of.303 ammunition.
- *October 11*: Five HNLC terrorists armed with AK-47 rifles kill Kilas Momin, a police personnel in Mawlai Nonglum, Shillong.
- *August 27*: An HNLC terrorist is seriously injured in

an encounter in Mawkriah village, near Shillong while another arrested.

- *August 24*: Two HNLC terrorists are arrested by the State police in Nongthymmai, near Shillong. The dead body of a suspected HNLC terrorist is found in Shillong.
- *August 15*: Security arrangements throughout Meghalaya are tightened to ensure the smooth celebration of Independence Day, following a 24-hour bandh (general strike) call given by the HNLC and the People's Liberation Front. Chief Minister F A Khonglam renews his invitation, on the occasion of Independence day, to terrorists groups in the State "to come to the negotiation table and sort out differences in a peaceful manner."
- *August 6*: Security forces in Meghalaya arrest eight HNLC terrorists from Mawlai, Shillong. The East Khasi Hills district police chief says those arrested are mostly teenagers and add that it confirms that the HNLC is recruiting teenagers into its fold.
- *July 1*: Meghalaya police arrest an HNLC terrorist from the 3rd milestone, Upper Shillong. An AK 47 rifle, a Smooth Bore Breech Loading (SBBL) gun, a country made revolver, ammunition and incriminating documents are recovered from him.
- *June 3*: Two HNLC terrorists are arrested in Shillong and another suspected HNLC terrorist in Nongthyllep village, near Mairang, West Khasi Hills.
- *May 13*: Meghalaya Director General of Police (DGP) L Sailo claims that the HNLC stood marginalised in the state.
- *May 8*: HNLC terrorists warn all outsiders doing business in Meghalaya to pay 'fixed taxes' and threaten them with 'severe punishment', leading to 'imprisonment and being driven out of the Hynniewtrep land' in case of resistance. The terrorist group also promises to negotiate with those businessmen who found it difficult to pay the 'taxes'.

- *April 2*: Meghalaya Deputy Chief Minister D D Lapang says the government is unable to spell the terms and conditions for talks with the Hynniewtrep National Liberation Council (HNLC) terrorist outfit as the latter failed to give any positive indication to the government's proposal.
- *March 27*: Eight HNLC terrorists, on their way to Bangladesh for arms training, arrested from Siatbakon Road..
- *March 18*: HNLC terrorist Mardor Bamon arrested by Shillong Police and the Special Operations Team (SOT) of Lum Jingshai in Shillong.
- *March 16*: HNLC terrorist arrested following a raid at Mawlai Umjaiw in Shillong.
- *March 6*: HNLC terrorists attack the East Khasi Hills district police chief's office.
- *February 16*: Three HNLC cadres killed in an encounter at Smit, East Khasi Hills.
- *January 23*: HNLC terrorist killed in an encounter and three others arrested at Riatmidi, bordering Mawlai Nangpdeng and Mawlai Motsyiar.
- *January 10*: HNLC terrorist escapes from Lumdiengjri Police Station.
- *January 9*: Suspected HNLC terrorist killed in retaliatory firing by the police at Lumshai, Shillong.
- *January 5*: Four HNLC terrorists, including a local 'commander', arrested after an encounter at Shangpung in Jaintia Hills disrtict. Three HNLC terrorists arrested after another encounter at Umsing in Ribhoi district.

2001

- December 21: HNLC terrorist arrested in Shillong.
- *November 12*: Two HNLC terrorists arrested by the Shillong Special Operation Team (SOT) at the seventh mile stone in Shillong.
- *November 11*: Suspected HNLC terrorists kill one of their own cadres at Panaliar, Jaintia Hills district.

- *October 23*: HNLC Chairman Julius K. Dorphang discloses that Ching Thangkhiew, the 'Commander-in-Chief' of the North East Red Army (NERA), now a defunct outfit, had been "eliminated" because he was assisting the security forces and the RSS against the interests of the HNLC.
- *March 28*: Two police personnel killed in an encounter with HNLC terrorists near Jaiaw Longsuing, in Shillong.
- *March 4*: Seng Khasi leader Rijoy Khongshah, was abducted earlier on March 1, 2001, killed by HNLC terrorists.
- *February 19*: The outfit, in a statement, opposes Census operations in the State and threatens to eliminate enumerators participating in the process.
- *January 19*: HNLC terrorists attack a police outpost in Shillong and kill two police personnel.
- *January 9*: Two security guards of a nationalised bank killed in an attack by HNLC terrorists at Mawsynram village.
- *January 5*: Five civilians killed and four others injured in an attack by HNLC terrorists on a business establishment in Shillong

2000

- *August 15*: Police personnel killed and another injured when fleeing HNLC terrorists fire at security forces.
- *August 14*: Three CRPF personnel injured as HNLC cadres fire around 600 rounds into the air and also in the direction of the CRPF camp in the State capital Shillong.

PEOPLE'S LIBERATION FRONT OF MEGHALAYA (PLF-M)

FORMATION

People's Liberation Front of Meghalaya (PLF-M) is a relatively new terrorist group operating in the Garo Hills of Meghalaya. Reports suggest that the outfit has been rechristened as the Achik National Council (ANC). When the Hynniewtrep Achik Liberation Council (HALC) split in 1992, it resulted in the formation of the Hynniewtrep National Liberation Council (HNLC), which represents the Khasis in Meghalaya, and the Achik Liberation Matgrik Army (ALMA), which wanted a separate Garoland State for the Garos.

The PLF-M is an offshoot of this Achik Liberation Matgrik Army (ALMA). Most of the ALMA terrorists surrendered in 1994, but a few formed the Achik National Volunteers' Council (ANVC) in 1995.

The PLF-M consists of some of these "surrendered rebels" of the erstwhile ALMA who returned underground after their rehabilitation scheme failed. The exact strength of the outfit is not known.

OBJECTIVES

The claimed objective of the PLF-M is economic development of the Garo Hills, as well as better educational opportunities for the Garo tribes in Meghalaya. It also demands a separate state for the Garos. In this regard, Chengku Momin, the 'minister for information and publicity' of the PLF-M had warned all the non-Garos, in March 2001, not to contest the State Assembly and district council elections slated for 2003.

Leadership

The chairman of the outfit is Vincent Sangma and Nimush Marak is the 'Commander in Chief'. Besides that L K Sangma is one of the 'area commanders'.

AREA OF OPERATION

The outfit is primarily active in Dainadubi, Williamnagar, in East Garo Hills, and Dalu in West Garo Hills. Among its activities include extortion of money to generate funds for its activities.

In July 2000, the PLF-M had slapped extortion notices even on some Member of Legislative Assemblies (MLAs) and including two ministers, from the Garo hills.

LINKAGES

The PLF-M reportedly maintains close connections with the Achik National Volunteer Council (ANVC).

2010

- *August 15*: The Police arrested three persons from Nengringittim in East Garo Hills for allegedly serving a demand note in the name of PLF-M. They were identified as Sengpang Sangma, Twisbirth Sangma and Milan Momin. According to Police, the accused had issued a demand note of INR 0.3 million to a person, Staforth Sangma, on July 22.
- *March 19:* The Meghalaya Governor R. S. Mooshahary expressed concern over mushrooming of militant groups in Garo hills and the activities of Assam-based outfits along the border. The Governor said that recent developments, such as reports on the formation of militant groups in Garo hills, were a cause of concern. Other militant groups active in Garo hills are LAEF, PLF-M, Achik National Security Defence (ANSD), Atong Liberation Army (ALA), and United Achik National Front (UANF). ULFA and NDFB are also active in Garo hills and border of Ri Bhoi District. The Governor said that the Government was committed to contain militancy at all costs. The Governor added that the security establishment of the State has acted swiftly to break up and contain the activities of the Hynniewtrep Liberation Front (HLF) in Khasi hills, and LAEF in the Garo hills. He said the activities of the local militant organisations like the HNLC and ANVC have been substantially controlled.

2009

- *February 28*: 45 militants, including a PLF-M cadre, surrender along with a huge quantity of arms and ammunition before Red Horns Division of Indian Army in a surrender ceremony organized at Rangiya of Kamrup District in Assam.

- *January 17*: Two militants, including the founder general secretary of the PLFM, John Jubilee D. Shera Marak, 34, are killed in an encounter with the Army at Hat Hati bridge near Singhimari village on the National Highway 37 in the Bongaigaon District of Assam. The Army said the encounter ensued when Marak, along with Biswajit Sharma, 22, another hardcore cadre of the outfit, was spotted by the troops in the Chowtaki area under Abhayapuri Police station. The Army later recovered a 9-mm pistol with three bullets, a 7.65 pistol with three bullets, an ATM card, a PAN card, a voter identity card, driving licence and a mobile handset from the slain militant's possession. The commanding officer of the Kumaon Regiment, Col S.K. Dutta, said, "Sharma, a man of Nepali origin, is also a hardcore activist. His driving licence was issued from Dudhnoi, but his voter card from Mekhiliganj under Cooch Behar district in North Bengal. We are cross-checking it with West Bengal police." Marak, hailing from Damas in East Garo Hills, founded the outfit in 2003. Though he was said to be involved in several extortions in Tura and its adjoining areas, he is reported to have shifted base to Dudhnoi in Goalpara and more recently to Bongaigaon.

2008

- *October 12:* The self-styled 'commander-in-chief' of the PLF-M, identified as Pollendro Marak, is shot dead by the East Garo Hills district police during an encounter at a forest of Bogakol village under Kharkutta police outpost. While around six other militants manage to escape, one Chinese made M20 pistol with five live ammunition and several incriminating documents are recovered from the encounter site.
- *September 29*: A school boy, abducted by PLF-M militants from his residence in Kharkutta 15 days

ago, is released by the militants in Dolonggiri area of West Garo Hills district.

LIBERATION OF ACHIK ELITE FORCE(LAEF)

FORMATION

The Liberation of Achik Elite Force (LAEF) is a Garo militant outfit that was formed sometime in 2005.

OBJECTIVES

In an appeal in the first week of October 2006, the LAEF outlined the reasons of its existence: "LAEF stands to fight for a separate Achik state after studying the scenario of the State. It is learnt that the citizens of our land have been ill-treated and discriminated in every field–socially, politically and economically by the Khasis and Jaintias of Meghalaya making our people lag behind in the development process." It also appealed to the Achik (Garo) people "to co-operate and join hands to fight for a peaceful movement for an independent separate Achik State."

LEADERSHIP AND CADRE

Darong Marak is reportedly the present chief of LAEF. He is believed to have taken over the reins of the outfit after his brother Peter Marak was killed. Darong is the main trainer and 'finance secretary' of the outfit. Peter Marak was a former Meghalaya Police commando. Marak was posted as constable in the Garo Hills during the latter part of the 1990s, and subsequently unsuccessfully contested the by-election for Meghalaya Legislative Assembly from the Songsak constituency as an independent candidate. Remsu Rema alias Chingkam is the 'chairman' of the outfit. Chingkam Marak serves as the 'Convenor cum Publicity Secretary' of the LAEF. The outfit, consisting of approximately 135 cadres, also has an unspecified number of 'secretaries'. According to police sources, the outfit has 12 AK assault rifles and other small arms.

AREA OF OPERATION

The outfit operates in the East Garo Hills district, South

Garo Hills district, Ri Bhoi district and East Khasi Hills district. The outfit's presence has also been reported from the Goalpara district of Assam. Police revealed that as many as 50 well armed and trained LAEF militants operate from the Garo Hills forests, according to Assam Tribune.

LINKAGES

According to a September 5, 2007-report, the LAEF is trying to regroup in the Garo Hills with the help of some other militant outfits, including the National Socialist Council of Nagaland-Isak-Muivah (NSCN-IM). Police sources said some of its cadres had fled to Dimapur in Nagaland and were in constant touch with the NSCN-IM leaders. Shortly after his arrest from Jorabhat, the LAEF chief Peter Marak was interrogated and as per his statement, the NSCN-IM had provided the LAEF with as many as 15 AK-47s, 25 automatic M20 pistols and three highly powerful Universal Machine Guns besides over a hundred hand grenades, Assam Tribune reported on August 23, 2007. He also claimed that all the armaments were paid for by his outfit.

A June 22, 2007-report stated that the outfit has established a link with the National Socialist Council of Nagaland – Khaplang (NSCN-K). Assam Tribune reported on August 23, 2007, that "the LAEF has since its inception in 2005 been rumoured to be patronised by members of a prominent political party from Meghalaya."

INCIDENTS

2010

- *December 16*: The 'chairman' of LAEF, Dimrim N. Sangma alias Ramen, surrendered before the East Garo Hills District SP S. Nongtnger along with four other cadres of the outfit in Williamnagar. According to the SP, the other four militants were 'sergeants' Rakshimbirth Sangma alias Rakrik, Ninja G. Mominalias Kakim, 'lance corporal' Akash G. Momin alias Bamrik and Tangrik Sangma alias Gilmat. "They deposited a 7.65 mm pistol with 10 rounds of live ammunition, a locally made lookalike of AK-47 rifle, an HE-36 grenade, a crude bomb, ten rounds of live MMG ammunition, their demand letters and receipt books," said Nongtnger, and added that all the five had undergone arms training in NSCN.

- *December 2*: The 'chief' of Garo hills-based militant outfit, the LAEF, Nikseng G. Momin, along with another cadre was killed in an encounter with Police at Darugre reserve forest in the East Garo Hills District. The other militant was identified as Rakbat Sangma. The Police recovered two pistols, a hand grenade and documents from the encounter site. Momin alias Dilkan and his gang were earlier involved in the killing of a Police commando, R.D. Sangma in 2008 after an ambush in the West Khasi Hills. According to the Police, the outfit mainly consists of deserters of other militant groups in Garo hills.
- *September 25*: An unidentified LAEF cadre was shot dead by the Police during an encounter at Shahlang in West Khasi Hills District. While a locally made revolver, a demand note of INR 7 00000 were recovered from the possession of the slain cadre, three other cadres managed to escape from the encounter site. Sources said the encounter ensued after the Special Operation Team (SOT) personnel got a tip-off about two traders from Shahlang going to deliver INR 7 00000 to the LAEF at Rongkhujre. With resumption of the coal trade for the season, the traders said, demand notes have started coming in from the LAEF.
- *September 18*: Three LAEF militants were lynched after a scuffle with villagers at Menadoba market in East Garo Hills District. They were identified as Arup Marak, Lucas Marak and Gneng Marak.
- *September 7*: The Meghalaya Police recovered three foreign-made pistols with ammunition, 69 rounds of live medium machine gun (MMG) ammunition

stored in a box, a laptop, a solar plate, two wireless sets and documents belonging to ULFA cadres after an operation against the militants holed up at Danal Dasik in the Songsak area in East Garo Hills District, reports Telegraph. The Police said there were around six militants belonging to ULFA's '109th battalion' in the hideout in Songsak, who managed to escape leaving behind the ammunition following counter-insurgency operations. The Police said ULFA's '109th battalion' is quite active in Garo hills which is being used by the outfit as a corridor to ferry arms and ammunition to Assam. The militants cross over to South and West Garo Hills from Bangladesh. The Police also fear that the militant groups active in Garo Hills like the Garo National Liberation Army and Liberation of Achik Elite Force (LAEF) which have links with ULFA, can use the weapons in Meghalaya to create law and order problems. "We are concerned about the stockpile but committed to check the trend as these arms may be used against soft targets in Assam," the Police official added.

- *August 2*: Suspected militants ransacked the office of the Prosecution Inspector's branch, which is housed in the same building as that of East Garo Hills Deputy Commissioner, and looted an unspecified number of sophisticated small arms. A senior unnamed Police official said they suspected the involvement of the Garo National Liberation Army (GNLA), led by Champion Sangma, who held the rank of Deputy Superintendent of Police before deserting the forces. He said the GNLA might have carried out the attack with the help of local goons. The Police are not ruling out the involvement of other militant outfits like the LAEF. But their primary suspect is the GNLA as it has a stronghold in Garo Hills and Sangma knows the Police armoury and the places the arms are stored with the East Garo Hills District administration.

- *August 1*: Two LAEF cadres surrendered before East Garo Hills District Police. "The ongoing police operation to curb on the outfit's criminal activities in the district has led to the duo's surrender," Superintendent of Police of East Garo Hills District Sylvester Nongtynger said.
- *August 1*: Two LAEF cadres surrendered before East Garo Hills District Police. "The ongoing police operation to curb on the outfit's criminal activities in the district has led to the duo's surrender," Superintendent of Police of East Garo Hills District Sylvester Nongtynger said.
- *June 25*: Two LAEF cadres were arrested by the Guwahati Police during a search operation in city in Assam.
- *March 19*: The Meghalaya Governor R. S. Mooshahary expressed concern over mushrooming of militant groups in Garo hills and the activities of Assam-based outfits along the border. The Governor said that recent developments, such as reports on the formation of militant groups in Garo hills, were a cause of concern. Other militant groups active in Garo hills are LAEF, People's Liberation Front of Meghalaya (PLF-M), Achik National Security Defence (ANSD), Atong Liberation Army (ALA), and United Achik National Front (UANF). ULFA and NDFB are also active in Garo hills and border of Ri Bhoi District. The Governor said that the Government was committed to contain militancy at all costs. The Governor added that the security establishment of the State has acted swiftly to break up and contain the activities of the Hynniewtrep Liberation Front (HLF) in Khasi hills, and LAEF in the Garo hills. He said the activities of the local militant organisations like the HNLC and ANVC have been substantially controlled.
- *February 7*: Meghalaya Chief Minister D.D. Lapang in the Conference of Chief Ministers on Internal

Security asked the Centre to go for a tripartite political and development accord with the ANVC to bring the ongoing peace process to a logical conclusion. He also stated that insurgent outfits like ULFA, National Socialist Council of Nagaland, NDFB and UPDS are not only supporting groups like LAEF, but also providing them arms, ammunition and training. He said that insurgent outfits both from the Northeast and adjoining Bangladesh were also using the peaceful State of Meghalaya both as temporary sanctuary and corridor. Lapang further claimed that both ANVC and HNLC have been largely neutralised with a sustained Police operation. But passive militancy is still a cause for concern, he further added.

- *January 16*: Two LAEF militants are killed in an encounter with Security Forces (SFs) in Songsak area in East Garo Hills District bordering South Garo Hills and West Khasi Hills Districts.

2009

- *January 16*: Two LAEF militants are killed in an encounter with Security Forces (SFs) in Songsak area in East Garo Hills District bordering South Garo Hills and West Khasi Hills Districts.
- *December 14*: Meghalaya Director General of Police S. B. Kakati said so far only the LAEF was active with a few cadres and weapons but its strength had been drastically reduced following successive operations by the State Police.
- *November 22*: The Meghalaya Police neutralized a hideout of the LAEF and arrested five of its cadres, including 'sergeant major' Kyndoh Momin, during a counter-insurgency operation at Byrnihat in the Ri-Bhoi District along the Meghalaya-Assam border. Police later recovered some letter-heads, demand notes and seals of the outfit. Police said the militants were involved in extortion in the State.

- *November 19*: The Inspector General of Police, B. L. Buam, said, "So far, the combing operation launched in State's Garo Hills region and West Khasi Hills district shown good results with the arrest of two LAEF cadres and seizures of arms and ammunition." He said, "Yes, we have made the breakthrough, but the flush-out operation against LAEF militants will continue to ensure peace and stability in the region." The LAEF maintains its linkages with the NSCN-IM, ULFA and NDFB. The militant outfit has set up its operational camp inside the Balpakram National Park, with the help of the NSCN-IM, to impart guerilla warfare tactics to the new LAEF recruits.
- *August 20*: An unidentified LAEF militant is shot dead by the East Garo Hills District Police during an encounter at Nengkra near Williamnagar. However, some other militants of the group manage to escape from the encounter site.
- *July 7*: Police arrested three LAEF militants at Sisobibra village in the East Garo Hills District while extorting INR 500000 from an unidentified local businessman. The trio was later identified as Demash M. Sangma alias Dema, Hamil T. Sangma and 'Lance Corporal' Sengba W. Momin.
- *March 24*: Meghalaya Police neutralise a camp of the LAEF outfit at Tajal area near Shahlang in the West Khasi Hills District. However, the militants manage to escape from the incident site.

2008

- *December 7*: A Special Operations Team constable, R.D. Sangma, and the 'commander-in-chief' of the LAEF, Kimrey K. Sangma, are killed during an encounter between police and militants at Damit village near Shahlang in the West Khasi Hills district. While an AK-47 assault rifle and some ammunition were recovered, other militants managed to escape from the encounter site.

- *November 28*: The 'area commander' and six other cadres of the LAEF, earlier arrested by the police personnel from Kadambari in the Ri-Bhoi district on November 18, are shifted to the prison at Williamnagar in the East Garo Hills district.
- *November 25*: Meghalaya Police said the ULFA and NDFB militants are using the LAEF cadres to make crude bombs. Police recover five crude bombs along with other arms and ammunition and incriminating documents from the nine LAEF militants arrested in the Ri-Bhoi district bordering Assam on November 18. They suspect that the LAEF militants were making a base in a forest area near Pilangkatta in the Ri-Bhoi district and were seeking logistic support from the ULFA and NDFB cadres. Meanwhile, a senior unnamed police official says LAEF militants usually go to Nagaland to procure arms from the NSCN-IM cadres. The NSCN-IM cadres also come to the Garo Hills and West Khasi Hills to help LAEF cadres with extortion and abduction. The report added that the LAEF had already set up two 'commands'—one in East Garo Hills and another in West Khasi Hills. The LAEF could not establish a third command in Ri-Bhoi as nine LAEF cadres were arrested by the police, when they were trying to set up camp in the area. The police claim that Naga militants are assisting LAEF cadres in East Garo Hills and West Khasi Hills districts. "While the NSCN (I-M) cadres supply arms to LAEF, the latter has to part with the major portion of extortion amount collected from coal laden trucks and businessmen in Garo Hills and West Khasi Hill," the police added. The police said though the strength of trained LAEF cadres is 50, the arrested militants claimed that the total strength, including the untrained cadres, would be around 200.
- *November 24*: A senior unnamed police officer said nine LAEF militants, arrested near Pilangkatta in the

Ri-Bhoi district on November 18, confessed during interrogation that the Garo outfit is recruiting computer literates and juveniles to widen its network. "Computer-savvy people were being employed to operate from inaccessible terrain to hoodwink intelligence personnel, while juveniles got the menial tasks done smoothly," mentions the police officer. "The arrested juveniles—Molin Sangma, 17, and Ranjit Marak, 15,—and computer expert George Sangma are new recruits," he says.

- *November 18*: Meghalaya Police arrested nine senior LAEF cadres, including an 'area commander', when they neutralised a newly set up militant camp at Kadambari near Pilangkata in the Ri-Bhoi district along Meghalaya-Assam border. The 'area commander' is identified as Sengrang Momin from a village near Williamnagar in the East Garo Hills district. He confessed that he was a student of the Umshyrpi College in capital Shillong. The Superintendent of Police of Ri-Bhoi District, M.K. Dkhar, said that Sengrang had travelled to various parts of the Northeast, including Nagaland. Police recover a US-made revolver, magazines, ammunition, wireless in local loop phones, five grenades, a laptop and several incriminating documents including extortion notes from the possession of the arrested militants.
- *November 10*: A LAEF cadre, Sail R. Marak, is arrested by Meghalaya Police from Nangalbibra in the South Garo Hills district. He belongs to Bhalukmari in the Goalpara district of Assam. A 7.65 pistol and a demand note for INR 5, 00, 000 are recovered from his possession. According to police sources, the demand note was meant to be issued to one Rajeev Bihari.
- *November 9*: Meghalaya Police said that the LAEF militants were collecting at least INR 10,000 from a truck per month in Shahlang in the West Khasi Hills

district and Nangalbibra area in the South Garo Hills district. Police reportedly come to know of the extortion drive of the Garo outfit during interrogation of its leader Arvind Sangma, who was arrested from Shahlang seven days before. "We are going all-out to stop the extortion drive of LAEF," Superintendent of Police of West Khasi Hills district H. Kharkrang says.

- *October 31*: A LAEF cadre, Arvind Sangma, is injured by the West Khasi Hills district police during an encounter at Rongkhugre village. While Arvind is arrested, five other militants manage to escape from the encounter site. A 9-mm Italian-made pistol, some ammunition and cash are recovered from Arvind's possession.
- *September 30*: A newly recruited cadre of the LAEF surrenders before the East Garo Hills district police at Williamnagar. The militant hails from Dolonggre area of West Garo Hills district.
- *September 13*: Meghalaya Police arrest one LAEF cadre, Sosing A. Sangma, during a search operation at Bajengdoba. One M-20 pistol and some live ammunition are recovered from his possession.
- *August 4*: In a joint operation, the East and South Garo Hills District Police neutralise a LAEF hideout and seize a huge cache of arms and ammunition. Police raid the residence of one person, Gilberth M. Sangma, in the Jadigittim area of South Garo Hills and recover one powerful US-made shotgun with six rounds of live ammunition, a.22 rifles, ammunition of.303 rifles and 9-mm pistol, a wireless walkie-talkie and a bundle of LAEF extortion notes.
- *July 11*: Meghalaya Police arrested one LAEF militant, Sengba W. Momin, from Tura in the West Garo Hills district. He confessed to his involvement in the abduction of a trader, Bendra Prajaparti, from Rongjeng in the East Garo Hills district on March 10. He is also accused of hurling a grenade at Wagesi

Weigh Bridge on May 26 and killing a person at Nonchram on the same day.

- *July 1*: Meghalaya Police recover the dead body of Nicheng Sangma, self-styled 'commander-in-chief' of the LAEF, near a camp of the outfit at Parasin in the East Garo Hills district. Police also recover three AK-47 assault rifles from the incident site. Earlier, police arrested two suspected LAEF cadres, Anju Sangma and Christian Sangma, from Pengkasot village. They confessed that Nicheng was killed by the LAEF cadres over the leadership issue.
- *June 30*: Two LAEF cadres, Anju Sangma and Christian A. Marak, are arrested by Meghalaya Police and Army during a joint search operation along Assam-Meghalaya border. Two Chinese grenades are recovered from them.
- *June 5*: An encounter between Meghalaya Police and suspected LAEF militants occurs at Thodmari in the West Khasi Hills district. However, no casualty is reported on either side. The encounter took place when a police team from East Garo and West Khasi Hills was returning after collecting the remains of LAEF chief Peter Marak's younger brother Darong T. Marak. Darong is suspected to have been killed by his fellow cadre after a clash over a share of money at Thodmari on December 21, 2007. Meanwhile, police sources say they recovered only ribs and bones of Darong from a gorge at a place in Thodmari.
- *May 31*: Intelligence sources said that seven former Naga insurgents, who deserted the NSCN–IM and NSCN-K, continue to maintain links with the HNLC and LAEF to extort money from coal exporters and other traders in the coal belts of West Khasi Hills and Garo Hills. "The Naga men normally go back to their State after collecting huge amount of money through extortion in Meghalaya," the sources stated. Intelligence sources also indicated that former NSCN

cadres involved in extortion in Meghalaya were planning to form a new militant outfit that could be more powerful than the NSCN-IM and NSCN-K. Many coal exporters from and outside the State have incurred huge losses due to the ongoing extortion drive jointly launched by cadres of the NSCN, HNLC and LAEF. Militants' threat is reported to have forced several coal exporters to leave the coal belt areas recently.

- *May 28*: The LAEF's new 'commander-in-chief' Daria Sangma, while speaking to the media over phone, reconfirms the Meghalaya Police's claim that the LAEF has forged ties with the Assam-based Black Widow (BW) outfit. He said that it was in the interest of consolidating LAEF to pursue its goal of a 'separate Garo state'. The report added that a group of five LAEF cadres recently returned from arms training organised by the BW in Assam. Daria also said the Garo outfit had recently held a general council meeting in the West Khasi Hills in which he was appointed the new 'army chief' in the presence of LAEF 'chairman' Darong T. Marak who, according to police, had been killed by his own colleagues long ago. The LAEF general council meeting is said to have also appointed one Khanam D. Shira as 'general secretary' of the outfit, besides a former ANVC cadre Nikseng Sangma holding an important portfolio within the group. Nikseng had deserted the ANVC and joined with former ANVC 'eastern area commander' Sohan D. Shira to help the LAEF during the early days of its formation. Following the killing of the then 'chairman' Peter Marak in the hands of police and subsequent surrender of Sohan before the government, Nikseng reportedly fled into the LAEF stronghold of West Khasi Hills. Daria also says tells the media that the general council meeting had taken up several resolutions one of which was to turn 'pro-active' in its operations against certain organisations aligning with the government to wipe out the outfit.

- *May 14*: The 'eastern commander' of the LAEF, identified as Daria Sangma, denies reports about the death of its 'chief' Darong Marak at the hands of a former cadre, and said that he was very much alive and safe. "Our leader is not in Garo Hills, but inside Bangladesh overseeing the operational command of the outfit. Police claims are completely false," said Sangma. The East Garo Hills district police and the Army, during a joint operation, had earlier arrested a LAEF militant, Walter Sangma, from Bajengdoba area following a tip off that the militant had fled the outfit after killing his own chief. The LAEF's 'eastern commander' claimed that Walter Sangma deserted the outfit shortly after the killing of the former 'chairman' Peter Marak and had never met Darong Marak. Meanwhile, the East Garo Hills district police informed that Walter Marak revealed during interrogation that Darong had indeed been killed, but, not by him. He, however, could not identify the man who killed Darong.
- *May 4*: Security forces arrested Walter R. Sangma, personal bodyguard of the slain 'chairman' of the LAEF Peter Marak, at Sarangkol village in the Bajengdoba area. He confessed to having killed Peter in a hideout near Songsak in December 2007 over an argument about the share of looted money.
- *May 3*: One LAEF militant, Satjeng M. Sangma, surrenders before the Williamnagar Police.
- *April 23*: Three persons, including two LAEF cadres, are booked under the Meghalaya Preventive Detention Act. They were recently arrested from Riangdo in the West Khasi Hills district for carrying out extortion drives in the coal belt areas. They are identified as Tipison G. Marak, Nihim G. Momin and Brimly Myrthong.
- *April 1*: One LAEF cadre, identified as Salman Sangma, is arrested by the Meghalaya Police from Shahlang in the West Khasi Hills district.

- *March 27*: Three LAEF cadres, Zwing D. Marak, Bilseng G. Momin and Lambor Puwein, were arrested during a search operation at Rongkhukre in the West Khasi Hills district. During interrogation, they confessed their involvement in many cases of extortion in the coal belt areas of district in the last few months. A.22 revolver, four rounds of live ammunition, two daggers and a torch were seized from their possession. Two persons, identified as Neston P. Sangma and Jingan R. Sangma, are arrested during a search operation at Riangdim near Borsora for providing shelter to LAEF militants who were extorting money from coal exporters in West Khasi Hills. The operation was carried out based on confessional statements made by two LAEF cadres arrested earlier from Riangdim.
- *March 26*: One policeman is wounded when LAEF militants opened fire on police personnel shifting their position for vehicle checking to another place at Dagal in the East Garo Hills district. One SBBL gun, one hand grenade and eight empty cases are recovered from the incident site.
- *March 12*: Militants of the LAEF demand INR ten million as ransom for releasing the abducted manager of a grocery shop, Devendar Prajati. A senior police official said, "The ransom note of the LAEF was found from the grocery shop. We are investigating the matter." Prajati was abducted from his residence in Rongjeng in the East Garo Hills District on March 10-night.

2007

- *December 21*: One extortionist claiming to be a LAEF cadre, Sucheng Marak, is killed and another was arrested by the Meghalaya Police in an encounter at Baghmara in the South Garo Hills district. One Chinese pistol, a revolver with six rounds of ammunition and INR 40,000 are recovered from the encounter site. Marak is the leader of a gang involved in extorting money from government offices in South Garo Hills. The gang had been collecting money in the name of the Achik force for the past month after serving demand notes to government offices. A few magistrates and block development officers also received demand notes, police say.

- *December 19*: Police in Tura said that the LAEF has served extortion notes on government officials based in the South Garo Hills district. The LAEF, which is believed to have close links with the NSCN-IM, is involved in extorting money from coal mine owners in Nangalbibra and coal exporters in the Gasuapara area bordering Bangladesh. "Now, the LAEF is even serving extortion notes, ranging from INR 5,000 to INR 20,000 to government officials in the district," South Garo Hills District Superintendent of Police (SP) H. Toi said. He, however, informed that the police had managed to contain the militant activities with the arrest of a suspected LAEF militant Sukar Momin alias Sulu Ralo and two government employees–Bainstan Momin alias Bes and Tarius Sangma - alleged to be the LAEF's linkmen from Baghmara. Police also seized a locally-made revolver and extortion notes from Sukar Momin's possession, he added. According to him, "The job of these linkmen was to serve extortion notes to the targets specified by the militants, collect the money and hand it over to the LAEF." Intelligence sources said that the NSCN-IM had provided the LAEF with as many as 15 AK-47s, 25 automatic M20 pistols and three highly powerful Universal Machine Guns, besides over a hundred hand grenades to carry out their operations in Garo Hills.
- *December 8*: The LAEF militants waylay a police convoy and snatch an automatic carbine gun and a pistol from Sub-Inspector M.L. Barman at a place near Songsak in the East Garo Hills district. Barman

is the officer-in-charge of the anti-dacoity camp at Dagal in Songsak. Police said that around six masked persons, carrying three AK-47 rifles and several pistols and appearing to be a mixed group of Bodos and Garos, were involved in the incident. Militants are engaged in extortion of money from trucks on the road near Songsak reserve forest.

- *November 15*: Meghalaya Police said that the LAEF militants are trying to regroup in the coal belt areas of the West Khasi Hills and East Garo Hills districts. "We have information about movement of LAEF militants in the two districts of West Khasi Hills and East Garo Hills," a senior unnamed police official said. The report added that the Meghalaya Police are clueless about the identity of 'chairman' of the LAEF, identified as Remsu Rema alias Chingkam, who had visited certain areas of Garo Hills in the past.
- *November 3*: Shillong Times reports that militants of the LAEF have asked for INR 500,000 from Monindra Rava, State Legislator representing Tikrikilla constituency in the West Garo Hills district, and threatened to kill his son and son-in law in case of his failure to pay the ransom within the deadline of November 5. Rava belongs to the Nationalist Congress Party (NCP).
- *October 17*: Meghalaya Police said that the Nagaland-based NSCN-IM and the LAEF have joined hands to extort money from the coal traders in the South Garo Hills district. B.K. Dey Sawian, the Director General of Police, disclosed that the NSCN-IM has set up a camp in the Balpakram National Park in South Garo Hills with the help of the LAEF to extort money from coal traders in the district. The report added that after the rainy season, coal export to Bangladesh will resume in November in the Nangalbibra area of South Garo Hills, where criminal activities, including extortion and abductions for ransom, occur on a regular basis. While commenting on the recent

counter-insurgency operations in the entire Balpakram National Park, Sawian says, "We, however, could not make much progress as the area where the NSCN (I-M) has set up the camp is inaccessible." Balpakaram area has been earlier used by many militant outfits for training and taking shelter. Following the killing of Peter Marak, 'commander-in-chief' of the LAEF, his younger brother Darong Marak has reportedly been trying to strengthen the outfit with the help of the NSCN-IM. Sawian mentions that the State Home Department has asked for intervention of the Union Ministry of Home Affairs in the NSCN-IM's activities.

- *October 12*: Meghalaya Police informs that there was movement of militants belonging to the NSCN-IM, ULFA and the LAEF in the entire Balpakram National Park of South Garo Hills district. Militants belonging to various outfits had earlier used the park for setting up training camps and also as a safe sanctuary against the troops, because of remoteness of the area and absence of large-scale human habitation along the park. With the annual coal export to start at Nangalbibra in October, militants are suspected to be indulging in a extortion drive.
- *August 30*: One LAEF militant, Jackius A Sangma, is arrested by Meghalaya Police from an unspecified place. He confesses that the NSCN-IM militants were providing arms and explosives to their outfit.
- *August 29*: Meghalaya Chief Minister D.D. Lapang has sought a report from police on the nexus between the NSCN-IM and LAEF. "I will seek the report from the police department and would act accordingly," Lapang said. Earlier, police said it would lodge a complaint with the Union Government against NSCN-IM for supplying arms and ammunition and imparting guerilla warfare training to the LAEF. The slain "commander-in-chief" of LAEF Peter Marak had revealed that NSCN-IM had provided them with AK

rifles, Universal Machine Guns etc, police said. The arrested LAEF cadre, Jackius A Sangma, was found to be involved in arms deal with the NSCN-IM in Nagaland, the police added.

- *August 23*: One LAEF militant, Lahat Marak, earlier arrested by police along with two M-20 pistols, 7.5 mm ammunition and 34 rounds of live ammunition of 9-mm pistols on August 2, is granted bail by a local court at Williamnagar. He is reportedly an active member of the ruling Congress party at Williamnagar.
- *August 22*: The chief of the Liberation of Achik Elite Force, Peter Marak, is killed in an encounter between militants and police personnel near a hideout of the outfit at a forest near Kalak village in the East Garo Hills district. One Liberation of Achik Elite Force cadre was injured in the encounter. He was reportedly killed while leading the police to one of the outfit's camps at Kallak, 30 kilometres from Williamnagar town, district headquarters of East Garo Hills.
- *August 21*: The chief of the Liberation of Achik Elite Force, Peter Marak, and two of his accomplices are arrested by the Meghalaya Police from an unspecified location between Jorabad and Khanapara in the Ri Bhoi district along the Assam-Meghalaya border.
- *August 7*: One cadre of the Liberation of Achik Elite Force involved in an arms deal in Nagaland was reportedly arrested at Shillong in the East Khasi Hills district on an unspecified date. The LAEF cadre, identified as Jackius A Sangma alias Jack, is a close associate of LAEF chairman Peter Marak. He had collected INR 100000 from a person at Williamnagar and taken the amount to Dimapur for purchasing arms.
- *July 4*: Two cadres of the LAEF, identified as Jonathan M Sangma and Junjun M Sangma, are shot dead by the Special Operation Team of South Garo Hills

police at Dimit in the East Garo Hills district. Two pistols and seven rounds of live ammunition were seized from the slain militants.

- *June 22*: Suspected militants belonging to the Liberation of Achik Elite Force lobbed two hand grenades at Tura town and the coal-rich belt of Nangalbibra in South Garo Hills killing one civilian, identified as Sapan Baraj, and injuring 11 others. In Tura, the explosion was triggered by a grenade lobbed into the main entrance of the Super Market by three LAEF militants. Similarly, in Nangalbibra the attackers lobbed the grenade at a shop and injured three persons.

The recruitment and training has been taking place since early 2006, the report added.

2006

- *December 12*: The on-going agitation programme of the Garo Students' Union, which is spearheading the demand for holding of the Winter Session of the State Legislative Assembly in Tura, has faced opposition from the LAEF. The outfit has warned the student body against disturbing the festive season. The outfit's 'Convenor cum Publicity Secretary', Chingkam Marak, said although the LAEF supported the demand for the session at Tura, yet, it should not be at the expense of the Garo people's wellbeing.
- *June 13*: The Garo Hills police conduct a raid at the residence of the leader of Liberation Achik Elite Front, Peter R Marak, at Songsak in the East Garo Hills district and recover one Chinese hand grenade along with some incriminating documents, including demand notes. However, Peter managed to escape from the incident site.
- *June 6*: Two LAEF militants, identified as Xavier P. Marak and Sylseng Marak, are arrested from Williamnagar in the East Garo Hills district.

4

Meghalaya Assessment—2010

Meghalaya has witnessed an almost continuous diminution in trends in militant violence since 2003, with a slight discontinuity in 2006. The years 2008 and 2009 saw the progressive marginalization of militant formations in the State, even as overall fatalities declined by 66 per cent, from an already diminished total. Militancy-related incidents decreased by 41 per cent, and there was a complete absence of any civilian or Security Force (SF) fatalities in 2009. A total of 4 militant fatalities were recorded.

Table. Militancy-related Fatalities in Meghalaya: 2001-09

Year	Incidents	Civilians	SFs	Militants	Total
2001	70	29	15	07	51
2002	84	28	14	24	66
2003	85	35	07	37	79
2004	47	17	08	22	47
2005	37	01	00	23	24
2006	38	06	00	20	26
2007	28	09	01	14	24
2008	79	00	01	11	12
2009	49	0	0	4	4

Militancy related incidents were reported from all of Meghalaya's seven Districts in 2009. While the East Khasi Hills was the most affected District, with 18 recorded incidents, Jaintia Hills reported 12 incidents; West Garo Hills, six; East Garo Hills, five; West Khasi Hills: four, Ri-Bhoi, three; and South Garo Hills, one.

The South Asia Terrorism Portal (SATP) database records that a total of 62 militants were neutralised in Meghalaya in 2009. Of these, 48 were arrested, 10 surrendered and four were killed. The proscribed Hynniewtrep National Liberation Council (HNLC), remains the strongest among surviving militant groups. Claiming to represent the majority Khasi tribe, the HNLC continued to operate in the Khasi-Jaintia Hills region in 2009. Extortion targeting local traders across the India-Bangladesh border constituted the bulk of HNLC's activities. Media reports in March 2009 mentioned that, after Police successes in curbing the HNLC's extortion drive, the group began targeting local traders in the border region. The HNLC has over 100 cadres, most of them located in Bangladesh. Difficult living conditions and the absence of facilities in the neighbouring country have provoked the surrender of many cadres in Meghalaya. According to the SATP database, at least nine HNLC cadres surrendered in Jaintia and East Khasi Hills District in 2009. One of them reveled that leaders of the proscribed outfit were leading a luxurious life, despite acute privations among the rank and file in Bangladesh.

On December 5, 2009, the Meghalaya Chief Minister D.D. Lapang appealed to HNLC 'general secretary' Cherishterfield Thangkhiew and 'commander-in-chief' Bobby Marwein to come over-ground and also offered them 'safe-passage.' The HNLC leadership, however, rejected the offer.

Purportedly representing the Garo tribe, the Achik National Volunteer Council (ANVC) has been under an extended cease-fire agreement with the Union Government since July 23, 2004. The ANVC has renewed its demand for a separate State of Garoland, after the Centre initiated the process for the creation of a new State of Telangana, bifurcating the south Indian State of Andhra Pradesh. The outfit's 'publicity secretary', Arist Sengsrang Sangma, on December 11, 2009, declared that, with the Centre taking steps to create a Telangana State, the ANVC's demands would also be justified in days to come: "Our demand is very much genuine and we are not asking for the sun or moon, but a separate State within India, unlike other militant groups, which are demanding sovereignty." Earlier, the Union Government reportedly rejected the outfit's demand for a separate Garo State, when the Joint Secretary (in-charge of Northeast) of the Union Ministry of Home Affairs (MHA), Naveen Verma, held a series of meetings with senior Meghalaya Government officials and discussed a rehabilitation package for the ANVC on September 10, 2009. Meanwhile, the Meghalaya Police sought the help of the ANVC to neutralise other militant groups in the Garo Hills. The ANVC leader Arist Sengsrang Sangma stated that the outfit was ready to help the Meghalaya Police. Since the cease-fire with the ANVC, several fringe militant formations had filled the vacuum in the Garo Hills, primarily with the intention of exploiting the lucrative extortion racket.

The Liberation of Achik Elite Force (LAEF) led the pack, maintaining linkages with the National Socialist Council of Nagaland–Isak-Muivah (NSCN-IM) in Nagaland, and the United Liberation Front of Asom (ULFA) and National Democratic Front of Bodoland (NDFB) in Assam. The Garo group had set up its operational camp inside the Balpakram National Park in the South Garo Hills, with the help of the NSCN-IM, to train new LAEF recruits in guerilla warfare tactics.

The Meghalaya Police have registered significant counter-insurgency (CI) successes against the LAEF in 2009. On March 24, the Police neutralized a LAEF camp in the Tajal area near Shahlang in the West Khasi Hills District. Again, on July 7, the Police arrested three LAEF militants at Sisobibra village in the East Garo Hills District, while they were trying to extort INR 500,000 from an unidentified local businessman. On August 20, an unidentified LAEF militant was shot dead by the East Garo Hills District Police during an encounter at Nengkra near Williamnagar. On November 22, the Police neutralized another LAEF hideout and arrested five cadres, including 'sergeant major' Kyndoh Momin, during a CI operation at Byrnihat in the Ri-Bhoi District along the Meghalaya-Assam border. Outside Meghalaya, on January 17, two cadres of another tiny armed Garo group, People's Liberation Front of Meghalaya (PLF-M), including its founding 'general secretary' John Jubilee D. Shera Marak (34), were shot dead by the Army during an encounter at Hat Hati bridge near Singhimari village on National Highway-37 in the Bongaigaon District of Assam.

Meghalaya's militancy flows substantially from activities of militant formations in the neighbouring States. Groups such as ULFA and NDFB in Assam have used the Garo Hills to travel between Assam and their base areas in Bangladesh. On June 5, 2009, a suspected NDFB linkman was arrested by Border Security Force (BSF) personnel from the Nokchi outpost in the West Garo Hills District, while trying to exfiltrate to Bangladesh. Similarly, on June 11, 2009, two ULFA militants were shot dead by a joint team of the Meghalaya Police and the Army at Bangalpara village in the same West Garo Hills District.

One of them was an 'area commander' of the outfit for the entire Garo Hills and was involved in the smuggling of arms and ammunition from Bangladesh through the Garo Hills border to Assam. Assam's armed groups also continue to engage in extortion in the Jaintia Hills region. On January 3, 2009, an NDFB militant, who, along with HNLC militants, was involved in an extortion drive in the coalfields of Jaintia Hills District, was arrested after being wounded in an encounter with the Police, in the Shohksih coal mining area. He subsequently succumbed to his injury.

A media report on January 16, 2009, mentioned that Assam's Karbi Anglong District-based militant groups, the Karbi National Volunteers and United People's Democratic Solidarity (UPDS), were engaged in extortion activities targeting civilians belonging to the Pnar tribe of Jaintia Hills residing in the Block-I area on the Meghalaya-Assam border. Several villages, including Mooluber, Psiar, Moojem and Deinler, were served demand notes ranging from INR 200 to INR 1,000 per household, depending on their family income. The Black Widow (BW) group in Assam, and the Kanglei Yawol Kanna Lup (KYKL) and People's Liberation Army

(PLA) in Manipur, also operate in Meghalaya. The 15th Parliamentary elections were held in Meghalaya's two constituencies of Shillong and Tura on April 16, 2009. While the HNLC called for a 24-hour general shutdown in protest against the visit of the Congress party president, Sonia Gandhi, to address a public meeting in capital Shillong on April 13, 2009, as much as 64. 41 per cent voter turnout was registered in the elections in the State.

An unfenced 65 kilometre stretch of Meghalaya's 443 kilometre-long border with Bangladesh continues to allow the inward and outward movement of militants. This is the principal reason for the persistence of the militancy, albeit at its lowest ebb, in the State. There is, however, projection for the complete fencing of India-Bangladesh border till 2010. Unless the security establishment in Meghalaya refocuses its strategy on this militant vantage point, the vestiges of militancy will continue to linger in the State.

NORTH-EASTERN INSURGENCY: PROBLEM OF ASSESSMENT

The decision of the Government of Manipur to de-notify the Armed Forces Special Powers Act (AFSPA) from two districts of the State against the wishes of the Union government is one of many such moves by different State governments of the northeastern region. As militancy in various States of the region show little signs of abatement, such decisions unveil a trend of assertive State policies on matters of security.

What followed the Manipur decision was a statement from N Rio, Chief Minister of Nagaland, where there has been an organised movement demanding the repeal of the Act. Speaking in Kohima on 15 August, Rio said "though the term of the Disturbed areas act was extended by another year, the government believes that the State could now do without it." Similarly, Assam differs in assessment of the security situation from the Centre. On 9 August, Assam State Minister for Home Affairs, Rockybul Hussain, in a statement in the Assembly, said that the State government has no direct evidence of the presence of ISI operatives in the State. In contrast, the recent Annual Report of the Union Ministry of Home Affairs (MHA), suggests that Pakistan sponsored terrorism "first appeared in Punjab and then in Jammu and Kashmir and it was later extended to the North-east by providing funds, training, equipments to terrorists and promoting infiltration."

The Assam Chief Minister, while speaking at the Independence Day celebrations in Guwahati on 15 August said: "Normalcy has returned to Assam after our government took over three years ago. The people have been able to move around freely after an era of fear and uncertainty that prevailed earlier had come to an end." In contrast, the MHA Annual Report categorises Assam as affected by high degree of violence. The report reads, "The level of violence in Assam was second only to Jammu and Kashmir and was highest in the North-east. The whole of Assam except Karimganj and Hailakandi district in Barak Valley are affected by insurgency in varying degrees."

Examples of such a trend are not few. Way back in the year 2000, the decision of the Union government to proscribe the two militant outfits in Meghalaya, the HNLC and the ANVC, was contested by the State government who termed the then prevailing situation as not too serious and the move of the centre as unwarranted.

The reasons of such different assessment are mostly rooted in the political ground. For example, in Assam, it is now an established fact that illegal migrants from Bangladesh have changed the pattern of politics in few of the districts and constitute an important segment in the State. Each of the political parties in the States needs to take their sensibilities into account while asking for support during elections. As a result, no political party can be seen as overtly anti-Bangladeshi, which can be easily interpreted, as anti-minority.

The second reason is the attempt by the different State administrations to boast of (nonexistent) peace as their achievements. It is this trend, which leads Chief Ministers and other authorities to announce the onset of peace long before its actual arrival.

Third is the pressure from the civil society and community based organisations in the State. In various States, such groups do exercise significant influence and are seen to be in favour of a political solution to the problem of militancy. As a result, in spite of spiraling violence, the State governments restrain themselves from declaring an all out war on the militants.

Fourth is the functioning of the intelligence agencies. The State level agencies are under instruction from their political masters to produce reports, which does not really contravene their public postures. As a result, their efforts end up suppressing the ground realities. However, the central intelligence agencies, who usually function independently from their State level counterparts, tend to take a detached view. There are, however, times when they have been found to have produced grossly inflated figures to suit certain political needs at the Centre.

A correct assessment is imperative for an effective counter-insurgency policy. Contrasting assessments not only lead to a friction between the States and Centre, but also act as a source of directionless policies towards establishing peace in the region. A middle ground needs to be evolved. The idea of a single, yet effective intelligence agency demands serious attention.

OPERATION LAUNCHED IN THE YEAR 2010 TO NAB FUGITIVE MEGHALAYA MILITANTS

Shillong, Dec 3 (IANS) A 53-member Special Weapons and Tactics (SWAT) team has been deployed in Meghalaya to conduct anti-insurgency operations, Home Minister H.D.R. Lyngdoh said Friday.

"The SWAT team is being deployed in Garo Hills to render quick and swift operation in the jungle against militants," Lyngdoh told legislators in the assembly during question hour. Garo Hills region, which comprises of three districts in the western part of Meghalaya, is home to more than five rebels groups fighting for a sovereign or autonomous homeland for the tribal Garos. The region, which shares its border with Assam as well as Bangladesh is also being used as a safe haven and hot corridor for various northeast-based militant groups including the National Socialist Council of Nagaland-Isak-Muivah) (NSCN-IM), the United Liberation Front of Asom (ULFA) and the National Democratic Front of Bodoland (NDFB).

The team has been trained in counter-insurgency and jungle warfare school of the Indo-Tibetan Border Police at Mahindanda in Uttarakhand and the Counter Insurgency and Terrorist School at Dergaon in Assam, Lyngdoh said. Operation launched to nab fugitive Meghalaya militants Shillong, Sep 27 (IANS) Two top commanders of the Garo National Liberation Army (GNLA) in Meghalaya are on the run after security forces raided their headquarters, and efforts are on to nab them, a top police officer said.

A combined team of Meghalaya Police and its Special Operation Team Sunday launched a massive combing operation code-named 'Operation Durama' and raided the GNLA's general headquarters and training camp inside Durama hill range. But no militant was arrested in the raid at the Durama hill range in Meghalaya's West Garo Hill district, about 350 km west of Shillong. "They (militant leaders) are on the run and we are putting extra efforts to nab these fugitives," Sylvester Nongtynger, the police chief of East Garo Hills district, told IANS.

Champion R. Sangma, a rogue Meghalaya police officer-turned chairman of GNLA, and the outfit's military wing Chief Sohan D. Shira escaped from the camop along with 50 cadres. "There was an exchange of fire between security forces and heavily armed militants but they escaped due to the thick vegetation," Nongtynger said.

A Chinese-made hand-grenade, a huge quantity of food rations, livestock and uniforms of GNLA cadres were recovered from the camp. The GNLA, fighting for a 'sovereign Garoland' in the western area of Meghalaya, has forged close operational links with other northeast-based insurgent groups like the National Socialist Council of Nagaland-Isak-Muivah (NSCN-IM), the United Liberation Front of Asom (ULFA) and he National Democratic Front of Bodoland (NDFB). The

GNLA's foot soldiers are deserters, mostly from the NDFB, the Achik National Volunteers Council (ANVC) and the Liberation of Achik Elite Force (LAEF).

According to police, the GNLA is reported to have made extortion demands ranging from ₹5 lakh to ₹1 crore from legislators, government officials and businessmen. Meghalaya, especially the Garo Hills region, is being used as a safe haven by various northeast-based militant groups, including the NSCN-IM, the ULFA and a faction of the NDFB, police say.

ROGUE MEGHALAYA COP DISMISSED

Shillong, Sep 4 (IANS) Champion R. Sangma, a Meghalaya police officer-turned-militant who floated the Garo National Liberation Army (GNLA), has been sacked, an official said. "The government has terminated Champion's service. He is no longer a policeman and is a free-bird now," Director General of Police S.B. Kakati told IANS. He said the order terminating services of Champion, a deputy superintendent of police, was notfified by the government about 15 days ago. Champion floated the GNLA in 2008 and fled to forests. Kakati said Champion was an indisciplined officer and his dismissal was sought on several instances.

"He (Champion) never attended work and remained absent for months, therefore, his post was never made permanent and his dismissal was sought after a departmental inquiry into his conduct," the police chief added. Champion, whose militant organisation is demanding sovereign Garoland in west Meghalaya, has forged a close operational relationship with other northeast-based insurgent groups such as the National Socialist Council of Nagaland (Isak-Muivah) (NSCN-IM), the United Liberation Front of Asom (ULFA) and the National Democratic Front of Bodoland (NDFB).

The GNLA's foot soldiers are deserters, mostly from the NDFB, the Achik National Volunteers Council (ANVC) and the Liberation of Achik Elite Force (LAEF). According to police, the GNLA is reported to have made extortion demands ranging from ₹5 lakh to ₹1 crore from legislators, government officials and businessmen.

Meghalaya, especially the Garo Hills region, is being used as a safe haven by various northeast-based militant groups, including the NSCN-IM, the ULFA and a faction of the NDFB, state police say. Meghalaya militant leader still a police officer in records Shillong, July 30 (IANS) Believe it or not: a Meghalaya police officer-turned-militant, Champion R. Sangma, is still a Deputy Superintendent of Police in the Meghalaya police records, a police official said Champion floated the militant Garo National Liberation Army (GNLA) in 2008 and took to the jungles. "I have recommended to the government that Champion R. Sangma is dismissed from service, but it has not been done so far," Director General of Police S.B. Kakati said. "I wasn't sure why the government has not dismissed his service. May be the legal angle to his dismissal is being looked into. I can't say anything on that," he added.

Kakati said Champion was indisciplined as an officer and his dismissal was sought on several instances. "He (Champion) never attended work and remained absent for months, therefore his post was never made permanent and his dismissal was sought after a departmental inquiry into his conduct," the police chief added.

Champion, whose dream is to fight for a 'sovereign Garoland' in the western area of Meghalaya, has forged a close operational relationship with other northeast-based insurgents groups such as Socialist Council of Nagaland-Isak-Muivah (NSCN-IM), United Liberation Front of Asom (ULFA) and National Democratic Front of Bodoland (NDFB). GNLA's foot soldiers are deserters, mostly from the National Democratic Front of Bodoland (NDFB), the Achik National Volunteers Council (ANVC) and the Liberation of Achik Elite Force (LAEF). The GNLA has slapped extortion demands ranging from ₹5 lakh to ₹1 crore on legislators, government officials and businessmen. "Champion has been teasing the state police and other security forces with his repeated SMSes about his weapons and his contacts," Kakati said.

One of his SMS went: "I am trying to get AK-47 from the NSCN (IM) in day or two and we will replenish our arms and ammunition", the police chief recalled. In a recent picture, some GNLA men posed with an LMG, Uzis and other weaponry. Champion even called up journalists here recently and boasted of having contacts in China, Myanmar and with other northeast-based militants.

Infact, the Meghalaya police earlier seized a machine gun, an Uzi sub-machine gun, grenades, bombs, a laptop and incriminating documents recovered from the GNLA general headquarters. The police recently zeroed in on one of the outfits' hideouts in South Garo hills jungles, but Champion and his men managed to escape. He left behind an Italian made Beretta pistol, extortion notes and a cap with "Champion" written on it. Meghalaya, especially the Garo Hill region, is being used as a safe haven for various northeast-based militants groups including the NSCN-IM, the ULFA and the anti-talk faction of the NDFB.

With the outlawed A'chik National Volunteers Council (ANVC) on a ceasefire agreement with the central government, the NSCN (IM) and the ULFA spawned several militant groups with the main intention of exploiting the lucrative extortion in the coal-rich areas of the Garo Hills region. Most people in northeast yearn for peace: Mooshahary

Shillong, May 1 (IANS) Meghalaya Governor R.S. Mooshahary has admitted that some people in the northeastern states still support insurgent groups but said the majority of the inhabitants yearn to live in peace and harmony.

Mooshahary, a former head of the elite National Security Guard (NSG), termed Meghalaya a "peaceful" state and said the police have cracked down on the insurgents. "Meghalaya cannot be termed as a disturbed place. By and large it's peaceful and police have been able to take prompt action against the spillover activities by ULFA (United Liberation Front of Asom) and NDFB (National Democratic Front of Bodoland). There has been no major incident in the state for so many months," Mooshahary told IANS.

Meghalaya, especially the Garo Hill region, is being used as a safe haven for various northeast-based militants groups including the National Socialist Council of Nagaland (Isak-

Muivah) (NSCN-IM), the ULFA and the NDFB, whose chief, Ranjan Daimary, was arrested in Bangladesh and handed over to India Saturday.

With the outlawed A'chik National Volunteers Council (ANVC) on a ceasefire agreement with the central government, the NSCN (IM) and the ULFA spawned several militant groups with the main intention of exploiting the lucrative extortion in the coal-rich areas of the Garo Hills region. The Garo National Liberation Army (GNLA), which is one among the smaller militant outfits, is believed to have been formed with the help of the NSCN (IM) to extort money.

Champion R.Sangma, a deputy superintendent of police turned rogue, is believed to be heading GNLA, whose cadres are deserters, mostly from the ANVC and the Liberation of Achik Elite Force (LAEF). Another outlawed outfit, the Hynniewtrep National Liberation Council (HNLC), has been demanding a sovereign Khasi homeland in Meghalaya is currently on the backfoot with most of its cadres, including its chairman Julius K. Dorphang surrendering to the government. According to the Meghalaya police officials, the HNLC is closely linked to the NSCN-IM and the National Liberation Front of Tripura.

On the birth of a new militant outfit GNLA in the Garo Hills headed by a former police officer, the governor said, "I don't think he (GNLA chief Sangma) has been able to make much headway. If he had any grievances, he should have aired the same to the concerned authority. It's a clear case of frustration and he is creating bigger problems for himself." He said Sangma will not be able to "create any large-scale movement" and will not have much following either. "One day he will have to come out in the open. It is difficult to survive as people do not want violence; they want to live in peace," Mooshahary said.

Downplaying the emergence of splinter insurgent groups, Mooshahary said: "The small groups that come up cannot be called as insurgent groups. They are merely a band of extortionists who are out to loot and plunder from others." He said that except for Manipur, the situation in the northeast has largely improved. "Nagaland and Assam have improved a lot in the law and order front, and the current trend in the region is towards peace," Mooshahary added. However, sounding a word of caution to the law and order authorities, Mooshahary said: "We should make sure that Meghalaya does not become a transit point for arms smuggling, but we have seen a lot of untoward events that have been prevented in the past."

He also stressed on the need to bring stringent electoral reforms to debar people with criminal antecedents from contesting the polls. "We need better electoral reforms and debar those (politicians) with criminal antecedents or having nexus with criminals from contesting elections," Mooshahary contended.

Top Meghalaya militant leader arrested in Siliguri: Shillong, May 16 (IANS) Founder and general secretary of militant outfit Garo National Liberation Army (GNLA) Novembirth Ch Marak has been arrested from Siliguri railway station in West Bengal, dealing a blow to the group's network, a senior Meghalaya police official said Sunday. "Novembirth is a prize catch for us in our operation against the GNLA," Superintendent of Police Dalton P. Marak, who is in-charge of the West Garo Hills district, told IANS.

Luxmary Sangma, the militant leader's girlfriend was also arrested while they were trying to board a train to Kolkata Saturday. Novembirth, the Number 3 man in the tribal Garo militant outfit, fell into the trap of the Meghalaya Police after a cash reward was announced for any information leading to his arrest.

On April 30, the militant leader managed to give police the slip—though not without receiving an injury—following an encounter with the Special Operations Team at the Bolchugre village and had since been hiding in one place or the other. Novembirth also exposed the linkages of the GNLA with other militant outfits, including the National Socialist Council of Nagaland-Isak-Muivah (NSCN-IM), United Liberation Front of Asom (ULFA) and National Democratic Front of Bodoland (NDFB).

"He (Novembirth) had held several meetings with an NSCN (I-M) leader for arms supplies and to impart guerrilla warfare training," the police official said. Not only that, the GNLA general secretary said that the outfit has a strength of 30 cadres and possessed two AK-47 rifles, a semi-automatic machine gun, 20 small arms, and 25 grenades besides country-made bombs. The GNLA, which is fighting for a 'sovereign Garoland' in the western areas of Meghalaya, is headed by Champion R. Sangma, a policeman-turned-rogue, whose cadres are deserters, mostly from the NDFB, A'chik National Volunteers Council (ANVC) and Liberation of Achik Elite Force (LAEF).

Champion also roped in John Robert Ch Marak alias Toding, a dismissed constable with the 1st Meghalaya Police battalion, who joined the GNLA as 'deputy commander-in-chief'. "On his (Novembirth) leads, we also arrested the outfit's finance secretary Solte Sangma and Martin Sangma from Williamnagar in East Garo Hills district and we expect more arrests in the days to come," Marak said. The GNLA had earlier slapped extortion demands ranging from ₹500,000 to ₹1 crore on politicians, petrol pump owners, coal dealers and businessmen in the coal-rich districts of Garo Hills.

A former minister in the previous D.D. Lapang ministry and a retired inspector general of police were among those who received extortion demands.

Militant outfit says Pakistan's ISI offered help: Shillong, May 22 (IANS) The Garo National Liberation Army (GNLA), a militant outfit in Meghalaya, has said that Pakistan's main intelligence agency and jehadi groups offered it help to take on the Indian state. "The ISI (Inter-Services Intelligence) and several jehadi groups extended help to the GNLA but I refused," GNLA chairman Champion R. Sangma told IANS over the telephone from an undisclosed location.

Sangma, a former deputy superintendent of police, deserted the Meghalaya Police and floated the GNLA due to alleged harassment by his seniors. The outfit's cadres are deserters, mostly from the National Democratic Front of Bodoland (NDFB), the Achik National Volunteers Council

(ANVC) and the Liberation of Achik Elite Force (LAEF). "We (GNLA) are not working against the interest of India but for the cause of Garo Hills within the ambit of the Indian constitution," Sangma said. He, however, boasted of having several "friends" in China, Thailand and Myanmar besides militant organisations from Nagaland and Manipur who were ready to help the GNLA. Asked why he floated a militant outfit, Sangma, who was trained as a police officer at the North Eastern Police Academy in Meghalaya, said he was "harassed" by his seniors.

"I submitted many representations to the government and the Meghalaya Police DGP (director general of police) but they never looked into my grievances. So I decided to float the organisation," he said. The militant group formed in 2007 suffered a major setback last week when its founder and general secretary Novembirth Marak was arrested from Siliguri in West Bengal. On Friday, five GNLA militants were arrested in Meghalaya's East Garo Hills district. Garo militant leader ready for talks, surrender Shillong, May 21 (IANS) Police officer-turned-militant Champion R. Sangma Friday said he is ready to surrender before union Home Minister P. Chidambaram but not before the Meghalaya government. "I will never surrender before the Meghalaya government, but I am ready to surrender before the government of India and that too before Chidambaram," Sangma, the Garo National Liberation Army (GNLA) chairman, told IANS over the phone.

Sangma, a former deputy superintendent of police, had deserted the Meghalaya police and floated the GNLA due to alleged harassment by his seniors. "The GNLA would sit for talks only with the centre and not with the state government. If we received a request from the union home minister, then only we will consider," he said. The outfit cadres are deserters, mostly from the National Democratic Front of Bodoland (NDFB), the Achik National Volunteers Council (ANVC) and the Liberation of Achik Elite Force (LAEF).

The militant group formed in 2007 suffered a major setback Saturday when its founder and general secretary Novembirth Marak was arrested from Siliguri railway station in West Bengal Saturday, dealing a blow to the group's network. The security forces busted a GNLA training camp at Durama Hill range in Garo Hills Wednesday and recovered a machine gun, an Uzi sub-machine gun, grenades, bombs, a laptop and incriminating documents.

Asked why he floated a militant outfit, Sangma, who was trained as a police officer at the North Eastern Police Academy in Meghalaya, said he was "harassed by my seniors". "I have submitted many representations to the government and the Meghalaya police DGP (director general of police), but they never look into my grievances. So I decided to float the organisation," he said. Asked about the GNLA demands, he said the group was only seeking a "Garoland" within the ambit of the Indian constitution. The GNLA is also not asking for a greater Garoland carved out of Bangladesh, Assam, Ri-Bhoi and West Khasi Hills districts of Meghalaya, like the ANVC, he said.

The ANVC is under a tripartite ceasefire agreement with the central and the state governments. The rebel group operating in Meghalaya's Garo Hills region is fighting for creation of Garoland Territorial Council.

MEGHALAYA REBEL CHIEF SURRENDERS

Shillong, Dec 17 (IANS) Dimrim N. Sangma, the chairman of Liberation A'chik Elite Force (LAEF), a separatist group operating in Meghalaya, has surrendered along with arms and ammunition. Four of Dimrim's aides - 'Sergeants' Rakshimbirth Sangma and Ninja G. Momin, 'Lance Corporal' Akash G. Momin and 'Private soldier' Tangrik Sangma - surrendered Thursday before East Garo Hills District Superintendent of Police, Sylvester Nongtynger. The rebels deposited one country-made AK rifle, one 7.65 mm pistol with 10 rounds of live ammunition, one grenade, crude bomb, ten rounds of live MMG ammunition and incriminating documents.

Dimrim gave up the armed struggle for an 'independent A'chik state' for the Garo tribals in western parts of Meghalaya following pressure due to the ongoing combing operations against militants in Garo Hills. On Dec 2, Nikseng G. Momin, the chief of the armed wing of LAEF was killed in a gun battle with the security forces in Darugiri forest in East Garo Hills district. "The surrender is a major achievement for us and we expect others (rebels) to toe the line," Nongtynger told IANS. He added: "Their surrender marks the end of LAEF outfit which had unleashed a reign of terror for the last five to six years."

The LAEF, which was one of the five Garo rebel groups, maintains closes links with the secessionist Naga rebel group, the NSCN (IM) and ULFA. Meanwhile, two Garo National Liberation Army (GNLA) rebels were arrested from Meghalaya Chief Minister Mukul Sangma assembly constituency, police said. Tricing D. Sangma and Namseng D. Shira were nabbed from Ampati area in Meghalaya's West Garo Hills district, district deputy police chief, Wallamlad Shabong told IANS. "We are still interrogating them to find out their plans," he said. The GNLA, one of the five Garo rebel groups, is fighting for a sovereign Garoland. It is headed by police officer-turned-rogue Champion R. Sangma, whose followers are mainly deserters of the outlawed ANVC and other rebel outfits.

MEGHALAYA POLICE OFFICER JOINS MILITANT GROUP

Shillong, March 18 (IANS) A deputy superintendent of police in Meghalaya has gone missing and has allegedly joined the militant Garo National Liberation Army (GNLA), a police official said. Champion R. Sangma was posted as assistant commandant of 2nd Meghalaya Police battalion at Goeragre in the state's West Garo Hills district when he went missing. "We have served notice to him for being absent from duty for a very long time. His salary has been stopped," Director General of Police S.B. Kakati told IANS. "We are making inquiries about Champion. We are hearing (he has joined a militant outfit) and waiting for the report," Kakati added. A senior Garo rebel leader claimed that Champion was now "commander-in-chief" of GNLA, whose cadres are deserters, mostly from the Achik National Volunteers Council (ANVC) and Liberation of Achik Elite Force (LAEF). Incidentally, LAEF was floated by another deserting policeman, Peter Marak, with the help of the National Socialist Council of Nagalim-Isak-Muivah. Marak was later killed in a crossfire while he was leading the police to a LAEF camp at Kalak in East Garo Hills Aug 22, 2007. The GNLA is under the police scanner for serving extortion notes, ranging from ₹5 lakh to ₹ 1 crore, to petrol pump owners, coal dealers and businessmen in the coal-rich districts of Garo Hills.

A retired inspector general of police was among those who received the extortion note. "Most of the rank and file of GNLA are mostly those who had deserted our organisation and members of the LAEF," ANVC spokesman Arist D. Sangma told IANS. ANVC, a Garo rebel group operating in Garo Hills region, is locked in a ceasefire with the central and state governments till March 31.

Meghalaya rebel group sends extortion demands to officials Shillong, July 16 (IANS) The Garo National Liberation Army, a militant group operating in Meghalaya, has sent extortion demands ranging from ₹30-40 lakh each to three government officials through mobile text messages, an official Friday said. The outfit has sent the extortion demands to the district transport officer and block development officer in East Garo Hills district, while a sub-divisional officer (civil) at Resubelpara received an extortion note signed by GNLA finance secretary Jagpil Sangma. "Police have registered a case following complaints lodged by the officials and a probe is on," East Garo Hill Deputy Commissioner Pravin Bakshi told IANS.

A cabinet minister in the previous D.D. Lapang ministry revealed in March that he had received a number of text messages from the GNLA asking him to "contribute to the organisation or face the consequences". The former minister, who did not wish to be named, claimed some Garo legislators too had received such text messages from the GNLA.

The GNLA had earlier slapped extortion demands ranging from ₹5 lakh to ₹1 crore on petrol pump owners, coal dealers and businessmen in the coal-rich districts of Garo Hills. A retired inspector general of police was among those who received the extortion note. Champion R.Sangma, a deputy superintendent of police turned rogue, is believed to be heading GNLA, whose cadres are deserters, mostly from the National Democratic Front of Bodoland (NDFB), Achik National Volunteers Council (ANVC) and Liberation of Achik Elite Force (LAEF).

- Police are hunting for Sangma, but so far without success.
- Five Garo militants arrested in Meghalaya

Shillong, May 21 (IANS) Five militants of the outlawed Garo National Liberation Army (GNLA) were arrested in Meghalaya's East Garo Hills district Friday, a police official said. The five were arrested from a hideout at Jagme village in the district and a 9 mm pistol with 9 rounds of ammunitions, one air pistol and ₹5,000 in cash were seized from them, district police chief Sylvester Nongtynger told IANS. "The ongoing combing operation against the GNLA militants has been successful and their top rung leaders are on the run," he said, adding the operations will continue till all its top leaders are arrested.

This has been the third set-back for GNLA in a week. Police arrested the outfit's general secretary Novemberth Ch Marak at Siliguri railway station last Saturday, and then one of its camps in Durama Hill between West and South Garo Hills districts was busted and arms, ammunition and incriminating documents seized. The GNLA, which is fighting for a "sovereign Garoland" in western Meghalaya, is headed by Champion R. Sangma, a policeman-turned-rogue, and its cadre are deserters, mostly from the National Democratic Front of Bodoland (NDFB), the Achik National Volunteers Council (ANVC) and the Liberation of Achik Elite Force (LAEF).

Hemmed in by the security operations, Sangma told IANS by phone Friday that he was ready to surrender before union Home Minister P. Chidambaram and hold talks on "Garoland" demand—significantly dropping demand for "sovereign Garoland". However, he defiantly said he would not surrender to the Meghalaya government. *Three GNLA rebels arrested*: Shillong, Nov 4 (IANS) Meghalaya police Thursday arrested three top rebels of the Garo National Liberation Army (GNLA) in western Meghalaya, police said.

Albin Ch Momin alias Gracepa, Johan T. Sangma and Rakesh T. Sangma, who are from the intelligence wing of the GNLA, were arrested from Williamnagar, the district headquarters of East Garo Hills. "All three are prized catch for us in the wake of the ongoing operation to rescue a transport official and his close-aide who were kidnapped by the GNLA," district police chief Sylvester Nongtynger told IANS.

He added: "Their task was mainly to observe the movement of security forces in Garo Hills and arrange logistic requirements of the GNLA cadres. Robinus Syngkon, district transport officer of East Garo Hills district, and his driver were abducted from his residence by five armed men of the GNLA Sep 30 in Williamnagar. The GNLA had earlier sent extortion demand of ₹60 lakh to Syngkon through text messages. However, Syngkon did not yield to the demand. "We are interrogating them and we expect that they will spill the beans on the whereabouts of the abducted official and his aide," Nongtynger said. The GNLA, one of the five Garo rebel groups, is fighting for a sovereign Garoland. It is headed by police officer-turned-rogue Champion R. Sangma, whose followers are mainly deserters of the outlawed ANVC and other rebel outfits. The outfit is believed to have links with the National Socialist Council of Nagaland (Isak-Muivah), the United Liberation Front of Asom (ULFA) and the National Democratic Front of Bodoland (NDFB).

Security forces bust militant camp in Meghalaya Shillong, May 19 (IANS) Security forces busted a training camp of the Garo National Liberation Army (GNLA) in Meghalaya and recovered arms and ammunition, a top police officer said. "A special operation team backed by the Central Reserve Police Force (CRPF) raided the GNLA's training camp inside Durama hill range," Superintendent of Police Dalton P. Marak told IANS. However, no militant was arrested in the early morning raid. The Durama hill range is located in Meghalaya's West Garo Hill district, about 350 km west of state capital Shillong.

"There was an exchange of fire between security forces and heavily armed militants but they escaped due to the thick vegetation. But they left some of their weapons behind," Marak said. A machine gun, an Uzi sub-machine gun, grenades, bombs, a laptop and incriminating documents were recovered from the GNLA camp. The GNLA, which is fighting for a 'sovereign Garoland' in the western area of Meghalaya, is headed by Champion R. Sangma, a policeman-turned-rogue whose cadres are deserters, mostly from the National Democratic Front of Bodoland (NDFB), the Achik National Volunteers Council (ANVC) and the Liberation of Achik Elite Force (LAEF).

The Meghalaya Police unearthed a mobile phone SIM card racket spread across Manipur and Nagaland based on the disclosures of arrested GNLA militant leader Novembirth Marak. Novembirth, founder and general secretary of GNLA, was arrested from the Siliguri railway station in West Bengal Saturday, dealing a blow to the group's network. The racket was unearthed at Tura town in West Garo Hill. "We have detained four agents of different mobile companies for questioning," he said. According to Novembirth, the mobile phone agents operating in Tura arranged for pre-paid SIM cards from Dimapur in Nagaland and Manipur. "They bring registered pre-paid SIM cards from Dimapur and Manipur and sell them to people, violating all telecom norms," Marak said.

The agents had demanded extortion money from various people through mobile text messages ranging from ₹5 lakh to ₹1 crore. The GNLA had made these extortion demands on politicians, petrol pump owners, coal dealers and businessmen in the coal-rich districts. A former minister in the previous D.D. Lapang ministry and a retired inspector general of police were among those who got extortion demands. The GNLA, a nascent militant outfit operating in three Garo Hill districts, has links with the National Socialist Council of Nagaland-Isak-Muivah, the United Liberation Front of Asom (ULFA) and the NDFB.

SEVEN INJURED IN MEGHALAYA BLAST

Shillong, Oct 10 (IANS) Seven people were injured in a bomb explosion at a crowded market in Tura in Meghalaya's West Garo Hills district, forcing authorities to sound an alert across the state, police said. "We have sounded general alert across the state following the explosion at a bakery shop," Dalton P. Marak, the police chief of West Garo Hills district, told IANS. The explosion took place at 6.45 p.m. when unidentified people lobbed the crude bomb from a moving vehicle at the bakery shop in Tura market, injuring seven people, Marak said.

Of the seven injured persons, four have been admitted in a government-run hospital, while the three were released after receiving first aid, the police official said. "The blast is mainly to create fear psychosis in the minds of the people. We are still investigating into it and we are not ruling out the involvement of militant groups," Marak said.

Though, no militant groups have claimed responsibility for the blast, intelligence agencies suspected the involvement of the Garo National Liberation Army (GNLA), a rebel group operating in the region. "It could be the handiwork of the GNLA militants to create fear psychosis and divert security agencies' attention in the wake of the combing operation against them," an intelligence official said. Security forces launched a massive combing operation in Garo Hills to rescue a transport official and his driver who were kidnapped by GNLA rebels Sep 30, even as their whereabouts are still unknown. Five armed GNLA rebels kidnapped R. Syngkon, district transport officer of East Garo Hills district, and his driver from his official residence in Williamnagar in west Meghalaya after he failed to meet their extortion demand of ₹60 lakh.

The GNLA, headed by police officer-turned-rogue Champion R. Sangma, who is fighting for a sovereign Garoland in western Meghalaya, is believed to have links with the National Socialist Council of Nagaland (Isak-Muivah), the United Liberation Front of Asom (ULFA) and the National

Democratic Front of Bodoland (NDFB). With the outlawed A'chik National Volunteers Council (ANVC) on a ceasefire agreement with the central government, the NSCN (IM) and the ULFA spawned several militant groups with the main intention of exploiting the lucrative extortion in the coal-rich areas of the Garo Hills region.

Condemning the incident, former Lok Sabha speaker Purno A. Sangma, the local legislator from Tura assembly constituency, asked the government to immediately find out the perpetrators and bring them to book.

Sangma asks police to probe mobile SIM cards racket: Shillong, Aug 8 (IANS) Meghalaya Chief Minister Mukul Sangma has asked the police to probe the SIM card racket in the state, expressing concern about mobile phone connections falling into the hands of militants. "I have asked the district authorities to probe as to how SIM cards land up with militants who use them under fictitious names," he said, after reviewing the law and order situation in the militancy-affected Garo Hills region of western Meghalaya Saturday.

Meghalaya Police busted a massive mobile phone SIM card racket spread across the state and Manipur and Nagaland as well, based on disclosures of an arrested top militant leader. The racket was unearthed at Tura, the district headquarters of West Garo Hills, following information obtained from Novembirth Ch Marak, founder and general secretary of Garo National Liberation Army (GNLA), who was arrested May 15 from Siliguri railway station in West Bengal.

According to Marak, mobile phone agents operating in Tura arranged for pre-paid SIM cards from Dimapur in Nagaland and Manipur. "They (agents) bring registered pre-paid SIM cards from Dimapur and Manipur and sell them to the people, violating all telecom norms," a police officer told IANS.

The GNLA, which is fighting for a 'sovereign Garoland' in the western areas of Meghalaya, is headed by Champion R. Sangma, a rogue policeman. It had demanded extortion money ranging from ₹5 lakh to ₹1 crore from various people through mobile text messages.

The messages were sent to politicians, government officials, petrol pump owners, coal dealers and businessmen in the coal-rich Garo Hills area. The GNLA, operating in three Garo Hills districts in the western part of Meghalaya, maintains links with the National Socialist Council of Nagaland-Isak-Muivah (NSCN-IM), United Liberation Front of Asom (ULFA) and National Democratic Front of Bodoland (NDFB).

Don't pay extortion to militants, Meghalaya officials told: Shillong, July 25 (IANS) Meghalaya Home Minister H.D.R. Lyngdoh Sunday asked government officials to inform the police about extortion notices issued to them by militants and threatened legal action if they complied with the rebels' demands. "We have received some information about GNLA (Garo National Liberation Army) sending extortion notices to some government officials," Lyngdoh told IANS, adding that police have started their investigation.

The GNLA, a tribal militant outfit operating in Garo Hills region in western Meghalaya, had sent extortion demands ranging from ₹30 lakh-40 lakh each to three government officials through mobile text messages. The outfit had sent extortion demands to the district transport officer and block development officer in East Garo Hills district, while a sub-divisional officer (civil) at Resubelpara received an extortion note signed by GNLA finance secretary Jagpil Sangma.

"The government has directed all government officials to report to the police on extortion notices served on them or else face legal action if the government found them complying to the militant demands," Lyngdoh said. East Garo Hill Deputy Commissioner Pravin Bakshi said that police have registered a case following complaints lodged by the officials and a probe is on to nab the militants.

A cabinet minister in the previous D.D. Lapang ministry revealed in March that he had received a number of text messages from the GNLA asking him to "contribute to the organisation or face the consequences". The former minister, who did not wish to be named, claimed some Garo legislators too had received such text messages. The GNLA had earlier slapped extortion demands ranging from ₹5 lakh to ₹1 crore on petrol pump owners, coal dealers and businessmen in the coal-rich districts of Garo Hills. Champion R. Sangma, a deputy superintendent of police-turned-rogue, is believed to be heading GNLA, whose cadres are deserters mostly from the National Democratic Front of Bodoland (NDFB), Achik National Volunteer Council (ANVC) and Liberation of Achik Elite Force (LAEF). Police are on the lookout for Champion R. Sangma.

5

Government of Meghalaya and its Vision 2020

OVERVIEW-SETTING THE CONTEXT

The Government of Meghalaya (GoM) has embarked on an initiative to formulate an IT Vision for the state which would lay the foundation for making Meghalaya an IT Destination and bring about an e-Governance culture in the state so that services are provided to all stakeholders in an efficient and transparent manner.

The envisaged span of this vision, called Vision 2020 will be till the year 2020. The vision is defined directly or indirectly by the various stakeholder groups (identified later in this document) with PricewaterhouseCoopers (PwC) playing the role of a facilitator. Vision 2020 requires its formulators to take a pragmatic approach and "looking forward to the future" and envision future quantum improvements in the state. However, the vision definition also needs to be tempered by the ability of the state to adopt change.

Hence, to develop a useful vision, the formulators must:

- Have the faculty of sight
- Know what is attainable in improvement terms
- Have unusual competence in discernment or foresight, to be able to develop a mental image of the future requirements and capabilities

VISION 2020 FORMULATION APPROACH

These provide the basic information for the vision formulation.

STAKEHOLDERS EXPECTATIONS

Stakeholders Expectation provides the most important set of inputs in formulation of Vision 2020.

The Stakeholders considered for formulating Vision 2020 are:

- Political Leadership of GoM
- Administrative Leadership of GoM
- IT Business Leadership of Meghalaya
- Residents of Meghalaya

Expectations from various categories of stakeholders are identified and graded to arrive at a prioritized set of expectation. Development Agenda The development agenda of the state reflects the thinking of the state leadership with respect to developmental issues and hence needs to be considered.

The current development agenda of the state has been sourced from the Tenth Five Year Plan of GoM. While reflecting the collective aspirations of the stakeholders, the vision must also have its focus. Therefore, the wish list needs to be filtered to ensure that it is in alignment with reality.

STATE PROFILE AND INFRASTRUCTURE

Relevant Data and statistics related to Profile of Meghalaya (both standalone and how it compares to other North Eastern states as well as nationally) and Infrastructure availability and issues are considered before arriving at a vision that is aligned with reality.

SWOT ANALYSIS

It is essential to understand the strengths of the state and identify the opportunities it can benefit from so as to prepare the state to overcome its weaknesses and threats.

SWOT analysis also helps us in understanding the constraints of the state which are acting as stumbling blocks in the path of the state govt in achieving its targets and expectations.

The final outcome of the envisioning exercise is Vision 2020 that is focused and aligned to reality while reflecting the stakeholders' aspirations.

PERFORMANCE MEASURE

Achievement of the vision must be measured against a set of performance measures and targets for each of the vision elements to ensure the vision is a real instrument of and inspiration for change that will be meaningful to everyone. Hence a set of Performance Measurement Parametres are defined against which achievement needs to be judged.

PERIODIC REVIEW

Any long term vision needs to be reviewed periodically to check against obsolescence. This is especially true for an IT Vision where the rapid rate of change of technology and trends has the capability of rendering a vision and consequently all its associated objectives obsolete within a relatively short span of time. Hence, it is imperative that the IT vision 2020 be checked for relevance and obsolescence periodically.

DETAILED PLAN—VISION 2020

Stakeholders Needs and Expectation During the process of drafting the vision of the State, needs and expectations of four major stakeholders and process participants were taken into account. These include citizens,business leaders, political leadership, and government departments and related establishments. In the subsequent paragraphs, needs and expectations of these four have been highlighted. After an initial round of meetings a draft report was finalised, this draft was again discussed with various stakeholders on July 19th, 20th and 21st and expectations were refined.

CITIZENS

Most of the people in the state live in rural areas and are dependent on farming and related activities for their livelihood. The citizens expectation are therefore related to better farm practices, better amenities such water supply, power, sanitation, health and education. Currently citizens have to travel all the way to district headquarters to avail of public services. In a few cases they need to travel up to Shillong to avail of Government facilities and even information about those facilities. Also the quality of service delivered is not of a good quality. Hence, the citizens' expectation is primarily related to improvement in the quality of service and also that they should be able to get information about Govt. services and schemes at a location closer to their place of habitation.

IT BUSINESS LEADERS

Interactions with business leaders primarily associated with the IT/ITeS sector in the state, revealed their expectation and concerns. Infrastructure particularly the telecom infrastructure of the state is inadequate. What they want is reliable, efficient and cost effective connectivity for their business. Improvement and optimization would be also necessary in road and rail network, energy and power sectors to ensure the growth of State's Industrial Infrastructure so as to enable businessmen a level playing field with their counterparts across the country Land acquisition policy is a major deterrent to expansion of existing businesses and also for setting up of new businesses in the state particularly for non tribal investors.

Another common issue raised by the business leaders was that while the state was making many new policies and rules, these were not available at the ground level. In the absence of information, many businessmen are confused as how to avail the rebates and subsidies mentioned in the policies. Businessmen in the state also feel that there is a need for handholding from the government as currently many of them doesn't have the technical expertise in the IT/ITeS sector. Many have burnt their fingers in the process of taking initiatives and are therefore hesitant without proper guidance and assistance.

GOVERNMENT DEPARTMENTS

Government Departments and related establishments all across the board would like to have access to contemporary and modern tools and technologies to aid in the process of plan and policy implementation, management and monitoring and bringing in transparency in the system. As per majority of the respondents, the lack of manpower resources and modern tools to transact the business are hampering the government officers to effectively manage their respective mandates and this is resulting in common citizens not getting the benefits of various plans and policies. Though some of the departments are yet to realise the benefits of IT, most

of the departments in the state are well aware of the benefits that their employees could reap from IT. Currently information technology is used in most government establishments for doing low-end jobs like typing letters and not for decision making or tracking and monitoring activities. Though the department heads appreciate the possibility of using ICT for such purposes, nothing much has happened on ground except in a few isolated cases.

POLITICAL LEADERSHIP

The political leadership of the state is targeting a growth of 8% of GDP and reduction of poverty by 5%. Focus is on providing basic social services like education, health, drinking water and sanitation. They are also expecting to provide economic and social opportunities to all individuals in the state and hope to reduce the economic disparities amongst the various sections of the society by providing gainful employment and increasing literacy rate.

DEVELOPMENT AGENDA

Govt. of Meghalaya has come up with developmental targets as part of the 10th Five Year Plan. However, many of these targets look well beyond the 10th Plan and consequently are important inputs for defining the vision.

These are:

- Reduction of poverty ratio by 5% by 2007 and 15% by 2012
- All children in school by 2003; all children to complete 5 years of school education by 2007
- Reduction in gender gaps in literacy and wage rates by at least 50% by 2007
- Reduction in decadal rate of population growth between 2001 and 2011 to 16.2%.

- Increase literacy rate to 75% within the plan period.
- Reduction in Infant Mortality Rate (IMR) to 45 per 1000 live births by 2007 and 28 by 2012.
- Reduction of Maternal Mortality Rate (MMR) to 2 per 1000 live births by 2007 and 1 by 2012.
- Increase in forest and tree cover to 25% in 2007 and 33% by 2012 ix. All villages to have sustained access to potable drinking water within plan periods.

To meet the above targets the developmental focus of the state will be in the following areas:

- Agriculture and land management
- Irrigation
- Poverty alleviation and rural development
- Social infrastructure like education, health and water supply.
- Economic infrastructure like power, transport and communications and road connectivity.
- Science and technology
- Forestry and environment programmes
- Increasing competitiveness of industries, particularly small scale industries.

Meghalaya is a land of young people. The above table shows that more than 65% of the population of the state of Meghalaya is below the age of 30. Therefore government needs to focus on these youths and provide better employment opportunities to them.

SWOT ANALYSIS

Strengths

- *Large Youth Population*: More than 65% of the population of the state is below the age of 30. Hence, the state has a large young working population giving it a huge benefit.
- *Capable female work force*: Meghalaya is the only state in India where a matriarchal society is prevalent. The women in the state are as much outgoing, hard working and entrepreneurial as the men. Meghalaya is among the best performing states in term of

Gender Disparity Index (GDI) and Gender Empowerment Index (GEI). This is particularly relevant in the context of IT/ITeS industries. Great potential exists for starting up all-women IT/ITeS industrial units in the state.

- *Availability of English Speaking manpower*: Meghalaya has been traditionally known for its education system during the British rule in India. As a result of which Shillong still has some of the best colleges in the whole of North East. These colleges have been producing graduates who have very strong English speaking capability. So voice based ITES companies would find a considerable pool of talented resource in the city.
- Prevalent western culture and cosmopolitan environment. Shillong has been known for its educational institutes in the whole of North East. This has attracted students from other north eastern states of India. As a result of which a cosmopolitan culture has developed in the city. Due to the influence of western culture the youth of Meghalaya are better accustomed to the western culture and accent. This is an advantage for youth planning to work in voice based call centres.
- *Low Attrition Rate*: Traditionally the Government has been the biggest recruiter in the state. Also traditionally the tribal people of Meghalaya are socially loyal. So the culture of switching jobs is not prevalent in the state. Hence the attrition rate would be low in the state.
- Availability of cheaper manpower in comparison to other states. Meghalaya has a fairly large pool of skilled, semi-skilled and unskilled labour. There is an adequate supply of secretarial staff in most parts of the State. A fair number of management and technical personnel have qualifications from recognised professional institutions and universities of India.

- *Good Climate*: The year-long moderately cool climate of Meghalaya is conducive to industrial development, particularly for hardware industry. It is also one of the cleanest and pollution free states.

Weakness

Landlocked and Limited Market

As a landlocked area, the state has to depend heavily on its road network which is to a considerable extent limited. Since it's a hilly terrain building railway network in the state is also difficult. The road network is under developed in the East and West Garo districts. Additionally a large rural population in the whole of North East coupled with low per capita income limits the size of local market.

- Poor communication and physical infrastructure. The whole of state has a low telephone density compared to national average. Though the telephone density in Shillong is higher than the rest of the state but reliability of connection is still an issue. Broadband connectivity is low, costly and unreliable. There are only two ISP providers in the state of Meghalaya and ISP market is limited to city of Shillong only. The state still has vast areas of underdeveloped land and some regions have been untouched by modern development. The road and transportation infrastructure is not well developed which results in poor connectivity between the various parts of the state.
- Poor Healthcare facilities in the state The death rate in the state is higher than the rest of the country. Life expectancy is also low in the state compared with the rest of India. This is reflected in the fact that only 0.77% of the population is above the age of 70. Healthcare facilities in the rural areas need to be expanded as well as developed.
- Limited availability of skilled manpower IT companies require engineering graduates while ITES companies look for arts, commerce and science

graduates. Voice based call centres look for people with good English speaking capability.Meghalaya or the other north eastern states don't have many engineering colleges to support the demand created by IT industry. Even the pool of good English speaking resources is more or less limited only to Shillong city. People in the remaining part of the state are not as proficient in speaking English as the people in Shillong. Meghalaya produces 3700 graduates every year. This talent pool is not enough to support big call centres.

- Education infrastructure not adequate to support growth of IT/ITES industry Absence of any engineering college in Shillong can be detrimental to the growth of IT industry in the region. The number of arts, science and commerce colleges in the state would not be able to support big KPOs and BPOs. The lack of adequate education infrastructure in the state is contributing to the brain drain.
- *Lack of Political vision*: Due to various local issues the political leadership has not been able to focus attention on attracting investments in IT/ITeS sector. However in the recent past the realization that these sectors have potential to generate substantial economic well being and employment opportunity has crept in and the political leadership is now keen on attracting IT investments.
- *State Image dented by insurgency in North East*: Even though insurgency in Meghalaya has been low for the last two years, other parts of North East have been facing this problem. As a result of which the outside investors are reluctant to invest in North East and hence Meghalaya is also suffering.
- Bandhs/protest: Though Meghalaya has been peaceful for the last 2 years with no incidence of major insurgencies reported in the state, there have been periodic bandhs and protests which have hampered the local business. In the past 72 hours bandhs have

paralysed life and business in Shillong and often local IT companies had to face huge business losses. Moreover such bandhs and protests create a negative image for the state which affects perceptions of potential investors, both inside and especially outside the state.

- Lack of technical expertise among local entrepreneurs Most of the local entrepreneurs don't have the technical expertise needed to setup an IT-ITeS industry. Meghalaya doesn't have any IT park as a result of which there is currently no big player. No national or international big player has ever invested in the state.
- *Negative perspective of local investors*: The local investors are quite hesitant and sceptical about investment in IT sector. IT Policy not enforced- Despite the formation of IT Policy in 2004, it has not been enforced.
- Level of e-readiness is low The level of e-readiness in the state is very low. Its rank has been categorized as Below Average Achievers by "India: E-Government Assessment Report 2004", a study done by

DEPARTMENT OF INFORMATION TECHNOLOGY, GOVERNMENT OF INDIA

- *Stringent tribal land transfer laws*: Being a tribal state, the land transfer and land acquisition laws are very stringent in Meghalaya. This has been a major hindrance in setting up of industry in many states and Meghalaya would also face the same problems. Govt. needs to look into this matter if it wants to attract investors from outside the state in the IT/ITeS sector.
- *Inadequate Social Infrastructure*: This results in lowering the quality of life that is demanded by employees associated with the IT/ITeS sector
- *High growth of urban population*: Meghalaya has a high rate of growth of urban population when compared

with the rest of the country. This shows people are moving from rest of the state to the urban centres for better livelihood. This will put pressure on the existing infrastructure of the urban areas. The Govt has to plan to meet the increasing expectations of these people as well as work towards reducing the migration of people from rural areas to urban areas.

OPPORTUNITIES

- *Ample funding agencies*: There are ample funding agencies like DoNER, NEDFi, NEC in Meghalaya who have financed IT initiatives in North East in the past. So getting funds for setting up IT/ITES companies in Meghalaya would not be difficult. The funding agencies and financial institutions have been discussed in details under "Present scenario of IT investment in the state", as well as under "Factors influencing investment in IT sector–Capitals/ Investments".
- Govt. of India "Look East" Policy and Proximity to South East Asian Market Government of India's "Look East" policy has helped in building cordial relationship with countries of South East Asia. This "Look East" Policy can also be looked at from a different angle - Reaching Southeast Asia via Northeast India. There is extensive government willingness to further develop the North Eastern India region and integrate it into the Southeast Asian hemisphere. The north eastern states hold great importance for India as they represent the key for achieving closer integration and gaining greater economic access to the other Southeast Asian nations. This has encouraged trade and cooperation between India and these countries. Meghalaya being nearer to these countries is in a better position to gain from this trade and cooperation. The state can attract investors from the South East Asian countries.
- Absence of IT/ITES companies in North East region

reduces competition in region Even though STP Guwahati has been set up in the North East, it has not been in the past able to attract many IT/ITES companies in the region. Assam could not capitulate on the first mover advantage in the region. Current competition from other states in the region is not expected to pose a serious threat.

- Non Resident Meghalayans willing to invest in the state People of Meghalaya who have left the state are willing to come back and invest in the state. NRIs are willing to invest in Meghalaya. These people not only have the finances but also the technical knowledge and expertise, as well as the entrepreneurships for start ups.
- *E-Government initiatives in progress*: Govt of Meghalaya is planning to start its e-governance initiatives. These initiatives once started should give a major boost to the IT investment in the state. E-governance initiatives would create a huge demand for software and hardware in the state which would draw IT companies from outside the state. Local entrepreneurs could gain from their association with these IT companies.
- *Different seismic plate from mainland India*: As per Seismic Zoning Map of India, Meghalaya resides in a different seismic zone compared to rest of mainland India, making it an ideal destination for Call Centre disaster recovery stations for Tier 1 and Tier 2 cities.
- *STPI Shillong coming up*: STPI Shillong, which is expected to come up soon, should boost the growth of IT/ITES investment in the state. This STPI would be acting as an incubator and facilitator for small and medium scale IT/ITES companies. The STPI would also solve majority of the issues related to communication and infrastructure. Govt of Meghalaya should persuade STPI to set up a satellite earth station to this effect.
- *IT/ITES companies shifting towards small cities*: IT/ITES

companies are showing increasing interest in setting up delivery centres in smaller cities and in cities not traditionally associated with the IT industry. The cities include Ahmedabad, Chandigarh, Mohali, Jaipur, Mangalore and Coimbatore. Moving into smaller cities has benefited the players by offering lower costs (both infrastructure and employee) and lower attrition rates.

- *Ample scope for Tourism Sector*: In the year 1994 154977 Indians and 577 foreigners visited Meghalaya. The figure increased to 268589 Indians and 3191 foreigners in the year 2002. Overall in these 8 years there has been 73% increase in Indian tourists and 453% increase in foreigners visiting Meghalaya, though the number of tourist places has not shown any remarkable increase. This shows that Meghalaya has tremendous tourism potential. It needs to market its tourism in the Indian as well as international market.

THREATS

- Future competition from Assam and other states in the region Assam is the gateway to North East. Even to reach Meghalaya, one has to go through Assam. A STPI has already come up in Guwahati. Though nothing much has been happening with respect to IT in Assam as of yet, but Assam can pose a serious challenge to Meghalaya in attracting IT/ITES companies. Not only Assam other states might also pose challenge to Meghalaya.

BRAIN DRAIN

Call centres all over India have a good percentage of employees who are from north east. Over the last few years Meghalaya has been loosing good educated youth to other Indian states. Due to lack of job opportunity in private or public sector in Meghalaya the youth of the state go out of Meghalaya for their livelihood. With more and more demand being created in other cities of India, more and more educated youths are leaving Meghalaya.

- *Future trends in IT/ITES industry*: Technological advancements in the field of computer telephony will result in decentralization of many Call Centre operational activities. Automated Call Distribution technology which underpins call centre operation may soon be upgraded so that it is also possible, using faster data telecommunications channels, to operate a call centre service using workers based at orkstations in their own homes. Limited use of home-based call centre staff has been reported in several countries. A report in the UK has recently suggested that 'virtual call centres' like this may be an idea which will become increasingly attractive for companies in future.
- Emergence of high-end KPO services may replace BPO as outsourcing trend There is a global trend in a shift in the nature of outsourcing activities up the "value chain". More and more high-end KPO services are being outsourced. Emergence of need of these highend KPO services may have a reducing (or even replacing) effect on overall BPO activities. Most of India's ITES-BPO work is for voice-based customer services. This service is at the lowest end of the value chain. Even though the revenues in this segment are increasing, the billing rates for these services are on the decline. In order to survive and grow, the sector needs to move up the value chain and start concentrating on high-end services like research and development, content development and data analytics. Companies also need to move towards providing end-to-end solutions to their clients. Required technical expertise to survive in this field is currently lacking in the state.
- *Competition from other Tier III cities*: Stiff competition can be expected from Tier III cities. When IT/ITES companies start looking beyond Tier I and Tier II

cities they would have the luxury of choosing from more than 10 cities which have better physical and communication infrastructure than Shillong. So to attract IT/ITES investment in the state, the state has to develop at a real fast pace.

- IT/ITeS sector may experience saturation/slowdown IT/ITeS sector has been showing high rate of growth in the recent past but as the market matures the rate of growth might slowdown and reach a plateau. We have also seen dotcom burst where many venture capitalists lost huge amount of money. If this happens then Meghalaya would find it difficult to attract outside investment as well as promote the local IT investors.

While it is absolutely essential to understand the weaknesses and threats, it is the aggregate of strengths and opportunities that infuses the State and its people with sense of optimism for the future.

SYNTHESIS OF NEEDS

In order to arrive at the Vision, it is necessary that needs and requirements of the State are synthesized and evaluated on the basis of the SWOT analysis and the Stakeholders' expectations as described in the sections above. The sector-wise needs for the State have been stated as necessitated by the SWOT and also as aspired by various stakeholders.

HEALTH

- Improve basic Curative and Preventive health Services
- Make health service modern, accessible, affordable and available in the rural areas
- Ensure co-ordination at inter-programme, intra-department and inter- agency levels

EDUCATION

- Take into account localized, contextual conditions during planning

- Make education available to all, contemporary and skill-centric with strong linkages to the changing regional and global scenarios
- Provide training facilities in ICT and BPO areas to enable the youth to get good jobs.
- Take industry needs into consideration while finalizing course for various technical and semi-technical courses
- Promote education as one of the main Revenue earning sectors

LABOUR AND EMPLOYMENT

- Create more work opportunities in different sectors and ensure better work conditions and adequate wages
- Reduce unemployment, underemployment and disguised unemployment in the rural areas by modernizing agriculture and setting up of agro-based industries
- Extend planning beyond the national perspective to acquire a more localized perspective

AGRICULTURE

- Increase productivity by assisting farmers to move to multi-crop farming.
- Provide better irrigation, fertilizers, use of HYV seeds and application of modern technology
- Encourage horticulture, cultivation of vegetables, plantation crops, spices,and orchids.
- Develop agro-based industries
- Facilitate a growth-rate in conformity with the Tenth Plan.
- Provision of sufficient information to the farmers for marketing and selling their produce.

RURAL DEVELOPMENT

- Empower institutions of local governance
- Tackle poverty and food insecurity

- Revive/develop village level productive resources

TRANSPORT

- Expand the reach and network of all operations of Road network in the State
- Ensure all weather connectivity to all villages of the State
- Stronger public transport

POWER

- Aim at increasing the generation capacity of the State
- Provide consumers with reliable and assured supply of power
- Provide electricity to all the villages of the State

URBAN DEVELOPMENT

- Increase the rate of urbanization to effective levels
- Create and empower Urban Local Bodies for development of cities and satellite townships
- Encourage private participation

INDUSTRIAL DEVELOPMENT

- Increase the rate of industrialization
- Create a conducive business climate for accelerated investment in industry and infrastructure projects
- Optimize the processes to facilitate industrial development Tourism
- Ensure the development of infrastructure that would aid in the development of tourism as an important industry for State
- Make accessibility easier for the pecple from other parts of the country and the world
- Improve Information availability about tourist destination
- Improve the image of the state through tourism

IT VISION

Based on the Synthesis of Needs as done in the previous

chapter and the inputs provided by the respondents during the survey carried out by the PwC team during the study, the IT Vision of Meghalaya for ensuring Good Governance practices and overall economic development reads as follows:

KEY THEMES

The vision statement clearly articulates the key themes of the Government's direction, which are:

- *Citizen*: This is an important focal point for the e-Governance initiatives which the state is likely to take in the next few years. This point establishes that the government's focus in ICT will be on the statutory requirements, like implementation of RTI Act and other central level schemes, so as to better serve its citizens in the rural hinterland as well as make information readily accessible. At the same time, the fall-outs of these efforts will also be derived by urban and the business community in the state.
- Information and Government Services While the common person may have a variety of needs, many of these could be improved by use of ICT. Delivery of these would require the government to focus on more convenient and reliable options rather than the standard option of citizen making visits to the Government Offices. The services should be measured on the following criteria
- *Accessibility*: Customers require a reliable access window through e-Governance to all Government information and services. Citizens expect that e-governance initiatives will minimize the time spent on repeated visits to government offices.
- *Flexibility*: Customer should be able to access the service through a variety of channels of his/her choice.
- *Quality*: The service should be timely and efficient. Correct and up to date information should be readily available.
- *Security*: The service and service delivery should be

trustworthy, both objectively and in citizen perception.

- *Transparency*: Information about mechanism of service delivery along with its associated cost should be readily available. Horizontal Scroll: "To incubate and harness the IT industry for growth of the state economy and employment generation for local citizens and To establish e-Governance with a view to empower the citizens by providing Govt. information and services in a transparent and streamlined manner at a place close to their habitation using ICT as an enabling tool."
- Service Delivery This indicates the intent of the Government to look at streamlining its procedures such that the number of visits a citizen has to make to the Government office to obtain any one service is reduced. At the same time transparency of the system would increase and it would be easier to monitor and manage Govt. projects and assets. It may necessitate the use of databases extensively so that the data once stored can be reused leading to saving in time and effort.
- *Accessibility*: Communicates the clear roles and responsibilities for all departments and staff with respect to delivering each service. This is also one of the requirements of the Right to Information Act, 2005. The citizens should be provided with easier access to information. This would require the transformation of the government making it more transparent, accountable and efficient. Accountability for delivering the various services and information should be clearly defined and communicated internally within the departments and externally to citizens. It would lead to greater participation by people in government by making it easier for those who wish to contribute. Mechanisms like citizen feedback, grievance handling systems, provision for citizen forums on the web portal and increasing the

number and breadth of access channels are some means of attaining this objective

- *Incubation*: The objective of an incubation programme should be as follows:
  - Nurture and motivate good ideas and brains Encourage entrepreneurship
  - Give a robust platform and infrastructure to start up for a kick start
  - Have common policy and regulatory framework for a even playing field
  - Put a structured approach in place to evaluate projects both long term and short term
  - Economic Development leveraging IT/ITeS

The economic development of the state is very essential for the improvement of the general well-being of the citizens as well as reducing the economic disparity in the state. The government aims to improve the standard of living of the people of the state and decrease the economic disparity in the state. The government wants to use the Information

Technology as a tool for generation of employment in urban areas. The welfare measures taken by the government are sustainable in the long run only if they are backed by the economic growth of the region. Government should support IT/ITeS sector in the state as this has the potential to generate employment for the urban youths as well as use ICT for the development of the rural people. Objectives Keeping in mind the above mentioned Vision, the objectives for Government initiatives can be grouped by the customer segment served. Encourage investment in IT/ITeS sectors with accomp-anied employment generation.

The initiative must achieve the following for the businesses:

- Reduce burden on business, provide one-stop access to information on rules and regulations and clearances
- Reduce the cost of compliance by reducing the instance on the business to report the same data, multiple times to multiple agencies.
- Help in the growth of the business and support IT

industries by providing them with necessary technical and financial help.

- Generate additional employment in the IT/ITeS sector Improve service delivery to citizens.

  The e-governance must achieve the following for the citizens:

  - Provide one-stop, easier access to information and services to individuals
  - Reduce the average waiting for the citizens to avail the services.
  - Provide the citizens with a transparent view of the government processes and timely response to applications. Improve Internal govt functioning: The e-governance must achieve the following for the internal functioning amongst the departments /its interactions with its employees:
    a. Assist the state and local governments to more easily work together to better serve citizens within key lines of business.
    b. Provide administrative savings for the government departments.
    c. Improving the way that information is shared among all levels of government
    d. Reduce the non-value added work for the workers in the government department.
    e. Providing enhanced access to high quality training and competency development for state employees through capacity building across departments.

Performance Measures To ensure achievement, a vision needs to be measured periodically against a set of well defined Performance measures. This will enable all the key stakeholders to ascertain the progress made in realising the vision.

In the instant case the following are the Performance measures that may be adopted:

- Increase in Service Delivery Points
- Increase in Service Delivery Channels

- Increase in availability of information on Govt services using e-Government framework
- Increase in number of Govt services being provided using e-Government framework
- Percentage increase in population accessing Govt information and services using e-Governance delivery channels
- Percentage increase in number of Govt personnel delivering information and services using e-Government framework
- Percentage increase in IT/ITeS related investments
- Percentage increase of contribution of IT/ITeS in State Domestic Product
- Percentage increase in employment in the IT/ITeS sector

REVIEW MECHANISM

As mentioned in the approach, a vision, especially an IT Vision needs to be periodically reviewed to check for its relevance especially in view of the rapid changes in technology to ensure the vision remains relevant. This is especially true for IT Vision 2020 as it spans a time period of fifteen years. However, any review of such kind needs an involved exercise and hence it is suggested that this review be done as part of the state Five Year planning exercise to ensure continued alignment of the vision with both the citizens' expectation as well as the development agenda of the state.

It is also suggested that the task of reviewing the performance measures as well as the Vision be carried out by independent entities like NASSCOM/consultants to avoid any bias and ensure neutrality.

CONCLUSION

The envisioning exercise clearly indicates that the State IT department needs to take up the twin initiative as highlighted below. These initiatives are detailed in the e-Governance Roadmap and the IT Investment Roadmap documents.

6

Integrating the Seven Sisters Including Meghalya

The ravishingly beautiful and picturesque landmass of our country, which adorns the mantle of the northeastern states, may distance wise be even less than Chennai or Trivandrum is from New Delhi, yet it remains emotionally detached from the rest of India. The reasons are more than intriguing. The perceived distance has more to do with the mindset of the average Indian rather than the actual physical distance.

For a plethora of reasons, perceived or otherwise, peace and normalcy remain elusive. Terrorism and insurgency have yet to recede fully although life continues as if normal. Not that it is normal by any standards but whatever the ground realities, life does go on. Probably in concert with the worldwide phenomenon of rising aspirations of human beings, Human Rights and civilised societal ways have taken a front seat and their denial or absence creates upheaval and discord.

Northeastern India continues to be in the grip of terrorism and insurgency for the last 50 years. The intensity, type, and level are different in different states. The time has now come for an absolute integration of this region with the rest of India. The Government has made concerted efforts to address the problems at different levels and the efforts have already started showing results. Due to these efforts, the ties and links with the rest of India are growing every day. It would be unwise to assume that the Northeast is being neglected in any way.

This has been made possible through a multi-prong approach. The problem has been tackled militarily up to the extent that it was required and also, politically, economically and socially. The resultant effect is amply manifest in an attitudinal shift, which is a positive deviation from the response hitherto. The great people of this region have understood that their future rightly rests with India. For this paradigm shift in the outlook of the people, one of the main reasons is India's growing prowess–economically, militarily and socially. The people have realised the futility of continuing with a struggle, which has lost direction and has misplaced aims and objectives.

Today, one finds people from the Northeast in appreciable numbers in all parts of the country, in every walk of life to include trade, government organisations, IT, media and defence. The numbers are increasing every day.

Electronic and print media have made them realise that despite their vast potential they are depriving themselves of opportunities, which can bring about a sea change in their economy and lifestyles. Wisdom has dawned that these seven sisters were always an integral part of India and will remain so for eternity. Today, one finds people from the Northeast in appreciable numbers in all parts of the country, in every walk of life to include trade, government organisations, IT, media and defence. The numbers are increasing every day. As a matter of fact, integration is almost complete notwithstanding traces of discontent and discord. It is a known phenomenon that insurgency may be completely eradicated but can never touch the x-axis. In other words, it can never be brought to zero. How did we achieve this stupendous task? There is a need for every Indian to know and to be proud of the fact that our sovereignty over this region stands vindicated notwithstanding a slow and steady pace with spikes of violence in between periods of peace, stability and prosperity.

Before we try to understand the genesis of the insurgency in the northeastern states known as the Seven Sisters, it would be prudent to identify the reason and causes which engulfed the proud people of this region in a human conflict resulting in self denials. Some call it exploitation of the have nots and a tampering with ethnicity. These are not the only reasons. These are certain irreversible causes, which have historical and geographical perspectives. In addition, political, economic, social, ethnic, and cultural reasons give a fillip to existing inadequacies, encouraging a movement to start and grow.

Partition further accentuated the problem. A psychological and a physical barrier was created. The creation of East Pakistan deprived the region of geographical contiguity with the rest of India. North East India had a land link only through the Siliguri corridor, 200 km long and 21 to 65 km wide. All our communication lines pass through this corridor. The only port of Chittagong which hitherto serviced the entire Northeast also fell prey to the misdeeds of partition. The entire region had become virtually landlocked. The lifeline of the Northeast states was now extended to over 1,600 km. Earlier, the distance between Calcutta and Agartala (Tripura) was a little over 400 km–this is one single factor that has very seriously affected the economy.

Typical of the British policy of divide and rule, this was yet another master stroke by them. This time a divide was created by placing a physical landmass, East Pakistan (now Bangladesh), between the people of India and the people of the Northeast. Compounding the problem further, British inner line policy created a rift between the people from the hills and the plains. The mistrust so created, fuelled discontent and human conflict. This coupled with mountainous jungle terrain and an unprotected International Border (IB) gave an ideal ground for insurgents to carry out their nefarious activities with impunity. There is a need for every Indian to know and to be proud of the fact that our sovereignty over this region stands vindicated notwithstanding a slow and steady pace with spikes of violence in between periods of peace, stability and prosperity.

Thus, it would be seen that relative geographical location is one of the main causes of this unrest and instability. This region is surrounded on three sides by foreign countries–Bangladesh from the south and west, China (Tibet) and Bhutan from the north and Myanmar from the east. The 4,960 km long IB constitutes 99 per cent of the periphery of these states. One of the main reasons for any insurgency to be successful is to have 'External Support', and this is an ideally situated region for the purpose. This aspect was fully exploited by China in the '50s through the '60s. Even now, China is adopting a typical Mao Tse Tung style 'Indirect Approach'. They have used the indirect approach remarkably well to keep us engaged on more than one front. As a matter of fact they have already achieved partial encirclement. We are fully engaged with Pakistan on our west. In the north the Maoist movement has created enough instability. The relevance of Nepal to the Northeastern states has increased over the recent years due to the recent upsurge in Maoist activities, the emergence of the Kamtapur movement in the Siliguri Corridor and the increased activities of the ISI in Nepal. The 1,800 km Indo-Nepal porous border is being extensively used by the ISI intelligence operations–this border needs to be sanitised.

The Maoist movement has not only threatened our states of Uttranchal, UP and Bihar with instability but has presented an opportunity for a 'Red Corridor', cutting through the states of UP, Chattisgarh/MP, Telangana (AP) to Kerala. Due to political instability, caste wars, and feudalism, Bihar–north of the Ganges–is an ideal ground for insurgency/naxalism to grow. To the southwest of the Northeastern states, Bangladesh has been propped up as yet another 'Terrorism Support and Export Centre' patterned after Pakistan. Bangladesh is believed to have 145 training camps of terrorist groups belonging to some of the Seven Sisters States on its soil, which is an ominous development. Their intentions are suspect and very evident from the fact that they have a serious objection to our fencing of the IB. Meghalaya, Cachar (South Assam) and Tripura have an IB with Bangladesh with the terrain and people being most inhospitable and hostile. The cruelty and barbarism practiced by Bangladesh has few parallels. This, however, should not deter us from countering this menace.

MEGHALYA

Meghalaya faces a major problem due to the illegal migration of Bangladesh Muslims into the state, in particular into the Garo Hills. The anti outsider feeling amongst the local populace often leads to violence. The aspirations of Garo, Jantia and Khasi hill tribes are soaring high with increased economic activity, due to large scale tapping of natural resources. These aspirations if not met adequately can lead to insurgency. It will be pertinent to mention here that the state is surrounded on all sides by active insurgencies. The thick forests of the state provide an ideal transit route for the underground groups. Meghalaya should be considered as a 'mountain of peace' and should be used as a platform for sending out peaceful vibes in all directions.

The alienation of the Northeast has come about due to the failure to recognise the social and cultural factors of each area with the common effect of isolation. The situation is further accentuated by the influx of foreigners giving rise to ethnic parochialism and an identity crisis...

As mentioned earlier, Tripura's 7/8th border is with Bangladesh. The insurgency in Tripura is mainly due to a large influx of Bangladesh migrants. The influx started with a demographic invasion and has now acquired the status of 'demographic inversion'. This has resulted in pressure on tribal lands. A nexus between major political parties and insurgent groups is very evident. These groups are easily aided by ISI through the 865 km porous border with Bangladesh. Bangladesh has also provided safe sanctuary to the militant groups.

Tripura has now emerged as one of the leading states to provide a safe corridor for smuggling of arms into the Northeastern states. In the year 2002, the Tripura Governor initiated a package of counter insurgency measures, which have started yielding results. However, Tripura will continue to be unstable as it is surrounded by Bangladesh on 7/8th of its periphery. A proactive policy is considered the only solution for lasting peace.

OTHER STATES

Tripura is yet another very vulnerable state. 7/8th of Tripura's boundary abuts Bangladesh and 1/8th with Cachar

(South Assam). Due to unfortunate geographical circumstances, its security considerations should never be neglected, delayed, postponed or pushed under the carpet.

Arunachal has an IB with Tibet and Myanmar. Nagaland and Mizoram have an IB with Myanmar. Apparently, we have no problems with Tibet but China refuses to recognise the McMahon Line, so the stalemate continues. Also, critical differences remain over the 90,000 sq km area of Arunachal Pradesh, though after death of Mao Tse Tung the Chinese involvement and support to militant groups has considerably reduced.

In any case, Arunachal is not known to have any effective indigenous insurgent group, although the people of Arunachal Pradesh are vulnerable to exploitation by NSCN groups using the lower slopes as safe havens. Myanmar has always been a friend to India but unfortunately, the writ of Burmese insurgent groups runs in the region bordering the Indian states of Mizoram, Manipur, Nagaland and Arunachal Pradesh. The terrain is ideally suited for infiltration and exfiltration by insurgent groups. We have the best of relations with the Burmese Army. Arunachal, more or less, kept itself away from any type of insurgency movement but any form of political machination can push this state also towards extremism.

Northwest Assam has a common border with Bhutan, which is a landlocked country. It also has border with Tibet. Presently, we have the best of relations with Bhutan. Joint operations against the ULFA and other insurgent groups located in Southern Bhutan are a testimony of regional cooperation against terrorism.

Sikkim, Bhutan and Arunachal Pradesh have an IB with Tibet (China). The development of a most modern infrastructure (roads and other allied facilities) in Tibet by China, although good for Tibet, could be a cause of concern to us. China has developed a road network right up to the IB and we are still far behind. We have got to develop these areas on priority. Mizoram has an IB with Myanmar and Bangladesh. It had the fiercest insurgency in this region under the militant leader, Laldenga, who later on became the first Chief Minister of Mizoram. Mizoram has been the most pragmatic state of our country. It realised the futility of continued unrest and opted out of insurgency and has been nurtured into a very dynamic, mature and buoyant democracy, especially so under the leadership of the present Chief Minister, Zoramthanga, a graduate of Imphal University.

Incidentally, Zoramthanga was No 2 to Laldenga while in the Mizo National Front when it was an underground organisation. Mizoram, to a great extent, has resolved its problems with Myanmar by having a free trading zone of 20 km but it has to guard against the drug menace from the east and the creeping invasion from the west.

Cachar District (Assam), which is to its west has been flooded with migrants and they are inching forward towards the less populated zone *i.e.* Mizoram. the demographic pattern of the state has already been affected. Today Mizoram is the most peaceful state of our country but it is better to avoid complacency.

The development of a most modern infrastructure (roads and other allied facilities) in Tibet by China, although good for Tibet, could be a cause of concern to us. China has developed a road network right up to the IB and we are still far behind.

Assam, the mother of all Northeastern states, is today in turmoil. The main reasons are basically two *i.e.* carving out of six states out of one and secondly its border with East Pakistan (now Bangladesh). It has common boundaries with all the six states. Assam was sparsely populated and this void was filled by a mass scale influx of refugees from erstwhile East Pakistan. This not only disturbed the demographic balance but in a number of districts resulted in demographic inversion. This has facilitated the emergence of a large number of insurgent groups including Muslim Fundamentalist Militia backed by the Pakistan Inter Services Intelligence (ISI). Currently, there are as many as 34 insurgent groups who have been identified, though the ULFA is the main player.

The ominous part of this development is the post 1990 mushrooming of insurgent groups along tribal, religious and cultural lines. We need to put a stop on further migration and de-recognise the status accorded to a segment of refugees who have migrated after a particular agreed upon date. Political expediency needs to be shown. To stop further influx of refugees, the border with Bangladesh is required to be very effectively policed. Notwithstanding the above, peace in Assam will always be contingent upon stability in the other six states.

Therefore, more teeth need to be given to the statutory coordinating body, the North East Council. Human Resource personnel with the requisite background, who have dealt with countering insurgency right from its inception, need to be inducted. We have very large numbers of ex Defence Services officers who have vast experience in this field, who understand the pulse and the ground realities. Induction of ex Defence Services officers in all disciplines in all types of cadres in civil administration can be the single most important factor for affecting an overall bonding and integration with rest of India.

Manipur has an IB with Myanmar, the interstate boundary with Nagaland to its north, Assam to its west and Mizoram to its southwest. The state has no major problem from Myanmar except that it has become the biggest transit hub for drugs. The main bone of contention of Manipur insurgent groups is the demand for a Greater Nagaland (Nagalim) by NSCN (IM) that includes Manipur's Ukhrul, Tamenglong, Senapati and Chandel districts. Redrawing of interstate boundaries at this juncture will only lead to further unrest and instability. In a coalition era, such an initiative will always be opposed from one quarter or the other. This is a typical problem of clash of ethnic interests. In a democratic and secular state there is need to shun caste and creed based politics.

The fallout is evident in these states. Although the Prime Minister has assured the Manipur Government that its state boundaries will not be redrawn, such ethnic and tribal contiguity will continue to be the bone of contention between Nagaland and Manipur. In case adequate statecraft is not exercised by the two states, a reverse flow of insurgency is very much on the cards.

Nagaland to its east has Myanmar, Manipur to its south, Arunachal Pradesh to its northeast, and Assam to its northwest. The Naga insurgency is the mother of all insurgencies in Independent India. It started in the mid fifties and continues till date, although in a state of suspended animation, with a ceasefire accepted by both sides and extended from time to time. The ethnic conflict between two rival factions of the NSCN remains one of the most intractable problems of Naga Insurgency and sporadic internecine conflicts between the two groups continue. The insurgency in Nagaland continues to thrive through safe-havens provided by Bangladesh and Myanmar to NSCN (IM). The key player to fuel insurgency in Nagaland was China till the late sixties and thereafter the indirect approach through East Pakistan was extensively used. The Naga people in general want their state to remain peaceful.

It is high time both NSCN groups reconcile. It is better to shun extra territorial demands. Another important reason was the lack of political imagination, which has been reasonably addressed, in the recent past. The Prime Minister has even offered to talk to any terrorist/insurgent group without any precognition. Unimaginative policies, indifferent attitude, ignorance and not respecting tribal ethos and customs by successive governments, in particular and the Indian people in general, have created a cultural divide between the Northeastern states and the rest of India.

It would be of interest to know that there are over 220 different clans and over 415 dialects spoken in the Northeast. The British attempts to Christianise and educate them were largely successful but old tribal affiliations and rivalries continue. After independence, the initial overtures of the government clashed with the interests of the tribal community. This ignorance of ethnicity and continued neglect of development slowly pushed this region into the grip of full-fledged insurgencies.

In this context, it is pertinent to mention Nehru's farsighted views during a discussion about statehood for Nagaland. He had said, "The traditional machinery of Naga self-governance at village, range and tribal levels should be strengthened." He even suggested that tribal names be given to the legislative assembly and the council of ministers. A top-heavy administrative system, as in other states, would be wasteful if adopted in Nagaland. The Nagas should be allowed to develop along their own lines; and select an organisation with tribal ethos.

Another glaring problem has been that the political boundaries do not coincide with the existing ethnic and social boundaries. If we take a look at the demographic mosaic of Northeast India it shows that this region is a meeting point of various races; Mongoloids, Aryans and Austeric ethnic races. The Northeast states have not been able to cater to the demands of all the ethnic categories clamouring for recognition of their distinctive identity. That the region has been split into seven states already since independence bears testimony to the fact that the Central Government is not wholly unaware of this fact and yet it has not come to terms with it, which led to the mushrooming of insurgency in the area.

The alienation of the Northeast has come about due to the failure to recognise the peculiar historical, social and cultural factors of each area with the common effect of isolation. The situation is further accentuated by the influx of foreigners giving rise to ethnic parochialism and an identity crisis, which is fomented by fear of cultural submergence, economic deprivation and social insecurity. Attempts to create ethnic identity in the region have suffered, making the people susceptible to insurgents' adaptations. The government, while showing excessive concern for the sensitivities of many ethnic and religious grouping, failed to bring them into the national mainstream. An unfortunate conciliatory approach adopted towards separatists was perceived as a sign of weakness and gave a fillip to secessionist and fissiparous trends.

A special service known as the Indian Frontier Administrative Service was established in 1957, to administer the Northeastern states. This service was doing a commendable job of adequately administering the Northeastern states with due regard to cultural and tribal sensitivities of the people.

For reasons best known to the government, the Indian Frontier Administrative Service was abolished in the later half of the sixties and replaced by a top-heavy Indian Administiative Service (IAS).

The genesis of the problem has been made amply clear and transparent. The need of the hour is to address the problems and reasons identified in a logical, compassionate and systematic manner. Prosperity and peace in neighbouring countries will automatically curb the menace. Sanitisation of the IB is a must by physical means and the creation of artificial obstacles wherever possible. Expediency and urgency needs to be shown to stop Islamisation emanating from Bangladesh in all directions. The Northeast should become a hub for a Look east policy. It should become a gateway for ASEAN countries. Good governance coupled with doing away with the notified area clause and extension of transfer subsidies by yet another five years is recommended. Tourism, health, and IT should be included in the concessional package.

The Kamtapur movement needs to be nipped in the bud. Any complacency will threaten the most sensitive lifeline of the Northeastern states *i.e.* the 'Siliguri Corridor'.

NORTH-EAST IS A GEOGRAPHICAL, NOT CULTURAL, CONSTRUCT

THERE seems to be a growing tendency among policy planners and social scientists these days to club together the different states of the north-eastern region of the country as the North-East. While there is no denying the geographical reality of the North-East, the complexities are bound to arise if the term is used as an umbrella connotation involving political and cultural aspects as well. It is true that the different states of India's "North-East" share a host of common problems ranging from communication bottlenecks to drug-trafficking, illegal infiltration and insurgency.

It is also true that several of the states which today make up the North-East were once part of the undivided state of Assam, and still happen to share certain commonalities. But it would undoubtedly be simplistic to view the problems of the different states through a common North-East perspective. For, these states not only possess distinct culturo-historical traditions, but economically too they are in different stages of growth. The present-day Assam, made up primarily of the Brahmaputra and Barak Valleys, for example, presents a very different picture when placed with the neighbouring states of Meghalaya, Mizoram, Manipur, Tripura, Nagaland and Arunachal Pradesh. Assam had a deep and wide-ranging cultural intercourse with the rest of the Indian subcontinent centuries before the other neighbouring hill regions came to know of the "mainstream". When most of the other regions were living on a subsistence economy, Assam was engaged in trade and commerce with neighbouring Bengal and state formation had taken place.

Of all the hill tribes, it was only the Khasis and the Jaintias who had a moderately developed economy, with the Khasis engaging in vigourous trade with the plains of Assam and with present-day Bangladesh, while Manipur also underwent the process of state formation from relatively early times. Politically too, all the states of the north-eastern region cannot be seen as one general unit, facing similar problems. Assam, for example, possessed a completely different political lineage and cannot be equated with other states of the north-eastern region, as a brief introduction to its history, culture and politics will reveal.

Today because of the rise of insurgency in the entire north-eastern region, "experts" tend to view the problem as a total North-East issue. But even when analysing the roots of insurgency in different states of the region, it would be advisable to take into account the history and economy of each individual state. For socio-economic factors which have given rise to insurgency in the different states cannot be put in one basket. Therefore, it is imperative that while dealing with the states of the north-eastern region of the country, the distinct history and culture of each people should be kept in mind and attempt to club all together as the North-East should be avoided. In matters of language and literature, culture and religion, the degree of Aryanisation or Sanksritisation, etc. the

Brahmaputra valley stands distinctly apart from other states of the north-eastern region.

Thus, the similarities that exist between different states of the region should not overshadow the different stages of socio-cultural and politico-economic development. This point was well illustrated during the Film Festival held in New Delhi in 1996. In the Indian Panorama section Assamese, Bodo and Manipuri films had been shown. But when it came to meeting the Press, all the directors belonging to the north-eastern region of the country were slotted together, whereas directors from other parts of the country were given exclusive time slots.

This was resented by Assamese film directors Bhabendranath Saikia and Jahnu Barua, both winners of several national and international awards, as they felt that the very purpose of interaction with journalists was nullified by such clubbing together. The Press Information Bureau of the Government of India, however, saw no problems in grouping all directors of the north-eastern region together. For it, the "North-East" was one single category. The Assamese and Manipuri directors boycotted the Press meet after making their point clear that in such matters they resented being grouped together.

Bhabendranath Saikia was making a strong case that though geographically, and also at times politically, it might appear to be convenient to refer to the region as the North-East, yet it would be wrong to steamroll the different histories and cultures of the people inhabiting this area under the blanket term "North-East".

The use of the illusive construct, the North-East, has not only led to discrimination in matters of financial allocation to resource-rich and larger states like Assam, but, more importantly, to serious administrative mishandling by the Centre of the complexities of the region. The tendency of the Indian state to treat this extremely diverse region as one unit has resulted in the growth of totally incomplete and often misconceived notions about the different states that make up the north-eastern part of the country. Such monolithic conceptions about a region, which stands out for its diversity of cultures and civilization, would only help to nourish the biases and prejudices which have marked the Indian state's approach to Assam and neighbours since independence.

The history of Assam, which is made up of the Brahmaputra and Barak Valleys, stretches back to the epics and the Puranas and mention of the region is found in Kautilya's Arthashastra. The political history of the Brahmaputra Valley could be traced to a period long before the foundation of the Varman line of kings of the fourth century AD. For instance, Amalendu Guha says: "The ancient history of the Assam plains could also be extended backwards beyond the fifth and fourth century AD. The Mahabharata and several Puranas that were rewritten between circa second century BC and the second century AD and the copper plate prashastis of the Kamarupa kings—all contain elements of late recorded oral history related to Assam's early Indo-Aryan settlers who were the carriers of the new civilization marked by iron, cattle, wet rice and the plough".

The process of state formation in Assam in the fourth and fifth centuries AD and epigraphic evidence show that the political chronology of Assam can be well traced to the fifth and the 12th centuries AD.

Assam had trade links with contries and regions lying to its north-east and to the west. One of the earliest references to commercial relations between Assam and China is to be found in the accounts of Chang Kien (200 BC) which have been highlighted in the works of Joseph Needham and P.C. Bagchi. There is a reference in the Shung Shu (AD 420-79) that a particular king of Assam sent an envoy to China. Initially, there seemed to have been one major land route to China through upper Burma but later on other routes were developed through Burma, Bhutan and Tibet. The Patkai Pass in upper Assam, through which the Ahoms came in the 13th century, must have been an important link in Assam's early relations with Burma and China. One text states that there were as many as 35 passes.

Most historians, however, agree that Assam's cultural and commercial relations with the rest of India have been closer. Chaudhury says that the most intimate contact which early

Assam had was with Magadha and that the earliest trade routes between Kamarupa and Magadha are to be found in Arthashastra. The Brahmaputra must have served as the main communication link between Assam and the rest of India and, compared to the river route, the land route through mountainous passes to Burma and China must have been a difficult one. Hence, the latter routes must have fallen into disuse by the time the British arrived on the scene.

The process of Sanskritisation and Aryanisation of Assam has been a long one. Suniti Kumar Chatterjee is of the view that the Aryanisation of the ruling classes in Kamarupa was completed as early as 400 AD. Chatterjee says that "by the early centuries of the Christian era, Assam as Pragjyotisa and Kamarupa had become definitely a part of Hindu India, although the masses of its people were probably still Bodo-speaking, as in the 16th century North Bengal among the Koches".

He further maintains that "by the end of the early medieval preiod, that is by 1200 AD, Assam, meaning specifically the plains-lands watered by the Brahmaputra, definitely appears to have become a part of Aryan-speaking India". The process of Sanskritisation gathered momentum during the period of Srimanta Sankardeva (1499-1568), the reformer-saint whose liberal brand of Vaishnavism brought thousands of tribal people of the Brahmaputra Valley within the fold of Hinduism. But the process of Aryanisation was heavily influenced by the tribal life-pattern of the region and this may be seen in the absence of the growth of professional classes or groups along caste lines.

The non-rigidity of the caste system and the relative egalitarian pattern of society were the direct result of the tribal influence. The lack of occupational specialisation in pre-Ahom Assam is also borne out by some of the inscriptions. Nonetheless, Brahminical culture, which was largely Sanskrit-based, made its presence strongly felt in ancient Assam and continued to be an important influence throughout medieval Assam. The impact of the process of Aryanisation was to be seen in the growth of wet rice plough cultivaiton in lower

Assam during pre-Ahom times and Guha says that "sali" cultivation in Assam plains was at least as old as the process of Sanskritisation itself.

The 13th century saw the coming into Assam of the Ahoms, a northern Tai or Shan tribe of upper Burma. Initially numbering only a few thousands, the Ahoms quickly assimilated with the local population. From 1228 onwards the Ahoms gradually extended their domain and ruled Assam till 1826 when by the Treaty of Yandoboo the British took over control of the region. Apart from their well-ordered system of administration, the Ahoms brought about a radical change in the economy of Assam by introducing wet rice cultivation in the upper reaches of the Brahmaputra valley and extending it by building hundreds of miles of embankments. Wet-rice cultivation, however, had been going on in lower Assam during the Kamarupa empire and must have produced enough surplus to sustain it.

The process of Hinduisation continued during Ahom rule and reached new heights in the 17th and 18th centuries. Thus "if the 16th century dominated by the expanding Koch kingdom was the formative period of Assamese society, the next one century and a half was the period of steady consolidation under the Ahoms. The extension of the plough at the cost of the hoe cultivation and of wet at the expense of dry ricelands alongside a general agriculture expansion - a process that was going on for some time in Upper Assam - led to a rapid increase in surplus produce. The consequent rise in population provided the Ahoms with the material base for their further economic and political expansion. Firearms, introduced in the area first in the 1530s, were increasingly put to use and, by the 1660s, excellent gunpowder, matchlocks and cannons were manufactured locally."

Compared to the well-documented history of Assam from the fourth century AD onwards, little is known about the hilly regions of the north eastern region which today forms part of the states of Nagaland Arunachal Pradesh, Mizoram, Tripura and Manipur. The lone exception seems to be Meghalaya, made up of the Khasi and Jaintia hills, where agriculture and trade were relatively developed, with primitive tribal organisations having been long replaced by a political organisation bringing together the different village republics.

Unlike Assam, most of the hill tribes did not possess the experience of state formation and continued to be governed by their own established tribal organisations. Guha says that "among the different tribes, it was only the Khasis who appeared to have moved towards statehood several centuries before the coming of the British". Most of the hill tribes maintained their autonomous existence. Village and kinship ties governed the average tribal's life; this being especially true in the case of the Nagas. Not only in the case of the Nagas, but with most of the tribal people of the region, the central political and economic unit was the village. So, it may be concluded that in matters of political organisation, the Nagas and other tribes did not go beyond the village and the immediate community.

A majority of the hill languages and dialects belong to the Tibeto-Burman group of languages and the absence of a script is common to most. Only the Khasis and Jaintias belong to the Austro-Asiatic group, though they too did not possess any script. As far as the hill tribes are concerned, it may be said that except for the Jaintias, there was no Sanskritisation or Hinduisation at all. Till the advent of the Christian missionaries, the tribal people of the region followed their own rituals and traditions. The traditional pattern of tribal society did not provide for specialisation of professions, though certain villages specialised in crafts.

It is in the complex mosaic of different nationalities at different stages of socio-economic and political growth that the Indian nation-state is today facing some of its gravest challenges, with the entire process of nation-building being questioned. It is here that the centralised authority of the Indian state is being repeatedly questioned, issues based on the uneven development of the socio-economic order raised, and the idea of the "mainstream" redefined. Time and again, the Indian nation-state has had to work out new strategies and adjustments to deal with the issues raised by the different autonomist and "secessionist" movements of the north-eastern region. Though the Indian nation-state's management of the problem of dissent and political identity has been commendable, especially when one takes into account the experience of most Third-World countries, yest there seems to be a long way to go. The idea of "one nation" which gathered strength during the country's freedom struggle and which was buttressed during the years immediately following the partition of the country and its independence, received its first jolt in the hills of the north-eastern region. This was an area which had been virtually untouched by the freedom struggle and also historically outside the pale of Indian civilization. Hence, it was difficult for those who believed in the unifying force of the Indian civilization to understand and appreciate the demands for autonomy that were raised in the Naga Hills and other areas soon after independence.

The success of the nation-state in providing a meaningful space within its system to the different nationalisties has not been uniform. Assam today poses a really grave challenge to the entire process of nation-building. With its really complex ethnic situation, the almost unsurmountable problem of influx and demographic change and the backward, almost "colonial" state of the economy, Assam has emerged as the problem state, next perhaps to Kashmir. The future health of the Indian state will depend on how well it can resolve the many problems which Assam today throws up. Many years ago, Ram Manohar Lohia had said that the struggle for Indian independence was being fought in the hills of Assam. That was said with reference to the first outbreak of insurgency in the Naga Hill district of Assam.

Today, the Indian nation-state is fighting not just insurgency in Assam and the other north-eastern states, but is fighting for the survival of those very values on which the Indian Union stands. This is bound to be a difficult struggle because the fight is not restricted merely to the swampy jungles of the region but is very much a fight on the plane of ideas. Moreover, it is a fight with its own people. The very idea of the Indian nation-state is being challenged by those who are fighting for an independent Nagaland and a Swadhin Asom. Will the nation-state be able to accommodate these recalcitrant nationalities within the framework of its Constitution? What are the structural changes in the Constitution that will have to be made for this? Success in dealing with the nationality issues being raised in the north-eastern region is bound to strengthen the Indian nation-state, while failure to check separationist tendencies in regions like Assam could have far-reaching negative effects on the country as a whole.

7

Khasi Nepali Ethnic Conflict in Meghalaya: Case Study

OLD DISPUTE

The dispute is not a new one. It has existed since the time Meghalaya was carved out of Assam in 1972. Occasional arson and crop-stealing belonging to members of the opposing community were common. The simmering tensions became international headlines on May 14 when the Assamese border police gunned down four Khasis, who were part of a mob that was attacking Gorkhas in the village and the police post. The Khasis, in turn, started venting their anger against Nepalis and Gorkhas throughout Meghalaya. A 70-year-old Gorkha, Loknath Bastola, was burnt alive in Badapani village, just below Shillong, the state's capital.

Nepali workers here believe there may have been more killings in the Jaintia Hills district that borders Bangladesh, where thousands of Nepalis labour in coal mines. "We believe the authorities may have buried some bodies to save their face," claimed a source in Ladrampai bazaar, the commercial hub of Jaintia Hills.

The government denies this. "We shouldn't go after rumours," said Mukul Sangma, the chief minister of the state. "We are investigating the matter. The truth will come out." After the Lampi incident, the Meghalaya government set up a police post in Lampi 'to protect Khasi people' under pressure from agitating Khasi organisations. The new post is just a few hundred metres away from the border outpost of 4th Assam police battalion. The village resembles a warzone where armed villagers patrol during night time. Meghalaya thinks Assam is encouraging Gorkhas to bring more people to the village so that its claim strengthens. "Apart from the Khasi and Garo population," Sangma said in an interview with me, "a certain number of families belonging to the Nepali community are residing in Lampi who speak fluent Khasi. But what has been recently an issue of concern for the local population are the new settlements. These settlements have come up with the help of Assam police. That has created a sense of mistrust and of insecurity among the population."

The Gorkhas feel they need to bring in more of their own from other parts of Assam so that the Khasis cannot intimidate them. "We have been living here for more than two generations," said Chakra Bahadur Chhetri, the village headman or gaunbuda. "Our grandfathers came from Nepal and settled here when no Khasi lived here. It was a jungle at that time and our grandfathers felt it was a good place for their cattle."

Most old Gorkhas in Lampi name one district or the other in Nepal to indicate the place where their grandfathers came from but they don't want to build on that connection for now. They have found an active and charismatic leader in Chhetri who takes their cause to the Assamese authorities. Chhetri, in turn, is thankful to the villagers that he has given a job that he likes the most. "I don't like working in the filed," the gaunbudha said. "I like talking and traveling. So our interests are compatible." That doesn't stop him from reflecting upon the situation when he is alone. "Sometimes I feel as though I have wronged my people," Chettri said "I wonder if I made them foreigners in this land.

Had I not been here, most might have returned back to Nepal and settled there. At the least they would have a country of their own. The other part of me debates do we ever get mato (soil) without struggle? Moreover, the government of Assam is helping us more than we need. With such pleasant weather, isn't it a good place to live in? Once the rasta is paved won't this place be better than Darjeeling?"

The rasta is not exemptfrom the rivalry between Assam and Meghalaya either. Once Assam started building the road to Lhampi, Meghalaya followed suit with an aim to link the village to a highway that goes to Shillong. Initially the Assamese border police, using local Gorkhas as pawns, created disturbance.Later they allowed the work to be continued considering it to be a development activity. That instance of agreement between the two states has done little to bridge the gap between the Khasi and Gorkha communities.

For instance, the Khasis of Lampi have no administrative relationship with Assam. The Khasis did not participate in the census administered by the Assamese side where as Gorkhas enthusiastically participated, with gaunbudha as the administrator of the procedure, ignoring the call by the Meghalayan government to halt census activity in the village. Khasis don't send their children to the primary and middle school run by the Assamese government in the village. The Meghalayan government has opened a Khasi medium primary school barely a hundred metres away. Assamese authorities have recognized Chhetri with annual best gaunbudha award of Kamrup district twice in recent years.

The animosity between the two communities continues in the playground that sees players from the two communities play with different balls in different parts of the ground. No sooner Meghalaya was formed; Khasis stopped Gorkhas from playing on a football ground forcing the Gorkhas to find a new one nearby. In recent months, Khasis have laid their claim to that ground as well, the Gorkhas allege. Some time back when a Khasi member of the Meghalayan legislative assembly from the region flattened the Gorkhas' playground bringing in a dozer Khasis asked Gorkhas to go back to their older playground. "Why should we go back and play in the old ground now?" asks the Gaunbuda. "Our boys (Gorkhas) play in one of the goalposts while Khasis play in the other. When we play a white ball they bring a black one, when we bring a black ball, they bring a green one."

Due to this animosity and sheer mistrust Gorkhas have started patrolling their neighbourhoods at night. They have deployed youths carrying khukuris, sticks and slings under the banner of Village Defence Person (VDP) which is a normal practice in the region. "Khukuri and sticks are our weapons," said Shivaram Sharma, 26, a VDP. "The slingshots belong to Khasis. Now we learn their weapon and defeat them in their own game." If this village goes to Meghalaya, which falls under a special Indian constitutional provision called the Sixth Schedule, the non-tribal population will have no right to land. "We will be homeless, landless," Chhetri said. "On the other hand, Assam is giving us every possible help. They are giving us roads, hospitals, drinking water." The Gorkhas hope it will be easier for them to bring in more people once the road is paved—expected to happen in two years.

Apart from the sense of security that the Gorkhas feel in Assam, cultural, linguistic and other social differences exist between them and the Khasis. Meghalaya is a Khasi-majority state that was created exclusively to look after the community's interest. Everybody else is an outsider here.

Khasis speak a language (belonging to Austro-Asiatic language group) which has no particular script like Devnagari on which Nepali, the language Gorkhas speak, is based. Almost all Khasis have converted to Christianity from their original religion of worshipping nature. Gorkhas are Hindus, and worship the cow, which Khasis eat. "Christian missionaries control the Meghalaya government," said a Gorkha leader in Guwahati, the capital of Assam. "They try their best to convert Nepalis to Christianity. When they can't, they target those who are unwilling to convert." This sentiment was echoed by several Gorkha leaders who said that the Church in Shillong keeps mum about the atrocities committed against the Gorkhas whereas "they create a lot of noise if someone throws a pebble on a church."

Khasis live in a matriarchal society where as Gorkhas are patriarchal. Sometimes conflict arises because these communities differ on how the land should be used. Gorkhas like to rear animals in open lands while Khasi prefer agriculture. Though Gorkhas claim they are the ones who taught Khasis how to cultivate. However, as the land is becoming scarce because of rising population, number of Gorkhas rearing cattle has reduced. The cattle owned by a typical Gorkha family don't number in dozens like in the earlier times.

Several factors, on the other hand, bring Gorkhas closer to the Assamese. Both communities speak languages that belonging to the Indo-Aryan group, practice the same religion and live in patriarchal societies. Assam faces the problem of land encroachment in other parts of the state from neighbouring states Meghalaya, Nagaland and Arunanchal as well. People residing in those controversial areas belong to ethnic community that is majority in the claimant states and are loyal to them, not to Assam. That has made it difficult for Assam to lay its claim over those disputed territories. In the border dispute with Meghalaya the Gorkhas of Lahmpi have become the citizen border police for Assam. "It isn't only Lahmpi that Meghalaya claims," Chettri said. "It wants Guwahati as well. The moment we leave this place Khasis will run down to Guwahati. So, we are securing the border of Assam as well."

Lampi dispute is a perfect example of how ethnicity-based federalism pits citizens against one another. The Assamese government encourages Gorkhas from other parts of the state to go to the village, settle and retaliate against the Khasis. Anyone wanting to go to Lampi gets land for free, I was told by the villagers, and the government has increased the pace of development activities in the area. Until two years ago, before a road connected the village to a highway, it used to take four hours to walk from Lampi to reach Guwahiti. Gorkhas are working on to giving a finishing touch to the 30-kilometre link road on which their future plans rest.

"Once this road is paved it will be easier to increase the number of our people (Gorkhas) here." said Dambar Bhattarai, 47 whom I found working on the road 10 km below Lampi village. "Anyone willing to come will be provided with land," he continued. "Our ancestors lived in this place. Why should we run away? We are ready for bloodshed but not to be chased away."

These differences, however, hadn't stopped the two communities from living side by side for more than two centuries. In Shillong and other parts of Meghalaya, Nepali men have married Khasi women and *vice-versa*. Gorkhas have mastered the Khasi language and many Khasis are fluent in Nepali. "These people are not that bad after all," said a Gorkha activist in Shillong. "Some vested elements are politicising the issue."

The activist was hinting at the recent change of guard in Shillong that saw Sangma, from the Garo community, replacing D.D. Lapang, a Khasi, as the chief minister (Both Sangma and Lapang were from the Congress as they are now. Government changes are frequent in Meghalaya. Only one chief minister out of 13 has completed a full five-year term in office since 1972). One influential former student leader Paul Lyngdoh wasn't included in the new cabinet. Nobody has produced solid proof but many believe the Lampi incident was the handiwork of Lapang and Lyngdoh who wanted to pull the rug under the new chief minister. "Some people are telling me some vested interests could have created this situation to create instability," said Sangma.

The name of powerful Assamese politician Himant Biswa Sarma also comes in the picture. Sarma is often considered a factor in the change of governments in Meghalaya especially the one which was formed one year ago that saw his party Congress takepower in Shillong. Some say he was also behind the recent change of leadership (from Lapang to Sangma). Sarma is also deeply involved in prodding Gorkhas in Lampi. He was the one who sent in money to build the road and inaugurated it despite the objections from the Meghalayan side. That the land area of Lampi has been identified as a source of uranium adds a new dimension to the power struggle. Some say the real cause of tension is the uranium that the politicians from both states want under their control.

If Sangma's detractors in Meghalaya were behind the recent chaos, then they were defeated. The chief minister handled the situation in a way that has won him accolades. "Thank God, 1986 didn't repeat itself this time," said Diwakar

Poudel, a Gorkha from Assam who lives in Ladrampai, referring to the year when thousands of Nepalis and Gorkhas were evicted from Meghalaya as part of the movement to flush out foreigners from north-eastern India. "The police acted promptly; though during the initial hours of the crisis, several Nepalis were beaten up, tortured and forced to flee." He said many Nepali-speakers stayed indoors or inside coal mines during the strike called by Khasi organisations in Meghalaya after the Lampi incident.

One of those who stayed in a shack near the coal mines was Shyam Prasad Pokharel. The 60-year-old man from Sindhuli does an unenviable job of carrying coal on his back from a 200-feet deep pit. "I remembered my ista-deuta (clan deity) that day. I asked for strength. I remembered my wife and children," he said. There's no exact data of how many Nepalis work in the coal mines in Meghalaya, but it's generally accepted that more than 100,000 Nepalis work in the mines.

In times of crisis, it is natural that rumours spread like wildfire, thereby creating panic. Some of them tried to flee overnight, while some hid inside pits and reportedly drowned to death as it rained particularly heavily that night. "It was terrible," said Pokharel. "We kept hearing this person was beaten up, that person was killed all day long. How can one live in such a situation?" The next day, his family from Sindhuli called on the mobile phone owned by the lady who cooks for Pokharel and other labourers in a mess near the mine. They asked him to return home immediately. "I felt like going back," he said. "But how can you travel at a time like this? Now the situation has become somewhat normal. I'll go in Dashain [festival]."

8

Vicious Circle of Insurgency and Under Development in North East

North East India comprising the seven States of Assam, Arunachal Pradesh,Nagaland, Meghalaya, Manipur, Mizoram and Tripura has earned the dubious distinction for persistent underdevelopment and growing insurgency. The fire of insurgency has been engulfing the region in such a way that there seems to be existence of a parallel authority of the insurgents in many parts of the region as rampant abductions, extortions and killings go on unabated. Consequently, normal life is often paralysed and all initiatives including the socio-economic ones are increasingly crippled as an air of fear and uncertainty pervades the region.

Nagaland has been the epicentre of insurgency in the North East. The Naga leader, A.Z. Phizo raised the banner of revolt at the very dawn of Indian independence, claiming that Nagaland had never been a part of India. Although the sub national State of Nagaland was created in 1963 in order to fulfill the political aspiration of the Nagas, the flame of Naga insurgency could never be doused effectively and now it affects almost all the North Eastern States in general and Manipur, Assam and Nagaland in particular as the Naga insurgent outfits aim at political union and independence of all the territories claimed to be

Naga-dominated areas and as these outfits are providing help and training to the insurgents in other States also. The National Socialist Council of Nagaland formed in 1980 (now split into two factions) is the most formidable insurgent outfit in the region. In Assam, the insurgency has grown out of mass movement over the foreigners' issue starting in 1979. The United Liberation Front of Assam (ULFA) which has been committing terrorist acts with their avowed objectives of forming independent Assam has created a serious internal security hazard. The Bodos are also up in arms under the leadership of the National Democratic Front of Bodoland (NDFB). In the North Cachar

District of Assam, the Dimasa Halam (DHD) is engaged in insurgency activities. While the declared political ambition of the Bodos is for separate statehood under the Indian Union to attain independence, the objective of DHD is not explicitly made known.

Thus, Assam faces a very complicated problem of insurgency. Manipur is plagued by triple problems. The valley faces the insurgency of the Meitei extremists while the hill areas are affected by depredations by the Naga militants on the one hand and inter-tribal clashes between the Nagas and Kukis on the other. The more prominent outfits operating in Manipur are the People's Liberation Army (PLA). People's Revolutionary Party of Kangleipak (PREPAK), Kangleipak Communist Party (KCP), Kuki National Organisation (KNO/KDF) and the National Socialist Council of Nagaland (NSCN).

In Tripura, the tribal-non-tribal socio-economic divide has been generating dissension from the very dawn of the State's accession to the Indian Union in 1948. Although socio-economic development of Tripura has traditionally been associated with immigration, the massive influx of the non-tribal refugees from East Pakistan (now Bangladesh) in the wake of the division of India in 1947 reduced the tribal people into a minority constituting less than one third of the population. As most of the immigrants settled in rural areas, the pressure of population on land was tremendous. The sense of being progressively marginalized gave rise to tribal insurgency in the State. In the 1980s the Tripura National Volunteers (TNV) was a formidable tribal terrorist outfit spreading hatred against the non-tribal and it was mainly responsible for the riots that took place in June 1980. At present there are about 20 tribal insurgent groups in Tripura, the two Prominent ones being the National Liberation Front of Tripura (NLFT) and the All Tripura Tiger Force (ATTF). In recent years the non-tribal are also being involved in anti-tribal violent activities.

Mizoram experienced rebellion of the Mizos under the leadership of Mr. Laldenga. But after the Mizo Accord of 1986, there has been no major wave of insurgency in the State. None the less, inter-tribe conflicts and suspicion against the non-tribal are not altogether absent in the State.

Meghalaya has been free from insurgent activities. However, for the last few years Hiniutrap Liberation Council (HNLC) has been organizing disruptive activities in the State on certain occasions in spite of the fact that they do not have mass support. Even Arunachal Pradesh which can be regarded as an island of peace in the whole of the North eastern Region is not totally free from trouble. The local tribal people refuse to allow the Chakmas to be absorbed in the State's population. A rising trend of ethnic separatism is also absorbed in the State.

As security is the primary infrastructure of economic activities and social stability and certainty about future are the essential prerequisite of investment, the persistent insurgency atmosphere has been the most important contributor to economic stagnation of the region. It is to be noted that the gateway to the North Eastern Region is the chicken's neck of Siliguri area in North Bengal and all flows to and from the Region on the surface routes have to pass through this neck and the Brahmaputra Valley of Assam, Guwahati being the grand nodal point. Therefore, any disturbance in the Brahmaputra Valley and/or its adjoining hills brings the activities in the whole of the N.E. Region to a stand-still position. Also, there is important spill-over effect of insurgency in one State on the contiguous States. Therefore, the problem has to be viewed and tackled in an integrated considering its regional external effects, uniformity in its basic nature and also the linkage between the insurgent outfits of different States.

So far as the economy of the North Eastern Region is concerned, the first casualty of insurgency has been its already weak infrastructure especially, its transport system. The subversive activities of the insurgents' damage rail tracks, cause accidents leading to loss of life and property, create terror among the travellers and throw the entire system out of gear. Similarly, vehicles in the State and National highways are often attacked, passengers and transport workers are killed or wounded and sometimes abducted for ransom; and goods are l ooted. As the region suffers from geographical isolation and faces ravages of

Nature in the form of floods and landslides during monsoon, the insurgents' attack on the transport artery represents the last straw on the camel's back. The next important target of the insurgents is the resource-based industries like petroleum and tea which form the core of the modern organised sector in the region. As the articulated economic grievance hovers around the idea of so called regional colonialism based on the alleged drain of rich resources of the region, any violent political movement makes petroleum and tea as its target. Oil pipelines are often blown up by the insurgents, tea gardens are targeted for extortion and sometimes, tea garden executives are abducted.

Tea gardens constitute the soft targets of the insurgents as these are in the vicinity of forests and away from the populous localities. It is easy to understand that disrupting industrial activities centreing on petroleum and tea are bound to block the wheel of progress in the region. The attack of the insurgents on tea and petroleum is bound to convey negative signal to the prospective investors. The potential of using gas reserve of the region will also be seriously hampered because of insurgency situation. It may be pointed out that in the post-liberalisation period there fierce competition between the States for attracting domestic and foreign investments. In this race, the North East which is lagging behind will face further hurdles.

The third, but first from long term point of view, victim of insurgency in the region is environment. On the one hand, insurgents damage forests by taking shelter there and on the other, anti-insurgency operations also lead to denudation of forests. This not only means that conservation activities and other forestry operations are hampered thus resulting in the loss of valuable natural resources but also that a grave threat is posed to the fragile ecology of the region.

Fourthly, insurgency has created serious problems for development of the interior areas. As is well known, the North East is predominantly a ruralised region characterized in many parts by hilly terrain and sparsely populated inaccessible and isolated human habitations. It is extremely difficult to build up rural infrastructure like roads and communication links, power grid, irrigation arrangements etc. It is also equally difficult to build up and administer schools, hospitals, agricultural extension centres etc in such a condition. In other words, rural-urban economic interaction in the hilly and interior areas of the North East has to cross a number of hurdles. The insurgency has aggravated the problem to such an extent that development workers of both the Government and NGOs are utterly discouraged from going to the hilly and rural areas as they face constant extortions and threats of abduction or death. Consequently, insurgency is pushing the backward areas of the region to the darkness of greater underdevelopment and is acting as a retarding force rendering disservice to rural poor especially the indigenous people whose causes they are suppose to uphold.

Economic development involves structural changes and organisation of new economic activities with new techniques of production. Participation of development organizers, experts and even workers from outside the traditional social boundaries becomes indispensable in the circumstances. The insurgents by breeding a cult of hatred against the supposed or real outsiders are blocking all inflows of resources, ideas, expertise and initiative to the societies of the North East. This is bound to tell upon the future of the region. It is a contradiction to grumble about the state of underdevelopment on the one hand and target the agents of development on the other in the name of protecting the interest of indigenous people. Why is this contradiction generated in the behaviour pattern of the insurgents? Surly, the insurgents cannot be regarded simply as disruptionists as they undoubtedly command some amount of popular support directly or indirectly as they get food, shelter and other assistances in their societies and as they derive inspiration from the autonomy movement in the region. In fact, the insurgents may be regarded to represent the violent stream of the ethnic separatist movement having roots in the socio-economicpolitical grievances. So, their behaviour-pattern has to be analaysed with the help of social theories which is attempted in the following section.

The origin and persistent existence of ethnic separatism as expressed through insurgency may be explained in terms of Amartya Sen's concept of *Co-operative Conflicts.* "In the social relations that inter-alias determines the entitlements enjoyed by different people, there tend to be a coexistence of conflict and congruence of interests. There are in most situations, clear advantages to be gained by different people through co-operation with each other and yet there are also elements of conflicts reflecting the partly divergent interests of the same people. Co-operative conflicts refer to this co-existence of congruence and conflict of interests providing grounds for co-operation as well as for disputes and battles". Co-operative conflicts may be illustrated from many different fields of social relations. An illustration provided by Dréze and Sen is as follows: Consider the relation between workers and industrialists in a particular industry. If production is disrupted, both the industrialists and the workers may lose, so that it is in the interest of both to co-operate with each other in the process of production. But the division of benefits obtained from production may also involve an extensive tussle between the industrialists and the workers.

Another illustration of the working of the theory of co-operative conflict is provided by the relation between different members of a family where co-operation is essential for living together and yet conflict arises in sharing of benefits. The theory of co-operative conflict is suitable for explaining the insurgency and social dissensions in the North East. On the face of it, the insurgency is organised against the Central Government located in New Delhi and the States are targeted because of their link with dependence on the Government of India. The non-indigenous elements of population who are considered as 'outsiders' to the region are also made the targets of attack. But the main grievance arises out of the iniquitous character of the development process which in spite of some measures of welfares for the indigenous people here and there has not been able to tackle their basic problems effectively.

On the one hand, the centralized character of planning has deprived the indigenous people of any meaningful say in determining the nature and contents of development (thus frustrating their aspiration for autonomy), and on the other, the predominance of the tertiary sector led by the Government Administration and creation of scattered and a few resourcebased industrial islands have left little scope for participation of the indigenous people in the development process and have seriously restricted their entitlements. Therefore, they do not find much gain in co-operating with the Government and the so-called outsiders in promoting development. Neither political stability nor economic development in the present milieu seems to have relevance to their interest as these aims at the development of the geographical areas constituting the North Eastern Region without ensuring significant uplift of the poorest of the poor who constitute the bulk of the indigenous population.

Therefore, although co-operation between different sections of the people and between the people and the Government could lead to development of the region, the political conscious among the indigenous people have chosen the path of non co-operation and violent disruption. What appears to be revolt against the Government of India for attaining either sovereignty or enlarged autonomy is actually a violent expression of grievance against a political and economic structure in which the indigenous people have little share in policy making and from which they do not benefit to the extent as would have satisfied their expectation. The turmoil is also a result of lack of co-operation between different sections of population. The broad pattern of social dissension takes the form of indigenous vs. the nonindigenous or tribal vs. non-tribal or autochthones vs. immigrants. But even within the different sections of autochthones, areas of conflict exist as all of them compete for scarce resources like cultivable land, use of forests, lakes and streamlets for economic purposes in a relatively stationary economic perspective.

While in a broad sense the problem of insurgency emanates from underdevelopment, it is the peculiar features of underdevelopment and development in the North East that are crucially important for understanding the causes of insurgency in this region. It is the distribution of burden of underdevelopment and costs and benefits of development among the different sections of the population that are causing dissensions and consequence revolt.What has been stated in the foregoing paragraphs may well be illustrated with the help of experiences of different States in the region. Let us take the case of Tripura.

Economic development of Tripura has been historically associated with immigration from the areas which now constitute Bangladesh. After the partition, refugee rehabilitation made the tribal, the autochthones minority in the State. Much of the political grievances of the tribal and the consequent tribal insurgency is ascribed to this factor. But the present state of affairs could be definitely avoided or at least mitigated if in the post-independence period the tribal economy of the State could be effectively linked with the relatively dynamic segment of economic structure of the State.

The tribal people found that as economic development gathered momentum; they were losing their traditional rights on forests and other natural resources. They also found that they would have extremely limited scope for wet rice farming if they opted for it by giving up shifting cultivation as arable land had already been scarce. They had little role to play in tea plantation industry as it had its own immigrant labour force. The tertiary led by public administration offered some scope to the educated tribal but their participation in this sector was limited by tardy progress in education and attainment of technical and entrepreneurial skill. The potential resource-based industries using natural gas also did not mean much for them. Naturally they could pin their hope only on the primary sector consisting of agriculture, horticulture, forestry, animal husbandry and fishery etc. Rubber plantation undertaken on family basis could be a growth-booster for the tribal society. But the relatively long gestation period, the skill gap, distrust of the market (generated by the past bitter experience of exploitation) and the urge for producing own food prevented the tribal people from taking advantage of it in a meaningful scale. Consequently, the tribal were left to the 'jhumia-cum-peasant' or 'pure jhumia' status (Jhumia refers to shifting cultivator). As they lagged behind, the anger accumulated finally bursting into insurgency. Assam, the major State of the region has been a classic example of economic development deeply influenced by exogenous factors. Development of Assam has been accompanied with massive immigration caused by both economic and political factors.

Her demography has a truly plural character consisting of the following broad social groups:

- Assamese-speaking Hindus
- Assamese-speaking Muslims
- Bengali-speaking Hindus
- Bengali-speaking Muslims
- Indigenous Plains Tribes
- Indigenous Hill Tribes
- Nepalese Settlers
- Population historically linked to Tea Plantation having heterogeneous religious ethnic and linguistic origin
- Businessmen, public servants etc coming from other States of India and
- Others.

Of these groups, the Assamese-speaking Hindus and Muslims with a sizeable middle class have been the dominant group politically. The anti-foreigners agitation mainly aimed against the immigrants from East Pakistan (now Bangladesh) was led by people from this group. The movement was apparently organised to protect the socio-cultural, economic and political interest of the indigenous population. But its economic roots lay in the economic stagnation of the State resulting in the fierce competition among the middle class people belonging to different linguistic groups (especially, the Assamese and Bengalese) for government jobs on the one hand and increasing pressure of population in the State in general and its valleys in particular. Later on, the formidable extremist outfit named ULFA was born with its avowed objective of session from the Indian Union. Gradually, the wrath of extremists also targeted the businessmen hailing from other States of India and the consequence is a threat to the very future of economic development of Assam.

It is to be noted that the plains and hill tribal people of Assam do not fully feel themselves identified with the movement led by the Assamese-speaking middle class. It is because of this that they have separatist movements of their own like the Bodo insurgency and political movements in the Karbi Anglong and North Cachar Hills districts.

The different segments of the population of Assam thus have their sectarian interests and their co-operative conflict ultimately expresses itself as a revolt against the local and central political establishments. In the case of Nagaland and Manipur, the problem of socio-cultural plurality in the population is not as intense as in Tripura and Assam. But the dualism involving the autochthones and the outsiders has gradually emerged as administrative infrastructure expanded and transport, communication and power development took place. The suspicion about the outsider and the peculiar coexistence of modernity and tradition (the former increasing consciousness about rights and the later forming walls of conservatism) made the indigenous people non co-operative with the central establishment. Thus, it is the failure of development policy to get concerted support from the population which has given rise to the insurgency problem. It goes without saying that it is not easy to break the vicious circle of insurgency and underdevelopment existing in the North Eastern Region. It can be nobody's claim that the problems can be tackled solely by administrative, political or economic measures adopted in isolation. It requires not only a holistic approach but also great deal of patience and understanding of the specific problems of different socio-cultural-ethnic groups residing in the region.

As we have already emphasized, socio-economic pluralism and inequality in the participation of the development process generating co-operative conflict lie at the root of the insurgency in the North East. Therefore, the distinction between economic development of the geographical areas constituting the region and that of its backward sections must be borne in mind by all those who seek solution to the problem. The conflict between equity and efficiency is very sharp in the region. If equity especially inter-group equity (group meaning a distinct socio-cultural-ethnic identity) cannot be ensured, development effort will be thwarted by social revolt. Therefore, development projects must be such as is able to receive social approval at the grass-root level, given the diversities of population. This means that it must ensure the participation of the masses of all groups in the development process with reasonable equity in the distribution of costs and benefits.

If we agree on the basic feature of development policy noted above, it follows that modernization of the primary sector and a vigourous programme of rural development should be nucleus of all development efforts. Although the region is industrially backward, stress on conventional pattern of industrialization will do more harm than good as this would largely bypass the indigenous masses at least in the short run. Instead, rural industries must be rejuvenated. If agriculture, animal husbandry, forestry etc are organised on modern lines there is scope for development of a number of processing industries in the region. It may, however, be remembered that growth of a modern middle class and change in taste and preferences of even the rural people may stand in the way of reviving some of the traditional industries like the tribal loin looms and handlooms. Their place has to be taken by processing industries connected with agriculture, animal husbandry, horticulture and forestry and also service industries related to the rural infrastructure like irrigation, rural electrification, transport and communication, marketing etc. Family plantation units in rubber and tea backed by processing units at corporate level will increase the spread effect of these industries. Another point to be stressed is that development in the North East must be ecologically sustainable and must not be eco-degrading. Even schemes for infrastructural development like construction of roads and railways and power projects must be so drafted as to involve minimal adverse effects on the ecology. Besides, special attention must be made while going for mining and cement industries. It must be remembered that in the North East the masses are overwhelmingly dependent on forests, rivers and other natural resources for their daily requirements. Even plans for environment protection must be chalked out with the consent of the people and keeping their interest in view.

Although statehood under the Indian federation cannot be granted to each subnational group or each socio-cultural-ethnic entity their distinct identities must be respected. The best way to ensure decision-making power to different groups is to decentralize the political and economic administration. Federal principle should be followed not only in the Centre-State relation but also in the relation between the State Governments and local-level political-administrative units. In the North East, the Panchayati Raj institutions, Autonomous District Councils, and Sub-State Regional Development Councils have not been able to achieve the objective of decentralization in decision-making process as they have lacked real power and modern outlook and efficiency. Serious thought must be given to the task of developing a decentralized power structure not only in the North East but also in the whole of India if separatism is to be fought effectively. For the region it is indispensable that the fear of the indigenous masses regarding loss of freedom and identity must be removed.

Lastly, it must be driven home to the people of the North East that they can never attain real political power and development if they depend on the outside funding in all important schemes as at present. Even while accusing the

Centre for neglecting the region one cannot deny the fact that most of the State Governments in the region are financially non-viable and they depend largely on the largesse of the Central Government for both plan and non-plan expenditure as evident from their annual budgets. The way to achieve greater financial and political autonomy and to avoid nonpriority expenditures or wastage is local resource generation for local development works. Of course, the resource-transfer from the Centre can never be totally dispensed with. But if Central resource-transfer is matched by significant amount of resource generation at local levels, it will not only reduce inequality and wastage of in the region but will also give the people the real taste of political power.

PROFILE OF INSURGENCY IN NORTH EAST INDIA

ULFA

Formation: Asom Sanjukta Mukti Morcha or the United Liberation Front of Asom (ULFA) was formed on April 7, 1979 by Bhimakanta Buragohain, Rajiv Rajkonwar alias Arabinda Rajkhowa, Golap Baruah alias Anup Chetia, Samiran Gogoi alias Pradip Gogoi, Bhadreshwar Gohain and Paresh Baruah at the Rang Ghar in Sibsagar to establish a "sovereign socialist Assam" through an armed struggle.

Leadership

Arabinda Rajkhowa is the 'Chairman' of ULFA. 'Vice Chairman' Pradip Gogoi was arrested on April 8, 1998, and is currently in judicial custody at Guwahati. 'General Secretary' Anup Chetia is under detention in the Bangladeshi Dhaka after being arrested on December 21, 1997. The outfit's founding member and ideologue Bhimakanta Buragohain, 'Publicity Secretary' Mithinga Daimary and 'Assistant Secretary' Bolin Das were arrested during the military operations in Bhutan in December 2003. Earlier, 'Cultural Secretary' Pranati Deka was arrested at Phulbari in the West Garo Hills district of Meghalaya. Other leaders are: Bhimkanta Buragohin, Pradip Gogoi alias Samiran Gogoi, Mithinga Daimari, Pranati Deka and Ramu Mech,Mithinga Daimary (real name Dipak Das),The cultural secretary of the Ulfa, Pranati Deka hails from Nalbari district. She is the wife of the group's finance secretary Chitrabon Hazarika. She was first arrested from a Mumbai hospital in 1996. Later, she was released on bail in 1998 only to be arrested again at Phulbari, Meghalaya in 2003 while trying to escape. The ULFA has a clearly partitioned political and military wing. Paresh Barua heads the military wing as the outfit's 'commander-in-chief'. Following the military operations in Bhutan in December 2003, most of its top leadership reportedly operates from unspecified locations. According to reports, ULFA is in the process of relocating its camps in Myanmar, Mon district of Nagaland, Garo hills of Meghalaya and Tirap and Changlang districts of Arunachal Pradesh.

AREAS OF ACTIVITY AND INFLUENCE

The ULFA's organisational structure is divided into four zones:

1. East Districts(Purb Mandal)
2. West Districts(Paschim Mandal)
3. Central Districts(Madhya Mandal)
4. South Districts(Dakshin Mandal)

SANJUKTA MUKTI FOUJ (SMF)

A military wing of the ULFA, the Sanjukta Mukti Fouj (SMF) was formed on March 16, 1996. SMF has three full-fledged battalions (Bn): the 7th, 28th and 709th. The remaining battalions exist only on paper - at best they have strengths of a company or so.

Their allocated spheres of operation are:

- 7th Bn (HQ- Sukhni) Responsible for defence of GHQ
- 8th Bn Nagaon, Morigaon, Karbi Anglong
- 9th Bn Golaghat, Jorhat, Sibsagar
- 11th Bn Kamrup, Nalbari
- 27th Bn Barpeta, Bongaigaon, Kokrajhar
- 28th Bn Tinsukia, Dibrugarh
- 709th Bn Kalikhola

Links and Camps

The ULFA sought shelter in the forests on the Indo-Bhutan border from the early 1990s and established several camps in the forest areas of southern Bhutan. Over the years, it reportedly developed linkages with several officers and personnel of the Royal Bhutan Army (RBA) and Police - which ensured, among other things, a steady flow of rations, logistical support as well as aid and contacts for money laundering. The ULFA's Bhutan set-up had a reported strength of around 2000 cadres spread across the outfit's 'General Head Quarters', it's 'Council Head Quarters', a 'Security Training Camp' and a well-concealed 'Enigma Base'.

Numbering around 13 in all, the major camps of the ULFA in Bhutan included:

- Mithundra
- Gobarkunda
- Panbang
- Diyajima
- Pemagatsel Complex
  - Khar
  - Shumar
  - Nakar
- Chaibari
- Marthong
- Gerowa
- *Sukhni (Merungphu)*: 'General HQ'
- Melange
- *Phukaptong*: 'Council HQ'
- Dalim-Koipani (Orang)
- Neoli Debarli

Most camps and other establishment of the ULFA were in Sandrup Jongkhar, a district in southern Bhutan that borders Assam's Nalbari district. The RBA is reported to have destroyed all the outfit's camps and observation posts during the military operations launched in December 2003.

In 1986, ULFA first established contacts with the then unified National Socialist Council of Nagaland (NSCN) and the Kachin Independence Army (KIA) of Myanmar for training and arms. ULFA linked up with the Kachins through the 'good offices' of the Naga rebels. It learnt the rudiments of insurgent tactics from the Kachins (who reportedly charged Rupees

100,000 per trainee). Subsequently, links were established with Pakistan 's Inter Services Intelligence (ISI) and the Afghan Mujahideen. Reports indicate that at least 200 ULFA activists received training in Pakistan and Afghanistan.

Bangladesh authorities arrested its leader Anup Chetia on December 21, 1997. He is currently under detention at the high-security Dhaka Central Jail. The main charges against Chetia include illegal entry into Bangladesh, possession of two forged Bangladeshi passports, possession of an unauthorised satellite telephone and illegal possession of foreign currency of countries as diverse as the US, UK, Switzerland, Thailand, Philippines, Spain, Nepal, Bhutan, Belgium, Singapore and others. Two other accomplices, identified as Babul Sharma and Laxmi Prasad, were also arrested along with Chetia.

ULFA gradually expanded its network to include operational control of activities and the receipt and shipment of arms in transit before they finally entered India. Owing to greater vigil along the known routes of ULFA arms flow, the group has, in recent times, been making attempts to set up bases in Meghalaya, especially in the West Garo Hills to coordinate the transit of arms.

ULFA has for long maintained close linkages with the Pakistan's ISI which procured several passports for Paresh Baruah and other ULFA cadres. Several ULFA cadres have also received arms training from the ISI at various training centres in Pakistan, close to the Afghanistan border. ULFA had also announced its support for Pakistan during the Kargil war. They described the Pakistani intruders - primarily Pakistani Army regulars and Afghan mercenaries - as 'freedom fighters'.

Reports indicate that the ULFA's mouthpiece, ULFA's a website newsletter Swadhinata also known as 'Freedom', receives editorial support from ISI inside Pakistan. It was in 'Freedom' that the ULFA first supported the Pakistanis during the Kargil war. The ISI has provided ULFA cadres with arms training, safe havens, funds, arms and ammunition. Training has been given at camps in Pakistan and Bhutan. At least 300 ULFA cadres were also trained at Rawalpindi and other locations in Pakistan. The training included courses in the use of rocket launchers, explosives and assault weapons. Paresh Baruah has been regularly visiting Karachi since 1992-93. He is also reported to have met Osama bin Laden in 1996 during a visit to Karachi. The ULFA leader was reportedly taken to a camp on the Pakistan-Afghanistan border, where he not only received assurance of military help in the form of arms and ammunition, but also assurances of co-operation and logistical support of all international organisations owing allegiance to bin Laden, including the International Jehad Council, the Tehrik-ul-Jehad, Harkat-ul-Jehadi-e-Islami (HuJI), apart from the Al Qaeda.

The ISI has also trained ULFA terrorists in counter intelligence, disinformation and use of sophisticated weapons and explosives. Pakistan has facilitated the visits of Paresh Baruah and other ULFA leaders to Singapore, Thailand and other countries, and a channel for the transfer of funds and arms has been created. The ISI largesse enabled ULFA to buy arms in Cambodia, paying for these in hard currency routed through Nepal. The ISI also 'introduced' ULFA to LTTE transporters who, for a fee, undertook to transport arms from Southeast Asia into Myanmar. In April 1996, Bangladesh seized more than 500 AK-47 rifles, 80 machineguns, 50 rocket launchers and 2,000 grenades from two ships off Cox's Bazaar. Four Tamils were among those arrested

Co-operation between various terrorist organisations in India's north-east and foreign groups was formalised with the formation of the Indo-Burmese Revolutionary Front (IBRF) in 1989. The IBRF was made up initially of the NSCN-K, ULFA, United Liberation Front of Bodoland, Kuki National Front (KNF) (all from India) and Chin National Front (Myanmar). Paresh Baruah is reported to have paid a substantial sum of money to the Kachins for the first large consignment of weapons from Thailand. Manerplaw in lower Myanmar on the border with Thailand is the stronghold of the rebel Karen National Union which, in 1993, is reported to have delivered, from the Cambodian arms market, AK-56 rifles, machine guns, rocket-propelled guns and anti-tank rifles to the ULFA. The organisation's cadres have identified an arms dealer as an ethnic Kachin and wife of an assassinated Manipuri rebel

Themba Song. The Communist Party of Burma is known to have gifted some weapons, mainly Chinese-made M10 rifles, to ULFA and Naga terrorist organisations.

Arrested ULFA cadres have claimed that Baruah used to smuggle heroin, procured in Myanmar into Assam as part of "a personal operation". According to surrendered ULFA cadres, the ULFA terrorists had also crossed over into China via Bhutan and established contact with the Chinese Army. The group, on the basis of these contacts, had a rendezvous with a Chinese ship on the high seas in March 1995 during which a weapons' consignment was transferred to them. A further consignment ultimately landed up in Bhutan in 1999, though it was actually acquired in 1997. ULFA also runs profitable narcotics business in Myanmar and Thailand. A close nexus between ULFA and the Liberation Tigers of Tamil Eelam (LTTE) had also been reported. The LTTE is reported to have trained various ULFA cadres in explosives handling.

ULFA AS A REVOLUTIONARY ORGANIZATION

United Liberation Front of Assam, ULFA, a revolutionary political organisation was born on the lawns of the historic Rang Ghar of Sibsagar on 7th April 1979.

ULFA'S AIMS AND OBJECTS

To liberate Assam, (a land of 78,529 square K.M.), through Armed national liberation struggle from the clutches of the illegal occupation of India and to establish a sovereign Independent Assam.

ULFA REPRESENTS

ULFA represents, as its name implies, not only the Assamese nation but also the entire independent minded struggling peoples, irrespective of different race-tribe-caste-religion and nationality of Assam. The struggle for national liberation of Assam never is a separatist or secessionist movement. Assam was never a part of India at any point of time in history. The fact is independent Assam has been occupied by India, and deploying occupation forces they are oppressing our peoples and persecuting them. ULFA itself and all freedom fighters of Assam are neither planning nor conspiring to break up India! We are not conducting any armed operation inside India. Freedom fighters of Assam are only trying to overthrow Indian colonial occupation from Assam.

The armed struggle for self-defence: The people of Assam are confronting with various problems. Among those, the National identity problem is basic. The communal riot that was followed by the partition of India and Pakistan was responsible for the influx of foreigners from the Indian sub-continent in large scale and thereby caused a real threat to the demographic composition of Assam. India has all along encouraged this influx because of a population base having ethnic affinity with main land India is always favourable to their long term security perspective. This is one of India 's major aspects of colonial occupation of Assam.

In economic sphere, India has been engaged in large-scale exploitation. Despite its rich resources, Assam remains one of the most backward states. Therefore, the question of real threat to the national identity of the people of Assam under the colonial occupation and exploitation of India has become the basic problem. As a whole, the problem has become a question of life and death to the people of Assam. The people of Assam confronted with the aforesaid problems such as influx of foreigners and massive exploitation of its natural resources and determined as national identity problem after summing up them. Against the gross injustice for sheer survival as a nation, as a people and as individuals, the people of Assam many times launched democratic and unarmed peaceful movement. However, India ruthlessly suppressed and crushed them ignoring the value of democratic movement. Though the people of Assam and leadership of the struggle have a strong stand for peaceful and amicable solution of the conflict, India has always been trying to force a military solution.

INDIAN MILITARY OPERATION IN ASSAM

The main intention of this operation is to suppress the legitimate aspiration of the people of Assam, and their basic and fundamental human rights *i.e.,* national self-determi-nation. There are endless lists of gross human rights violations during this period by Indian occupation forces. They have killed hundreds of innocent people, hundred more have disappeared in their custody and many of our womenfolk have been raped while many more hundreds have been severely tortured to become handicapped. It is the reflection of direct consequence of colonial repressive policy of India. Today, Assam is an occupied country under Indian's martial law and an undeclared war inside Assam is running on. Any thing may happen at any time inside this war theatre. Colonial India 's this repressive policy compel to the freedom fighters of Assam to take up arms for self-defence. So, armed national liberation struggle of Assam is a democratic struggle for the survival of a Nation.

ULFA COMMANDER PARESH BARUA

One of the 'most wanted' north-east terrorist leader, the 45-yr-old ULFA 'commander-in-chief' Paresh Barua is a versatile radical who has been successful in evading Indian forces for long despite non-stop efforts by the latter. Wanted for a series of robberies, killings and extortions, he is believed to be currently based in Bangladesh or Bhutan. Trained in guerrilla war by ISI, Kachin Independent Army (KIA) of Myanmar and NSCN, he can handle all kinds of weapons, travels on forged passports and identity cards and lives on money obtained from extortion or robbery.

Also known as Paban Barua and Pradip Barua. He, he is 173 cms in height, has black hair and black eyes, a scar on the palm of his right hand. On May 10, 1985 he and some others raided a bank in Guwahati and shot the manager and stole a sum of ₹27, 549.62 in cash. Often dubbed as 'braveheart' by many ULFA sympathisers, he has had brush with death several times, including in Dec 2000 when he was seriously wounded in a factional gun-battle in the Chittagong Hill Tracts in Bangladesh. But there is other side of Barua story too. Born on May 1, 1957, he is a very good football player, can speak a number of languages including English, Bengali, Hindi, Naga and Singpho and of course Assamese, his mother tongue.

MAJOR INSURGENT OUTFITS IN NORTH EAST INDIA

ARUNACHAL

- National Liberation Front of Arunachal: Koj Tara Dragon Force (ADF)

ASSAM

- United Liberation Front of Asom (ULFA):Paresh Baruah,
- Arbinda Rajkhoa,
- Anup Chetia, Daimari, Pradip Gogoi
- National Democratic Front of Bodoland (NDFB)
- United People's Democratic Solidarity (UPDS)
- Bodo Liberation Tiger Force (BLTF)
- Dima Halim Daogah (DHD)
- Karbi National Volunteers (KNV)
- Rabha National Security Force (RNSF)
- Koch-Rajbongshi Liberation Organisation (KRLO)
- Hmar People's Convention- Democracy (HPC-D)
- Karbi People's Front (KPF)
- Barak Valley Youth Liberation Front (BVYLF)
- United Liberation Front of Barak Valley

MANIPUR

- United National Liberation Front (UNLF)
- People's Liberation Army (PLA)
- People's Revolutionary Party of Kangleipak (PREPAK)
- Manipur People's Liberation Front (MPLF)
- Kangleipak Communist Party (KCP)
- Kanglei Yawol Kanna Lup (KYKL)
- Manipur Liberation Tiger Army (MLTA)
- Iripak Kanba Lup (IKL)
- People's Republican Army (PRA)
- Kangleipak Kanba Kanglup (KKK)
- North East Minority Front (NEMF)
- Kuki National Front (KNF)
- Kuki National Army (KNA)

- Kuki Revolutionary Army (KRA)
- Kuki National Organisation (KNO)

MIZORAM

- Hmar People's Convention (HPC)
- Hmar People's Convention- Democracy (HPC-D)
- Hmar Revolutionary Front (HRF)
- Zomi Revolutionary Army (ZRA)
- Zomi Revolutionary Volunteers (ZRV)
- Indigenous People's Revolutionary Alliance(IRPA)
- Kom Rem People's Convention (KRPC)
- Chin Kuki Revolutionary Front (CKRF)
- Bru National Liberation Front

MEGHALAYA

- Hynniewtrep National Liberation Council (HNLC)
- Achik National Volunteer Council (ANVC)
- People's Liberation Front of Meghalaya (PLF-M)
- Hajong United Liberation Army (HULA)

NAGALAND

- National Socialist Council of Nagaland (Isak-Muivah) - NSCN(IM)
- National Socialist Council of Nagaland (Khaplang) - NSCN (K) Naga National Council-NNC (Adino)

TRIPURA

- National Liberation Front of Tripura (NLFT): Biswamohan Debbarma, Nayanbashi Jamatia
- All Tripura Tiger Force (ATTF): Ranjit Debbarma
- Tripura Tribal Volunteer Force (TTVF)
- Tripura Liberation Force (TLF)
- All Tripura Volunteer Force (ATVF)
- Tripura National Army (TNA)
- Borok National Council of Tripura (BNCT)

WEST BENGAL

- Kamtapuri Liberation Organisation (KLO)

9

Northeast Violence: An Overall View

Brahmaputra, Imphal and Surma valleys with surrounding mountains and hills are the geo-political boundaries of Northeast India. Comprising of seven States Assam, Nagaland, Mizoram, Meghalaya, Arunachal Pradesh, Manipur and Tripura, with a collective area of 255,088 sq. km. (about 8% of the country's territory) include two third of hills and forests and one third plains. Bounded by Bhutan and China (Tibet) in north, Myanmar in east and south and Bangladesh in south and west, the region is connected with about 4000 sq. km of porous international borders and touching the two ends of only a 20km wide corridor (Siliguri Corridor) in west with the rest of India.

With a combined population of about four crores (38,495,089 -2001 Census), which includes 209 Scheduled Tribes (Arunachal Pradesh -101; Manipur -29; Assam - 23; Nagaland - 20; Tripura - 18; Meghalaya - 14; and Mizoram 53) - Northeast is a most diversified region.

States with overwhelming tribal population are Meghalaya, Arunachal Pradesh, Nagaland and Mizoram whereas those having more than one third tribal population are Manipur and Tripura. Contrary to the general perception these tribes constitute below 30% of the population of the entire Northeast.

While Assam, Tripura and Manipur are dominated by about 60% of non-tribal population, the rest of the states are having a tribal majority ranging from 60 to 90 per cent. The area being the abode of various ethnic groups like Ahom, Naga, Lusai(Mizo), Meitei, Garo, Khasi, Koch, Hajomg, Rabha, Kachari, Tippera, Chakma, Abhor, Bodo, Miri and hundreds of other tribes for centuries - remained the isolated corner of Indian sub-continent and away from the larger civilizational masses.

Contented in forests and hills, the tribes of the Northeast viewed anyone entering in their territory as outsiders. With a definite territory, kinship, social structure, distinct tradition and mostly having non-monarchical character, they remained away from the influence of Sanskritisation for centuries and preserved their exclusivity till the annexation of their territories by the British in the nineteenth century. Except for Nagas and the Mizos most of others were however, under the domain of some princely kingdoms like Ahom, Manipur, Tripura and Khasis. Nagas and Mizos were constant problems for these rulers.

The British annexed the Northeast at different points of time like Assam plains (1826), Cachar plains (1830), (Khasi Hills (1833), Jaintia plains(1835), Karbi Anglong or Mikir Hills (1838), North Cachar Hills (1854), Naga Hills (1866-1904), Garo Hills (1872-73) and Mizo Hills (1890). All these areas formed parts of Assam Province of British India. But the colonial power with a view to keep them excluded from the ministerial jurisdiction of Provincial Government declared these hill districts as Excluded Areas under the exclusive administrative control of Chief Commissioner of the province. They introduced inner line permit to prevent the entry of outsiders in this area without valid permit.

This permit system debarred the hill people from interaction with the larger masses of Indian mainstream and from the socio-political influence of the outside world. Manipur, Tripura and Khasi States (Now Khasi Hills in Meghalaya) remained as Princely States under Brtish control.

The Christian missionaries followed the British and established their foothold in the region. Converting the tribes from their indigenous faith to Christianity, they robbed off their traditional identity and imposed on them a new socio-religious identity based on Christian traditions. Such socio-religious transformation was though contrary to their respective ethnic traditions, over the years the converted tribes accepted it as the generic identity. Christianisation and basic education helped some of them to get middle to lower level jobs in Church and British administration which gave birth to a middle class; a new social phenomenon in tribal society. This new class of people, who came into contact with the people outside their area - gradually developed identity consciousness. The social reformers of mainland India practically remained indifferent of this development and did not make any effort to counter it. Similarly, the leaders of freedom movement due to lack of rapport with hill people - failed to instill among them any emotional feeling towards India. Thus, in the absence of socio-cultural intercourse with the plains of India the isolated tribes developed a centrifugal tendency against mainland Indian sub-continent.

In the backdrop of the historical reality, when freedom knocked the door of the country and the British declared the lapse of its paramountcy over Indian States, it placed the national leadership in a complex situation. Being confronted with the problem of preventing further balkanization and the task for integrating 562 Princely States - they failed to appreciate the new political awakening in tribal society.

The tribal masses accepted many imposed changes, which were against their self-governing character and heterogeneous system of pristine institutions but had not anticipated their future political identity because of non-participation in the freedom movement. Therefore, even with provision in Indian constitution for preservation of their traditions a section of vested interest with the investigation of foreign forces sought independent existence outside India. Ironically, those, who with a view to preserve their independent identity had fought decades after decades against the British before their subjugation - were in the forefront of secessionist demands on a plea of imaginary danger to their forcibly imposed religio-cultural identity. But the Mizos under the influence of Mizo Union, Garos under the banner of Garo National Council and most of the other tribes favoured integration of their territories with India with more tribal autonomy and thus, the entire region of the northeast became the integral part of Indian Union.

It is a known fact of history that in a federal polity the national objective cannot be achieved without regional support for which the Indian core was expected to appreciate the unique geo-social problem of the region. It needed an organic relationship with its diverse ethnic groups particularly the hill tribes. The national leadership however, failed to develop any mechanism for their emotional integration with the national mainstream. In stead of breaking the legacy of imperialist rule, undoing the arbitrary and irrational British method of administration and formulating a coherent nation-centric policy to build up an organic relation between the tribal masses and rest of people in India, they took them for granted. Ignoring the alienated mindset of these people, they provided opportunities to the forces of vested interest to fish in troubled water.

Taking advantage of the situation, the imperialist forces while establishing their operational bases in different parts of South East Asia began playing the divisive game in Northeast. (Insurgency in Northeast India by S. K. Sareen, 1982). While China with its eye on this oil, tea and mineral rich region tried to unite its people for an umbrella of Mongoloid movement, Pakistan and Bangladesh with Muslim League agenda of 1906 for Islamic expansionism promoted Muslim infiltration in the region and helped the secessionist forces against India. Church is regarded one of the four arms of western powers besides Infantry, Air Force and Navy (Dr. J. C. Kumarappa's quote from 'What ails Northeast' by Bhanu Pratap Shukla) and hence the Christian Missionaries, with a view to maintain religio-cultural hegemony in the region also helped them through western powers.

Against the background of the unique situation, India has been facing the challenge of autonomist and secessionist demands at different places in Northeast at different points of time but ethno-political violence in the the region was often greatly exaggerated in the media. India is a country where caste, creed, language and religion dominate the political discourse and therefore, the centuries old isolated region cannot be an exception. If we look into the on going movements and revolts in number of regions in the country, it appears that entire India is passing through a whirlpool of competitive and violent politics as seen in Northeast. Maoists, Sikh extremists and the movements for new States like Telangna, Bundelkhand and Harit Pradesh are nothing but a continuous search for new political identity by the diverse groups in the country.

In absence of a sense of pan-Indianism among them, hill people of Northeast, who had more proximity with the people and cities across the international border than rest of India, were not expected to overcome their political confusion overnight. With arms left by Japanese army in the region during Second World War the Nagas under the banner of Naga National Council led by Angami Zapu Phizo therefore, fired the first shot for liberation of this territory from Indian occupation just on the eve of Independence on August 14, 1947. Though, the revolt was suppressed and Phizo was arrested in 1948, his arrest made him the supreme leader of the Nagas. Gradually he succeeded in accomplishing Naga unity irrespective of their division in over a dozen of sub-tribes. He even consolidated the Nagas residing in the contiguous areas of Assam, Manipur, Arunachal Pradesh and even in foreign territory of Mynmar and now the insurgents are demanding Greater Nagaland, which includes all the Naga inhabited areas. The poisonous virus of Naga revolt disturbed the political climate of entire Northeast and subsequently encouraged other ethnic groups like Mizo, Bodo, and Meitie for similar demands.

The Unique geo-political situation of Northeast with long international border is vulnerable from the security point of view. Moreover, instigating hand of foreign enemies further complicated its problem. The British granted political asylum to Z. A. Phizo, the legendary Naga rebel and extended helping hand to Mizo insurgent Laldenga. Pakistan, China and Bangladesh on the other hand were supplying arms to various insurgent groups regularly. Baptist Christian Missionaries like Michel Scott meddled in tribal politics. These known misdeeds of foreign forces are enough proof to suggest that had the Indian establishment countered the evil designs of foreign adversaries effectively, the on going insurgency would not have persisted. Forced migration of Hindu refugees from East Pakistan reduced the aboriginal natives of Tripura to minority and Assamese also became scared of similar fate due to the politics of Muslim infiltration. Despite these developments the national leadership remained contended and paid little attention to study the problem dispassionately. Even re-organisation of states in mid 1950s was carried out without looking into this dark area.

The dialogues maintained by different insurgent groups in northeast with Government of India is continuing since independence. In the process some of them gave up their secessionist demand and also joined the politico-economic mainstream of the country. But there are still a sizeable number of insurgents particularly in Nagaland, Manipur, Assam and Tripura where widespread ethnic conflict has kept the entire northeast disturbed for decades.

Over the years the Government of India with a view to pacify the secessionist and autonomist ethnic groups, reorganised Assam and created Nagaland (1963), Meghalaya (1972), Mizoram (U.T. in 1972 and full-fledged statehood in 1987), Manipur (1972), and Arunachal Pradesh. Creation of smaller States on the basis of ethnic groups opened a Pandora box as the state leadership in the region have not fulfilled the political aspirations of over 200 hundred tribes, who have been in inter-ethnic conflicts for centuries. In Manipur various aboriginal ethnic groups like Meithi, Nagas, Kukis, and Hmars are fighting against each other under their respective insurgent leaders. In Meghalaya too, Garos and Khasis do not have smooth relation. In Assam the Bodos, Kacharis and a number of other tribes are demanding their separate States or independence. Even though peace is restored in Mizoram, Chakmas in this State are not at all comfortable with the Mizos.

The background of all the secessionist movements in Northeast is different but ironically, a section of media, academics and social scientists are trying to combine them together and have made the problem more and more complex. Blaming the Centre for the neglect of the region they plead that the former is treating its people as if they are not the citizens like rest of India. Mahasweta Devi, a well-known litterateur while answering to a question on unrest in Northeast said, "I think the area has been neglected for years. We have not treated them as part of India so it has resulted in unrest" (Pioneer dated January 16, 2006). Such academic assessment suggests that the genesis of the trouble has emanated from the neglect of the region.

Movement for preservation of ethnic identity in India has been an important issue of political discourse for decades. There is nothing wrong if such discourse is meant for the progress of the society without negating the nation building process. In Northeast it is however used by wide network of self-serving and anti-people corrupt politicians, Government officials, drug and arm smugglers and lumpen elements with the help of instigating hands of neighbouring countries.

The educated elite among the hill peoples with their share in political power emerged as a new feudal class that changed the socio-economic scenario in the in tribal society. Usurping the traditional right over land and forest of their own people and dividing the tribal society between rich and poor, they created class rivalry, which was unusual for tribal society. Ironically, despite the deep-rooted inter-tribe contradiction, tribal intelligentsia, who failed to share political power, is in unending search for larger identity on the plea of ethno-nationalism, which is the common ideology of all the secessionist groups. Their so-called quest for identity related insurgency is simply a pressure tactics for more and more political concessions.

The State leaders are saleable commodities at the hands of the ruling party at Centre. They change their loyalty overnight if there is change in Centre as they are more interested in seeking Central fund than to change the secessionist tendencies of the people. The national leadership overlooks the siphoning of public fund to the insurgents for the sake of their respective party's interest. Media reports suggest that the insurgents extort huge amount from ruling party leaders in their respective States. "The Outlook magazine carried a story that Ibobi Singh, Chief Minister of Manipur paid ₹ 1.5 crore to some Revolutionary Peoples' Front. Former Governor Lt. Gen. (Retd) V. K. Nayyar levelled similar charges against two former Chief Ministers in the State, besides a number of other politicians" (Pioneer dated February 9, 2006). In spite of the known nexus between the various anti-people forces and the insurgents, to put blame only on Centre may not be fair.

Above all, the ground reality also suggests that the failure of the Central Government to manage the international boarder with firm hand to counter the unfriendly designs of our neighbours is the prime reason behind the unrest. Except Bhutan no other country across the border took tough action against the insurgents. If trans-border migration of insurgents is prevented, they may not survive for long. Ever Since Jawaharlal Nehru, the first Prime Minister of the country was trapped in the 'Hindi-Chini Bhai Bhai' slogan and faced humiliating defeat in 1962, his successors continuously maintained soft attitude towards undesirable developments along the northeastern borders. Failure of the Centre in 1962 War gave rise to centrifugal forces in Northeast to accelerate secessionist demands.

The insurgents groups have covered a long way in fighting for the independence of their territories and some of them strengthened their striking power due to the sanctuary and help from across the international border but the common masses are not with them. They are fed up with the disturbances, which have only increased their miseries. They are more interested for development than to support them. It is a historical fact that rise of any country is closely linked to the emotional integration of its diverse regions and accordingly, contrary to the general academic perception the post-colonial leadership of India always accepted the people of the region as equal partners in nation-building process. But it is unfortunate that they are facing the trauma of insurgency for over half a century at the hands of a group of their own people. As discussed above, their owes are factually linked with the deep nexus between the insurgents and corrupt politicians and State officials, who allow unabated black-marketing of essential commodities and drug smuggling and not with identity crisis as is often highlighted by the media.

One can understand that the hill people of the region were under historical isolation from the socio-cultural interaction with the larger civilizational masses for centuries and were therefore apprehensive against the imaginary danger to their ethnic identity. But had such historical background been reason behind insurgency, why did the Assamese, who had centuries old socio-cultural link with the rest of Indian sub-continent and had taken an active part in freedom movement also now pose challenge against their assimilation with Indian State?

In view of the multiplicity of large number of ethnic groups, who are now aspiring to have their respective independent States or sovereignty on the plea of their pre-British status and separate nationality, the problem is getting multiplied day by day. The belief of the hill people that they were sovereign entity before their annexation by the British is applicable to a number of ethnic groups in the country. After departure of British over five hundred Princely states which had sovereign status merged under one democratic geo-political boundary and the Hill districts of Assam also became a part of Indian Union. Thus, harping on Pre-British status will only add to the prevailing socio political tension in the region. With growing number of militant outfits, if independence were granted on the basis of ethnic identity, there would be endless fight for hundreds of States or nations in the northeast. This is neither practicable nor feasible. However, being a region of competing ethnicity of a large number of tribes and sub-tribes, Northeast needs a lasting solution in totality through a revolutionary nation-centric policy.

Academics, political analysts, social scientists and tribal intelligentsia are pondering over only the economic neglect of the region and their pre-British identity as primary reasons behind the insurgency. But if one looks into the overall economic structure of the country Northeast is also in the continuing process of development particularly in fields of education, communications, rural electrification and cottage industries. The level of development in this region may not be at par with relatively higher developed states like Punjab, Haryana, Maharashtra, Gujarat, Karnataka and Tamilnadu but in comparison to BIMARU States, from where crores of populations are migrated for search of livelihood, Northeast is much better off. An ambitious plan of a grand Asian high way to connect India to Myanmar, Thailand and China through Assam, Manipur and Nagaland is already in pipeline, which will provide economic boom to the region once it is through. Thus, the blame on Centre for economic neglect of Northeast may not be fair. In fact the Indian establishment provided respectable and proportionate place in the political map of the country also to the people of Northeast. But with greater number of western educated people than many of Indians in plains, they expect larger share in political power.

Despite political and administrative corruption, the increasing participation of the people of Northeast in the development process of their respective States and significant changes in their socio-political behaviour have sent a positive signal that they are working as equal partners in the nation-building exercise. Sending larger number of their representatives in Parliament from national parties like Congress, BJP and CPM and participation of the people of entire region in elections prove their commitments towards the core of Indian Union. Laldenga, the Mizo rebel leader ultimately joined the mainstream politics under India's constitution and Mizoram is practically free from the menace of insurgency. Similar is the case of Meghalaya and Arunchal Pradesh. Therefore, the apprehension of the dismemberment of Northeast from India through the so called co-ordinated challenge to the Indian core is far from the ground reality. Only some misguided sections in Nagaland, Manipur, Tripura and Assam are working for India's inimical neighbours and anti-Indian forces only for their self-serving interest. They need to be handled with a strong political will as the rise of a sovereign state depends upon the integration of its diverse regions under a centripetal pull. Once the forces of disintegration are allowed to grow it will be the beginning of its decline.

INNOVATIVE METHODS IN FIGHTING INSURGENCY IN NORTH-EAST INDIA

State initiatives to fight insurgency and restore law and order in the North-Eastern region of the country has experienced a paradigm shift. The concerns with security and the erstwhile socio-economic conditions which prevailed over the democratization processes in the state bringing more powers to the police and the Army were diluted towards citizens' satisfaction. In contrast to the Armed Forces Special Powers Act an innovative initiative has addressed the problem of insurgency through positive means of partnership of the government with people on one hand and with related government agencies on the other.

The focus of fighting insurgency has shifted from merely arming the state machineries to a strategy of agreements and negotiations alongside improved counter-insurgency measures. It is with these innovative methods in fighting insurgency that the State aims to restore normalcy in the region. The regional challenges to the innovative strategy: The North Eastern region of India, occupying 8.06% of the Indian landmass, comprise of the eight States of Assam, Arunachal Pradesh, Manipur, Meghalaya, Mizoram, Nagaland, Sikkim and Tripura. Except for the States of Mizoram and Sikkim, the North East is widely known as one of the most disturbed areas in the country. The whole of Manipur (except Imphal Municipal area), Nagaland and Assam, Tirap and Changlang districts of Arunachal Pradesh and a 20 km. belt in the States of Arunachal Pradesh and Meghalaya having common border with Assam have been declared 'Disturbed Areas' under the Armed Fo rces (Special Powers) Act, 1958 as amended in 1972. The Governor of Tripura has declared the areas under 28 Police Stations in full and part of the area under 6 Police Stations as 'Disturbed Areas (Ministry of Home Affairs, Annual Report - 2008). Thus, in the remaining North Eastern states, fighting insurgency constitutes the priority of governance.

Origin of the initiative: The initiation of the innovative methods in fighting insurgency in the North-East can be traced to the signing of the Ceasefire Agreement with the National

Socialist Council of Nagaland (Isak-Muivah)/NSCN (IM). Since then, Ceasefire Agreements have been signed with:

- The National Socialist Council of Nagaland (Isak-Muivah)/NSCN (IM) on August 1, 1997.
- The National Socialist Council of Nagaland (Khaplang)/NSCN (K) on April 28, 2001. Like the Ceasefire Agreement, similar armed suspension agreement framework termed the
- Suspension of Operation (SoO) has been initiated.
- Suspension of Operation (SoO) has been signed with
- Kuki National Organization (KNO), Manipur in August 2008.
- Tripartite agreements between the Government of India, the Government of Assam with the National Democratic Front of Bodoland (NDFB) on April 24, 2005.
- Achik National Volunteer Council (ANVC) Meghalaya on July 23, 2004.
- Dima Halam Dagoah (DHD) in the North Cachar Hills area, Assam since January 1, 2003.
- United Peoples Democratic Solidarity (UPDS–in the Karbi Anglong Area of Assam) on August 1, 2002.

PROBLEMS ADDRESSED

The signing of the Ceasefire Agreement or the Suspension of Operations indicates very important developments. As the name suggests- Ceasefire Agreement or Suspension of Operations- once signed between the State and the insurgent outfit or a tripartite agreement between the Government of India, the State Government and the insurgent outfit, a certain code of conduct or ground rules is agreed upon.

The code of conduct entails that:

- The insurgent groups will not engage in violent armed conflict, live in designated camps or cordoned off sites mutually agreed by both the State and the group,

- Not engage in any illegal activities like extortion, kidnapping etc., and put weapons in double-lock mode. Thus, the agreement provides the State Government with opportunities such as:
- Firstly, the air of uncertainty as to when and which armed group is going to attack or pose threat to the people is cleared to an extent.
- Peace process is initiated with the insurgent group,
- Increase counter-insurgency measures on the other militant groups operating within the State.
- Maintain vigil over the outfit currently observing ceasefire/suspension of operations.
- The State can focus attention on the more important and pressing needs for development

The New Samtal area in district Chandel in south Manipur, which had continued to be infested with insurgency, was largely cleared during the year, and action is underway to reactivate the civil and developmental administration and activities in this area. The enforcement of the ground rules under the Ceasefire Agreement or the Suspension of Operation necessitates certain arrangements: Institutional: Certain institutional mechanisms are set in place to ensure that sustained dialogue is possible. Like in the state of Nagaland while at the level of the State, a State Level Strategy Group is formed under the Chief Secretary, at the district, the District Level Monitoring Groups, comprising of civil society representatives like the church are established. Similar other institutional mechanism like the Unified Command under the Chief Minister is formed in the States of Assam and Manipur, respectively.

Organizational: The implementation of the code of conduct is also periodically reviewed by a Joint Monitoring Group comprising representatives of the Government of India, State Government, Security Forces and the concerned outfits. For example, while a Ceasefire Monitoring Group headed by a Retd. General as Chairmen is set up for monitoring developments of the NSCN (IM) agreement, in the case of the NCSN (K) a Ceasefire Supervisory Board, comprising of members of the different NSCN factions and State Forces. Likewise, similar other supervisory boards are respectively established. Procedure for the signing of a Ceasefire Agreement: One such important accomplishment of the agreement is the singing of the memorandum of settlement between the Government of India, the Government of Assam and the Bodo Liberation Tigers (BLT) in February 2003, which led to the laying down of the arms by the outfit The initiative has many breaks from the past; Partnership: Partnership - between the Ministry of Home Affairs, State Government, paramilitary forces and even the willing insurgent group - plays a pivotal role for the success of the Ceasefire Agreement or the Suspension of Operations.

Though the basic law and order maintenance is entrusted and carried out by the State authorities the Ministry of Home Affairs provides all needed support, whether infrastructure, financial, manpower or guidance to the State, to maintain law and order. Further to help the State maintain law and order in the region 40 Indian Reserve Battalions have been sanctioned.

- Of the 40 India Reserve Battalions (IRB) sanctioned,
- 8 each for Assam and Tripura,
- 7 for Manipur,
- 5 for Nagaland,
- 4 each for Arunachal Pradesh and Mizoram,
- 3 for Meghalaya and 1 for Sikkim.

The State Government through the local media and civil society actors and groups calls the willing insurgent group to come forward for peaceful talks and redressal of grievances. This olive branch is then accepted and welcomed by any interested insurgent party. Transparency: The process of dialogue creation and the signing of the Agreements/ Suspension of Operations are open to public viewing. The presence of a strong effective press/media and civil society pressure groups also reinforces transparency in functioning.

Replicability: The first ceasefire agreement was singed with the NSCN (IM) in 1997. Since then, similar framework of agreement like the Ceasefire/Suspension of Operations has been introduced in the other states- Assam, Manipur,

Meghalaya and Tripura. Sustainability: The aspect of sustainability varies. While with the NSCN (IM) the Ceasefire Agreements have been sustained over the years the issue of sustainability arises with the other groups. One such example is with the UNLF in Assam - in 2006 the Suspension of Operations was utilized by them for consolidation and reorganisation of their cadres, there was an increase in violence, particularly in areas of upper Assam and Guwahati city (Ministry of Home Affairs, Annual Report 2008). However it would be wrong to completely state that such talks are not sustainable as the on-going talks between the NSCN (IM) and the constituted Group of Minister (GoM- assisted by Shri K. Padmanabiah, Government of India's representative) point to the sustainable nature of dialogue generation. Innovativeness: Fighting insurgency is a prolonged continuous exercise. However, with the adoption of two pronged approach- of fighting the insurgents and engaging in dialogue with the interested groups - the new strategy offers the space for peace initiatives. Challenges for Implementers:

The initiation of talks and the signing of Ceasefire Agreements and of the Suspension of Operations however does not imply that long lasting peace efforts prevails. Sporadic instance of violent armed conflicts do arise. Thus, there are both improved changes as well as setbacks. However, it is important to note here that the nature of violence has changed. Armed conflict between the State forces and the insurgent group party to the agreement is relatively reduced. Therefore it would be erroneous if the opportunities provided and secured by the agreements and talks are ignored. Such agreement's act as a breather for the State forces, the Union Government and the insurgent group. It allows the space for re-organization, for developing new improved strategise for law and order maintenance, engaging in counter-insurgency operations against other warring groups and importantly, brings the party insurgent groups within the ambit of State purview.

Many challenges and anxieties are mentioned below:

- The framework of negotiation can be introduced only if the insurgent groups are interested.

- Scope of civil society or citizen participation in the operational framework of the agreement is limited. Presently, such participation is in the form of pressure groups.
- Better policing strategies based upon collaborative plan actions involving civil participation must be adopted.
- The agreements do not address the issues of increasing inter-factional conflict. Such as, factional fights between the NSCN (IM) and the newly formed NSCN (U) are on the rise or even the attacks on civilians by the insurgent groups.
- Governance and capacity building mechanism need to complement the initiatives to improve the overall state of insurgency and development.
- The signing of Ceasefire agreements or of Suspension of Operations is based upon mutual acceptance of the ground rules and the willingness of the insurgent group. Hence, it cannot be impressed upon the group by the State, as seen in the case of United Liberation Front of Assam (ULFA) - who could not be swayed even after three rounds of talks were held with the People's Consultative Group (PCG) and the Government.

RUMBLING ON THE NORTH-EAST STATES–INSURGENCY, PARALLEL GOVERNMENTS AND WIELDING POWERS

The ceasefire agreement in Nagaland has been extended. After weeks of speculation the National Socialist Council of Nagaland (IM) has withdrawn its opposition to the Congress led government's Common Minimum Programme document. The CMP has said that the territories in the North Eastern states will not be tampered with. The group read this as a rejection of its demand for the integration of all contiguous Naga inhabited areas in the Region. The Convenor of the group's ceasefire monitoring cell, Phungthing Shimrang, has said that they had decided to ignore the contents of the CMP since that was an internal matter of the government. He added that if the new government wanted to discontinue alteration of existing boundaries that was their internal problem.

Though the main rebel group has softened its stand against the new central government there are still dark clouds ahead. The rival Kaplang group has threatened to withdraw from the ceasefire because the Assam Rifles were raiding their camps to search for ULFA rebels. The group has confirmed that it is helping the Assam rebel group to reorganize it's after it was badly mauled in Bhutan.

Intelligence sources claim that the chance at the Centre had caused misgivings among the Naga insurgent groups about the future of the ceasefire. The main insurgent group the National Socialist Council of Nagaland, Issac Muviah (NSCN IM) had forged excellent relations with the Vajpayee government. The insurgent are reported to have helped the saffron party to gain a foothold in the hills states in the Region. It is a commonly known fact that the NSCN (IM) had helped the BJP gain a foothold in the Nagaland Assembly helping it to win six seats.

In Arunachal Pradesh it was responsible for bringing about the fall of the Mukut Mithi led Congress and the installation of the first BJP government in the Region under Geogang Apang. With S.C.Jamir, one of the strongest opponents of the NSCN (IM), as Congress Chief in Nagaland, the insurgents were unsure of the attitude of the Congress led government at the Centre.

In its effort to continue the peace effort in the Region the new government has agreed to continue with the Mizoram Chief Minister Zoramthanga as one of the negotiators in the peace talks. Jamir has been removed from the scene by his appointment as the Governor of Goa.

Like its predecessor the present government at the Centre is keen to end insurgency in the Region. It is being increasingly realised that insurgency has been the main cause of the backwardness of the Region. Leaders in the Region point out that with permanent peace real economic development is not possible in any state of the Region.

Over the years, and particularly since the late 1970s, the number of insurgent groups in the Region has multiplied. Almost every state in the Region, especially Manipur, Nagaland, Assam and Tripura, are insurgency hit. In army parlance the scale of conflict in these states have been categorized as low intensity wars, conflicts wherein fatalities are over 100 but less than 1,000 per annum.

While these four states are severely affected, Tirap and Changlang districts of Arunachal Pradesh face the spillover effects of insurgency from the neighbouring states of Nagaland, Assam and Manipur. In Meghalaya two outfits, the Hynniewtrep National Liberation Front (HNLF) and the Achik National Council (ACNC) is spreading terror. The only state in the region which is largely insurgency free is Mizoram.

Insurgency has flourished because of the close nexus of politicians and bureaucrats with various militant groups, a fact which is recognized in various reports of the Union Home Ministry. A recent Report says "Insurgency has given birth to an entirely new "genre" of mischievous politics wherein politicians of all hues thrive by hobnobbing with one or the other militant outfit. The entire administration is sucked into its vortex. Budgetary funds, even DRDA funds of the Central Government are being diverted into the coffers of the militants. The administration too seems to have a vested interest in such a situation because that way it can evade its basic responsibility of maintaining peace and work for development."

Successive governments at the Centre have tried to fight the scourge of insurgency through a system of 'money pour'. Despite this heavy money pour the targeted groups have remained out of the purview of the benefits acquiring from economic development while the nexus of politicians, bureaucrats, businessmen/contractors and the militants have enriched themselves.

Insurgency has developed into a small scale industry with new groups mushrooming at regular intervals. According to Ajai Sahni, Executive Director, Institute of Conflict Management, "a substantial proportion of the proliferation of armed groups is the result of the demonstration effect of the 'successes of other groups in the past. Such 'success' is not necessarily measured in terms of any political gains but, increasingly in terms of financial gains of widespread criminal operations by all militant groups in the Region."

The elimination of terrorism does not seem to be a serious policy agenda of the various state governments. A growing body of evidence shows that insurgency not only benefits the various militant groups but also politicians, bureaucrats and contractors. In all the four main insurgency hit states the underground run parallel governments. These wield greater power and influence than the democratically elected governments. They enjoy the power of taxation which unlike in the case of state and central levies is paid by the different sections of the population without protest.

In Nagaland and Manipur government servants have to pay a uniform 25 per cent of their salaries to the underground on a regular basis. Senior officers, especially IAS officers and heads of Department are expected to pay not only the 25 per cent but also ensure the regular diversion of public funds into the coffers of the underground. All over the Region the militants levy a road tax on all trucks and commercial vehicles, which sometimes adds up to almost 25 per cent of the cost of the goods being transported.

A Senior Army Commander has revealed "Extortion is rampant in all disturbed states of the region and so is funding of militant outfits by government officials, traders and big business houses. But what is most worrying for us is that huge amounts of money released by the Centre for welfare projects are being siphoned out to the coffers of militant organizations. Militancy will continue to thrive unless there is a full stop to extortion. The administration needs to be strengthened to handle the situation better. It is argued that increased financial allocations will help curb insurgency and ensure that the 'misguided youth' lay down arms and join the mainstream. Lack of funds, however, is not the main cause for the lack of development in the Region or the cause for insurgency. Evidence points to the fact that with every increase in allocations to the Region there has been an increase in militant activities and in the number of insurgent groups. Often referred to as the Land of the Seven Sisters; the North East accounts for just 8 per cent of the total geographical area of the country, with about 4 per cent of the total population. Broadly three distinct groups inhabit the Region: Hill Tribes, Plain Tribes and Non Tribes. Almost one fourth of the total population of the Region is made up of Tribals though they are in majority in the hill states of Arunachal Pradesh, Mizoram, Meghalaya and Nagaland. There are 160 scheduled tribes belonging to five different ethnic groups.

States in the Region arc categorized as special category states which entitle them to received 90 per cent of the plan assistance as grants and only 10 per cent as loan. Other mainland states get only 30 per cent as grants and the remaining 70 per cent as loan. The National Development Council sets aside 30 per cent of its entire allocation to finance development plans of the special category states. In addition to liberal finance from the Planning Commission these states receive preferential treatment in the sharing of Central Taxes from the Finance Commission. In addition every department at the Centre has set aside 10 per cent of its total annual budget for schemes in the North East Region. These states, as such, have not suffered because of lack of resources.

Gulshan Sachdev, who has undertaken an intensive study of the economic development of the Region, has indicated that the Region has received funds in abundance from the centre. "The main task has been simply to find ways to utilize central funds in a routine manner." According to his estimate the Region has received over ₹60,000 crore during the 1990-2000 decade. Of this Assam alone received ₹25,000 crore while both Manipur and Arunachal Pradesh got ₹5500 crore each. Nagaland and Mizoram got ₹6600 crore and ₹4800 crore, respectively while Tripura and Meghalaya received 7000 crore and ₹5000 crore, respectively.

It is interesting to note that the per capita Central assistance to the states in the Region is the highest in the country. Arunachal Pradesh heads the list. In the Eighth Plan against the national average of ₹1,080 the state received more than ₹36,237. Similarly Nagaland and Mizoram received ₹ 23,177 and ₹32,567 respectively. Sikkim received ₹33,486 and Tripura ₹8,476. Other special category states like Himachal Pradesh and Jammu and Kashmir and even Assam got a much lower share. According to available data Himachal Pradesh received ₹5,921 per capita while Jammu and Kashmir and Assam got ₹9,754 and ₹3,161 respectively. The economically poorest state of the country, Bihar got a paltry ₹876 while Uttar Pradesh received ₹789 per capita.

Despite these liberal allocations the condition of the common man in the Region has not improved substantially. The impact on the targeted population has been almost negligible due to the massive corruption and violence prevailing in the Region. In fact much of the investment has ended up financing militancy through a network of extortion and collusion. Government sources have revealed that subsidized essential commodities made available to the states are diverted into the open market. The conversion of the PDS quota into slush funds is done in a very simple manner. The entire stock of essential commodities, rice, wheat, sugar and kerosene oil, is diverted to the open market where they command a premium, through designated businessmen. The profits made are shared by the nexus of politicians, bureaucrats, businessmen and militant groups. The common people for whom the allotments are made pay open market prices to procure their requirements.

In Assam a regular source of finance for the militants, both underground and over ground, is the funds allotted for rural development. One estimates points to the fact that almost 70 per cent of the allotment to the government of Assam is siphoned off to the insurgents on a regular basis. During 1992 and 1998 of the ₹11.65 million allotted under this head only ₹4 million was used to finance legitimate schemes.

A Report on Integrated Rural Development (IRDP) held the upsurge in insurgency in Assam responsible for practically no development activities in the rural areas. In June 2001 the then Union Development Minister Venkiah Naidu, following a meeting of Rural Development Ministers of the Region, had warned that "the centre would stop disbursing rural development funds to states, where the bulk of the funds go to the coffers of the extremist outfits."

The theory that increased investments is the best way to curb insurgency no longer holds good. In fact with every increase in allocations acts of terrorism and violence have escalated. The S P Shukla Commission appointed in 1996 had said "it would be simplistic to believe that development by itself can end insurgency and restore tranquility." What is required is good governance which will ensure that the benefits of planned development percolate to all sections of the populations. Growing insurgency provides the states government an excellent excuse for non performance.

It cannot however be denied that insurgency has restricted the ability of the state government to undertake development activities. Increasing security related expenditure has constricted the availability of funds to undertake development activities. The ratio of development expenditure to non development expenditure has declined despite increased devolution from the Centre. The state is spending almost 70 paisa per rupee on administrative expenses.

Government estimates indicate that the two main factors which have caused an increase in the non development expenditure of the states are administrative services and interest payments. Of the administrative expenses policing consumes up to 70 per cent of the total. Though this might seem a reasonable expenditure, given the level of insurgency prevailing in the region it needs to be understood that the brunt of the counter insurgency operations are carried out by the Army and Para-military forces of the Centre. The state police play a very restricted role.

Bibliography

Ahuja, M. L.: *General Election in India,* Bangalore: Geological Society of India, 2002.

Chaube, S. K.: *Hill Politics of Northeast India,* New Delhi: Oxford University Press, 2000.

Datta, P. S.: *Autonomy Movements in Assam,* Madras: University of Madras, 1999.

Ghosh, S. K.: *Echos from North Eastern India,* Agartala: Benign Hills, 2004.

Horam, M.: *India's North* , Bangalore: Geological Society of India, 1996.

Kumar, Amrit: *Department of Tourism, Government of Meghalaya,* Manson: Manson Publishing, 2004.

Kumar, M.: *Women and Changing Power Structure in Northeast India,* Madras: University of Madras, 1997.

Mishra, U.: *The Periphery Strikes Back—Challenges to the Nation,* Mumbai: Manaktalas, 2003.

Sarin, V. I. K.: National Family Health Survey, Mumbai: Manaktalas, 2003.

Sen, A.: *Hunger and Public Action,* Delhi: Oxford University Press, 2002.

Sinha, A. C.: *North-Eastern Frontier of India,* Mumbai: Manaktalas, 1999.

Sreen, S. K.: *Insurgency in North—East India,* New Delhi: Oxford, University Press, 1999.

Index

I

M

N

P

S

U